And Two Were Chosen

*A Novel of Political and Biblical Intrigue
based on Fact and Truth*

Karen Sweetland

PublishAmerica
Baltimore

Hardcover 978-1-4560-5523-3
Softcover 978-1-4560-5522-6
PUBLISHED BY PUBLISHAMERICA, LLLP
www.publishamerica.com
Baltimore

Printed in the United States of America

To Craig…

…Smart…Handsome…Talented

The Son I Wish I Had

To Holly Boyd
Like a Loving Daughter

Daisy and Earle   May They Rest In Peace

In Appreciation

Sandra Bossert for the original conceptual inspiration
My friends who have provided support over this long and arduous
process
Patriots and Constitutionalists who inspire and motivate me to seek
the truth

PROLOGUE

This intriguing and implausible story is a work of fiction based on fact and truth; a story that could not have been created were it not for the plotted events of the past several years. No matter how adept at the written word or how grand one's imagination, it's unlikely anyone could have imagined this plot, this cast of characters, or the implications of their combined actions. So I offer the usual 'disclaimer'—I have changed the names—to protect the guilty.

This is the story of two insightful, delightful women of disparate backgrounds, who discover, by way of a door opened by God that the two Witnesses in Chapter 11, Book of Revelations, are here now. The Witnesses are using their celebrity to warn the world of the existence of the Antichrist, and his age-old plot to foster mayhem and chaos around the world. They also warn of the rise of the beast from the sea, and urge people to a final call to repent.

The stage is set for an insidious series of events that attack the very fiber of American culture, even life itself, resulting in economic ruin for America. The two women in this story gain access to information and participate in events that span the period from the 2007-2008 presidential campaign to 2012, and they encounter an evil force unequaled in modern history. America and the world are at a pivotal time of change, where the lessons of history are colliding with the realities of the present. Could the fall of America topple most of the rest of the world? Could that be the end; could that be Armageddon?

If students of history look closely at a series of events in the early 1900s during the days of Woodrow Wilson, they will see that today's issues were being discussed even then. Terms like 'One World Order' and 'progressive movement' were on the tongues of many of this country's business and political elite at that time. The beliefs and attitudes of that era paved the way for today's thinking and actions.

This story is rooted in Biblical text, with historical comparisons between ancient times and today; and in the relentless pursuit of truth. The Witnesses were charged with reporting on current events and Biblical truths, much like the Witnesses of ancient times, Elijah, John the Revelator, and others, in a final call to repent.

Witnesses Eli Gabriel and Patrick Hennessey bring us full circle from early days of unrest through a cataclysmic conclusion. They keep an eye to the future, and show how current events might play out in a global setting, amid tragic occurrences intended to awaken those who worship false Gods or none at all. "There shall be no Gods before Him."

True believers turn to the Bible not only for solace in time of trouble and crisis, but also for the insights into the future from Biblical prophecies. Non-believers may lack faith in the Bible or God, and be unaware that the role of repenting is to heal; yet they have no less desire to make sense of today's issues to better understand tomorrow's events.

TRUTH

"I am the way, the truth, and the life. And no one comes to the father but through me." Whether one believes it or not, if anyone adds to or takes away from the truth they will be damned. There will be a final call to warn the masses to change. It's a change of heart, not a change of false gods. There is only one real God and he is about to call everything to order, and that is the truth.

The Witnesses

CHAPTER ONE

*I don't believe in accidents. There are only encounters in history.
There are no accidents.*
Elie Wiesel
1928-, Rumanian-born American Writer

The sky was black from smoke; choking and suffocating smoke.
The pilot of their helicopter circled over the area of devastation. They
were at low altitude and from the lights of the copter they could see
the people stumbling amid the debris, tears streaming down their
faces, children crying, people calling out the names of their missing.
The moon in combination with the remaining flashes of light, cast an
eerie glow over the other-worldly scene of mass destruction, and as
they flew over downtown it appeared there were no buildings standing
amid the rubble. The copter moved on in the darkness, broken only by
an occasional, barely visible flashlight or candle.

They made their way north from Portland to the Seattle area, enroute
to a remote airfield and waiting plane. But for the beams of a solitary
vehicle moving slowly, the darkness below showed no clue of what
had transpired, or what now existed. They finally reached the metro
area of Seattle; the familiar tall buildings—mostly gone. The pilot
circled lower. They could hear sirens and see thousands of people
silhouetted in the moonlight on a stretch of highway. Flying lower,
they saw apparent strangers embracing each other, looks of terror on
their upward turned faces.

The people had been warned! Oh yes, they had been warned!

As they watched this sea of frayed, anxious humanity slowly moving
about in disbelief and fear, unsure of what to do, Mackenzie's thoughts
drifted back to the beginning.

Neither Katherine nor Mackenzie could ever have imagined what
was ahead of them as they formed their new friendship. Had anyone

9

suggested that the crossing of their paths would lead them on a journey filled with danger, with global implications and a cast of evil characters with an anti-American agenda, they'd have thought them loons.

Mackenzie was not unaccustomed to dicey situations or intrigue, but their journey proved far beyond her wildest expectations. Threats to their lives, attempted kidnapping and stalking are but a few of the dangers they faced. At stake was the fate of this nation's citizens and their souls, their Constitution and freedoms. Their decision to get involved, after inadvertently learning of a diabolic plot against America, was prompted by their fears of what would happen if people were not alerted; what would happen to America's Judeo-Christian values, or to the people of the world?

To understand what has transpired, we must go back to the time when Katherine Justice and Mackenzie Honor first met, a time when Americans and others around the world were distracted with economic woes and life's travails.

For Mac, being the political junkie she was, she'd usually go through her daily routine with her ears tuned to news of all sorts, especially during political campaign seasons. She went about her life trying to balance its various demands, but she longed to extricate herself from the anxieties experienced in her secret life. She feared someone from her past would reappear and create problems for her, or worse, she'd get pulled back in. Little did she know what was in store, and where her nose for news would lead her, or the dangers she'd encounter.

At the same time, Katherine was busy building her business, involved in family projects, and Bible studies. Life for Kate was full and happy, marred only by the occasional 'child' rumble. So when a client invited her to go to a conference she was helping organize in Seattle, Katherine thought it might be good to expand her horizons. Besides, a couple of days away from the salon would be a welcome respite. Kate too had no inkling of how this conference would be life-changing, or the adventure she would embark on in the coming months.

Through Mackenzie's ongoing networking, she learned of the same conference that featured presentations by a variety of global economic and political experts. She was invited to introduce one of the speakers with whom she had served on a committee, and leapt at the opportunity to reconnect with some colleagues she saw infrequently.

While Mac was relieved to not be fully involved in the dramas of her past, she did have occasional wistful pangs, missing the excitement and some of her former associations.

It was at this 2004 Seattle conference that Katherine Justice and Mackenzie Honor first met. They ended up at the same table, and quickly realized that they shared a number of interests and points of view, though they came to them from very different backgrounds. They had the added benefit of great chemistry, so they decided to meet outside the conference and get better acquainted. At the time Katherine said, "God arranges meetings such as this for his own purpose. In time we'll know what it is."

Mac too believed there were no accidents—that everything happened for a reason. One never imagined how convoluted things could be that served destiny. This chance meeting proved over time to be the definition of success—recognizing a door slightly ajar and taking the time to enter, ready for whatever might come their way—opportunity and preparation converging at the same time, while trusting the unseen and unknown.

Their friendship evolved over the next few years. They lived in different cities, Kate in Portland, Mac in Seattle, so chances to get together were infrequent. However, as Mackenzie's situation changed she decided it was time to leave Seattle for Portland. She had been called on to carry out a secret research project and Portland was a good place, and would enable her to be close to where her beloved son lived.

Kate and Mac managed to get together a couple of times a month, often to talk for hours about what was going on in the world. They found mutual stimulation in approaching world events from their different perspectives—Mac's the political, Kate's her relationship with God. They held different spiritual beliefs but shared very similar views on family, friends and some social issues. They were both patriots and devoted to America.

They knew that for another shining moment in history, Americans were as one, in defiant and patriotic unity against those who wished us dead. 9-11 brought out the best in us. But as time heals all wounds, it also clouds over the tragedy and pain. Americans thought less and less of the event and potential threat to their lives, and eventually resumed life as normal. Even though the outrage and urgency lessened, as time went by they realized all was not well.

These two women regarded the nation as out of control, spiraling downward into poverty and chaos, with mounting debt, a government spending too much, two wars and a stock market on the down-slide. Katherine often commented that evil had a grip on many vulnerable souls.

Now and then Kate and Mackenzie would take a short trip for some R & R. On one such occasion they took a train to Seattle for an Indian summer weekend of shopping, food and Pike Place Market.

While there the two women ended up attending a fund raising event benefitting a favorite charity of a close mutual friend. The event included a silent auction at which they each placed a couple of bids. It turned out that Katherine won a week's trip for two to New York and Mac won a spa day for two at Elizabeth Arden. They decided to combine their winnings and go to New York together. What better time than mid December, perhaps before the snow but with all the holiday decorations. They eagerly anticipated their upcoming trip.

Mackenzie made plans to do some in-person research and digging around for some rather illusive information needed for her secret project while in New York. She put in a call to her supervisor, "Hi Jack, Mackenzie here. I wanted to let you know that I'll be going to New York in December for a week. I was thinking it would be a great time to do some of my research while there. So far I've been able to use the phone and various ploys, but in New York I need a good cover. Any ideas? I'll be traveling with a friend, who won a trip to New York for two."

Jack's voice sounded pleased, as he said, "Mac Hi. I was just thinking about you. Was at a meeting this morning and your name came up, folks wondering how you are doing on the project. I told them it was a slow process, but you had found some good information. Now as to New York, and you're there with a friend you say?

"Can you be there a bit early, like in three weeks? The reason I ask, the timing could not be more perfect. There is a super secret meeting going on and our friend will be there, along with many of his cronies. I can get you in, if you can make use of it. And yes you would need a good cover. Can you get your friend to go along with a plan; is she very nosey?"

"Hmm, well I think we can arrange the trip for three weeks out. Kate is easy going, though we were planning on going a little bit later, in early December, my personal favorite, but what's a week or two! So what would be a good cover, and what is this meeting?" Mackenzie asked.

"Excellent," Jack declared. "I think you should be two ordinary friends, vacationing from Oregon, but in business together with an idea to create a social entrepreneurial venture, perhaps supporting global wildlife, or the poor in Africa, or some similar global objective."

"Oh yes, you asked about the meeting. I'll send you some information by email, along with your invitation. Make the most of this, and be on your toes. Our buddy and his goons will be there in full force, emerging from their holes all over the world. The conference is part of a group of meetings and is deadly serious, with some of the big players attending. Be very cautious Mac; listening will be far safer than commenting. Dig?" Jack urged.

"Jack you know little gives me pause, but this guy is one exception. I can imagine my knees rattling or buckling in front of him. You saw my last report. Yes, I surely do dig," Mac sighed.

Jack cajoled her, saying, "Come on now girl, you can do it. Just be careful, alert, and call me if you find out any important information or need anything."

She said, "Okay Jack. I'll be in touch. Bye."

Mackenzie sat for a moment, staring off into space. A chill ran over her body, as she imagined actually sitting next to this man. It was like bellying up to the bar with the Devil. She heaved a huge sigh and decided to call her son before she went on about her business.

"Hi honey, Mom here. How are you? I've not seen you all in weeks and you've been on my mind. I'm going back to New York shortly.

I'll be gone about a week. I hope we can get together before I go, but certainly after I get back."

Jamie responded, "Hi Mom. I'm fine, we are all fine. We are busy, just no free time. When will you be back? Maybe you can come for dinner in a couple of weeks. Got something to show you. Hey Mom, I've gotta go, being paged. Have a safe trip. See ya."

Mackenzie smiled but there was sadness in her eyes. She never expected they would be tied closely to each other, especially after he married. She always wanted him to be his own man, to be independent and do well with his life. But since he married she rarely saw him or heard from him and it broke her heart in ways she could not express, or would even allow herself to ponder. She knew she just had to buck up, and hope one day things would improve.

She set about making lists and preparing for the trip to New York. A day at the spa would be heaven; and there were several theatrical productions she was eager to see. She called Kate to advise about the date change because she had business to do at that time. Kate was not concerned and agreed to the change.

The two women arrived in New York on their auction winnings. It was late November of 2006 just after Thanksgiving; the weather was lovely and brisk. It was great to be in the hustle and bustle of the great city of New York.

Once settled into their suite at the 'W' they started talking about what things they wanted to do while in New York.

"I think we should do the spa day on our last day so we are totally relaxed to head home," Mac said.

"Exactly, and tonight let's play it by ear and check out one of Bobby Flay's restaurants, and then go someplace for coffee and music after," Kate replied. "I read an article about his restaurants and watch him on the Food Network, so I promised myself I'd check at least one out if I ever got to New York."

The women got dolled up and headed out to Mesa Grill, foolishly without calling ahead. The wait was too long, so they decided to check out Nobu, a place about which they had heard a good deal of buzz. It was stunning, and after a brief wait they were seated at a table with a great view of the room. Nobu , partly owned by Robert De Niro, evoked the ambiance of a Japanese country home and the food—well it gave fusion a whole new meaning. They decided to take their time and order many little plates to sample the splendid array of textures and flavors.

The room was full of upscale customers, warmed by soft lighting, and an ample supply of quality wine. The two women had an animated conversation with the couple at the adjacent table, finding New Yorkers far friendlier than most believed. After bidding their new friends goodbye, they headed to one of Mac's favorite places—the Café Carlyle where Bobby Short once held court at his baby grand piano. It was still charming and intimate, but not like when Bobby was there. Back in the day an intimate crowd gathered around the glorious Carlyle piano to listen to Bobby belt out Cole Porter songs. He had a Southern drawl, easy manner, and it was obvious how he'd become so well entrenched in the upper social strata of New York, and given the nickname "the darling of Café Society."

Mac and Kate slept in the next day, still on West Coast time, but their list of "musts" had grown during their conversations the previous night. They bounded out of bed, not wanting to waste any time; they got through the morning routine and prepared for their day-long adventure.

The sun was shining brightly, the air brisk in anticipation of late November's chill. During the taxi ride Kate decided to call her husband. "Hi, it's me. The flight was fine. We had dinner last night at De Niro's restaurant. It was delicious, as raw fish goes. Right now we are headed to the tour boat for a cruise around Manhattan, and then going exploring. Oh John, no I won't go crazy spending money. I am going to pick up something for the grandkids. Did you get hold of Mikey? Be sure he brings the equipment back. Did you call the bank? Yes, you need to call them today. I know, but I am not there, so you need to follow up on it. The paperwork has been there for more than a week. It's just a phone call honey. The information to give them is written on the pad by the phone in the kitchen. Good grief, these taxis go fast. John I'd best go now. Love you too. Bye."

Katherine, having gone along with Mac's choices the night before, declared "Today is my plan. I have things I have wanted to do forever, so humor me, as it is going to be a whirlwind. First up, the Circle Tour boat around Manhattan; then let's go to South Seaport and grab some lunch and wander around."

"Terrific," Mac said. "I've wanted to check out Seaport too. But before we do anything, let's decide on where we want to have dinner so we can make a reservation. Any ideas, like a place you have always wanted to check out?" Mac asked her.

Kate smiled, "Now that you mention it, yes there is one special place I have heard of all my life and I'd die to go there. Its way out of my budget, but what the heck, John won't know, so let's do The Four Seasons Restaurant!" Katherine was clapping her hands together like a girl, so of course they had to go there. "I feel guilty being so selfish and demanding, but I want to see just why everyone refers to the Big Apple as the Greatest City on Earth. It makes me think of the dreaded bite into the apple in Genesis that caused the downfall of man, the Great City and the final call to repent in Revelations."

"You know, Chapter 11 in the Bible?" Kate pressed. "I guess you wouldn't. Well, it talks of a great earthquake in modern times that will kill many thousands of people in mere minutes. That day will come, and affect so many people. I look around here and imagine what would happen then and it is so sad."

Mackenzie rolled her eyes and pleaded, "Let's talk about happier things, okay? Is everything okay at home? No worries or problems?" Mac inquired.

Kate hesitated briefly and then said, "Oh, John is always worried I will spend too much money. He makes good money and so do I, but he seems to forget that I bring in a good income so should have the option of doing with it as I choose, at least a part of it. We are in pretty good shape financially, having saved all our married life, plus we help the kids out, and we have our new vacation home in Arizona. I think because he wants to retire, he is afraid something will go wrong. I wish he'd relax a bit. But let's not dwell on this stuff."

Kate agreed to stick with happier topics, knowing Mac's sensitivity to matters of the Bible. But she had faith—knowing that God works in mysterious ways and of his own timing. She knew that Mac would one day hear God's message and would embrace Jesus, but for now Mac was resistant. AMEN she thought to herself.

Sunny brisk weather made for a perfect tour around Manhattan, save for the stark and somber reminder of the missing WTC towers that once defined the skyline. The empty hole in the skyline brought back that fateful day of 9/11 and the horrific images broadcast for days. Mac had been glued to the television for four days barely sleeping, until she could handle no more. Today she felt a knot in her throat as her eyes filled with tears when looking out at the huge hole in the skyline.

It was always different experiencing a city from the water and this was no exception—it was grand. After the tour and another wild taxi ride down to the Lower end of Manhattan, they entered Seaport. They spent the next few hours in a whirlwind of browsing, shopping, snacking, watching performers and wandering. It was all great fun and a perfect respite from any worries.

They returned to their hotel for some much needed rest and a cup of tea, elated over their purchases, exhausted from their feet up. They mulled over the sights and experiences of the day, their purchases and contentment as they lounged in front of the fire in their suite. Each slipped into a brief nap and later they got all dolled up for their special night of dining at the tres chic Four Seasons.

Mac had gotten ready before Kate. She was a sophisticated woman in her early 60s though she appeared younger. She was tall, at five feet eight inches, and had a rather substantial figure, neither fat nor thin, but sturdy. Her hair was dark brown with a few touches of gray, worn short with a trendy kick to her style. She had a youthful, round face, large green eyes, smooth unwrinkled skin, and was regarded as very attractive in most circles. That night Mac wore a dark green wool dress with a lovely antique broach on one shoulder, dark brown leather and suede boots with modest heel. She was turned out with makeup artfully applied, well manicured, elegant and classy, but just slightly understated. She could easily pass for a chic New Yorker, and usually did whenever visiting the City.

She sat watching the news on television, waiting for Kate to emerge from the bathroom, hoping she'd be ready soon. Kate was giddy about going to the Four Seasons, and decided to go all out.

Kate was a few years younger than Mac, in her mid fifties. She was petite in stature and body shape, and still had the same figure she had when a teenager. She was proud of her body and she liked to show it off. She often wore skin-tight clothes, very short skirts with boots or heels. Kate no longer had the dark hair of her youth, having opted for bleached blonde long hair worn in a tussled fashion. Without makeup she looked like the girl next door, but she hated to be seen without makeup, opting for thick dark liner around her eyes, dark brown brows (in contrast to the blonde hair), and very pale lipstick. She was a tanning addict and kept a dark tan all year long, either from being in the sun, or from the tanning bed in her home.

Mac had once mentioned how good Kate looked without all the makeup, but Kate would hear none of it. Mac realized that telling a hairdresser anything about fashion, cosmetics and hairstyles was not a great idea and was not well received. Mac did not have the heart to tell her that it was time for her to drop the dated look and to adopt a bit more understated style becoming of her age. So Mac had decided to leave well enough alone and to embrace Kate, no matter how much makeup.

Kate finally came into the sitting room announcing she was ready. Her makeup was a bit darker than usual, hair orchestrated into clouds of blonde anchored by lots of hairspray. She had on a short black skirt and low cut black sweater cinched at the waist with a glittery belt. Forgetting the cold weather, Kate was in heeled sandals without stockings, and had on a fluffy short coat with lots of yarn strands flitting about. It was one of her favorite outfits, too dressy for normal wear in Portland, and Mac knew Kate felt very dolled up.

Mac said, "You are looking might sparkly there girlfriend. Don't you worry you'll get cold without stockings or a heavy winter coat? There is a chance of snow tonight."

Kate smiled, shaking her head, "Oh heavens, we'll be in a taxi; how cold can it get? I'm starving. Let's go!"

Mac grabbed her gloves, scarf and mink coat and headed for the door. They were quite a contrast these two women, in ways obvious and not so much. Light dark; short tall; tailored frilly. When they left their room, they were eager and excited about the evening, oblivious to anything but having a marvelous evening, unaware things would change forever that fateful night. Dressed to the nines in their own way, ready for the luxurious environment of The Four Seasons, they left the hotel. The doorman hailed a taxi, that delivered them at 8:45 for their reservation.

The restaurant, a classic in New York, remained elegantly understated and traditional. It was an architectural wonder of floor to ceiling glass windows, sheer draperies that offered a gauzy glimpse of the bustling street outside and flattering, perfectly dimmed lighting. The focal point of the main room was a large white marble pool and trees positioned at the corners of the pool that were changed seasonally.

They were taken to their table adjacent the pool, a prime spot to observe the crowd and ambiance. Kate beamed and strutted her way through the tables, as if a starlet waiting to be discovered. Mac strode with confidence; as if she was accustomed to the luxury and crowd. While waiting for their drinks to arrive Mac began looking about the room. There were some familiar faces, among them Mikhail Baryshnikov with a small group; Tom Brokow with a couple of other gentlemen; a noted Broadway actress and her husband. No sooner did their drinks arrive than a group of three men was seated at the table next to them. Katherine and Mac were busy chatting, studying the huge menu, marveling at the mammoth wine list and commenting on some of the patrons, too busy to notice the group of men next to them.

Mac urged Katherine "Look over there—see the woman with the red hair? She is a wealthy socialite and business woman. Look at the jewelry! Hundreds of thousands of dollars on her neck alone. And those shoes—simply to die for!"

"I arrived feeling chic and smartly dressed, but there are so many stylish people here. Not like back home," lamented Katherine. "This is even more amazing than I expected. Did you see Baryshnikov over there? I'd love to run over and get his autograph."

"Don't you dare," Mac chided.

Kate laughed, and then said, "Isn't that Cora Lamia over there? Who is she with; do you know that old geezer she is making over? I wonder what she's doing out of Washington? And without an entourage, fancy that! Hey, what do you think she is up to? She is never without a posse."

Mac turned and looked in the direction Kate indicated, "Gee, I am not sure about the old geezer as you put it. I really can't make out his features well enough in this lighting. The other man is her husband I believe; I have no idea who the other couple is, and you know my eyes and vision are getting horrible."

Before long a tall somber man in a dark suit strode up to the table next to the two women. He looked foreign, austere and rather sinister. Mackenzie studied his face and determined that he was either Middle Eastern or perhaps Slavic. He was well dressed, seemed humorless, and was apparently peeved with someone at the table to the point of almost making a scene.

Katherine started to talk, but Mac raised her hand to silence her so they could listen.

"Johann, I got a call from him this morning. You let us down. You did not come through with the information you promised and he is upset. No make that damn mad. What the hell were you thinking?" the tall man was saying, as he pulled out the empty chair and sat down.

A waiter rushed over and took a drink order for the table, as the conversation continued. Mac moved her chair to get a better look, and to her utter amazement she recognized one of the men at the table. There sat the billionaire Ivan Schwartz. Kate pointed out that he was the man huddled earlier with Cora Lamia. Knowing what she did about this man, an involuntary shiver took over her body as she realized that this was very likely an unholy alliance seated at that table. She knew she had to hear the details of their conversation.

Mac leaned over the table to whisper to Katherine, "We need to hear what is going on at this table. Let's inch our table toward theirs just a bit. Then when you go to the lady's room I am going to switch seats so I can move my chair a bit closer."

"But I don't need to visit the lady's room" Kate complained.

"Just go" Mac softly prodded. "You have no idea who these people are and what they represent. We need to listen to their conversation. Now go," Mac whispered.

They did a bit of a shuffle, then, bewildered, Kate excused herself. Mac dropped her glove to give herself a chance to stand up, and when she sat back down it was in the seat next to the adjacent table.

The men were sipping their cocktails as the conversation continued; this time Ivan Schwartz began speaking in a low stern voice with a thick Eastern European accent. "He's a SOB, but he is MY SOB. I want this whole deal to come off without further glitches. You and your dipshit aides have bungled things one too many times. Damn it, I have a lot at stake here. I'll not allow some amateur to squander this opportunity, or for that matter, go against my plan in any way. I have too much at risk, do you hear me?" His face was obviously red, even in the dim light.

The man called Johann said, "Mr. Schwartz, I assure you that they are all onboard and wish to be of help. I am sorry. I will get my core group together later tonight after my conference call, and make sure that everyone is totally clear on what they need to do. I have 250 teams organized. They are getting their training; a few are done now, and are ready to be dispatched to the field. He knows that things are going according to plan and by the way, I thought they had through this year to get fully organized? We've have been keeping him and his people informed almost daily. I saw you chatting with Cora Lamia. Are we meeting with her this evening? If so I need to adjust my schedule."

Katherine leaned over and said "Who do you think they are talking about? She handed something to Mac and said "Use this. I use it all the time for my Bible studies class. It works great, and we'll have some record to listen to later."

With that, Mac took the tiny tape recorder, turned it on and clipped it to her coat collar draped over the chair next to her.

"Listen Ivan, you want their support. You have made demands on us that will create a good deal of havoc in a couple of years. Well, they are willing and able. But if you think they are going to impact the whole country, be on notice that a lot more money will have to change hands. Does that work for you? I'll not have my leadership or my people second-guessed. I'll not sit around waiting to pick up the pieces from a mess created by one of your groups. And speaking of groups, what the hell are those people in DC doing holding a press conference now? It will be much too easy for some nosey media hack to connect the dots. Things are going your way Ivan, such that you can come out in the open now. But you don't need media sniffing about," bemoaned the tall man.

Ivan Schwartz growled, "The media will do what I want them to do. Don't question me. As for the schedule, yes they have through the year, but I want trial runs on special community projects carried out to be sure there are no bugs, no buffoons to mess things up. Are we clear? Let me add this, and hear me well. I do not want to be questioned, or second-guessed, not now, not ever. This plan has been in the works for many years. I know what I am doing, I know what I want and when, and I expect you to follow orders, period."

The third man, who had sat silently till now, said, "Ivan, I have raised over \$137 million for your pet project and so far I've not had a single word out of D.N. There are many people around the country who are worried they have hitched their hopes to the wrong horse. Isn't that how you say it? Hopes and horses?"

Ivan interrupts, "All of you keep your voices down. None of this should be discussed here in public. I am going to the conference tomorrow. Joe I want you to go too. You show up alone. There will be no interaction between us. Got that? The meetings end at 4PM. There is a suite in the Ritz Carlton where there will be a cocktail party. It's a safe place, people we know. We can all meet there. I've got a teleconference set up there with the two in Asia."

"The hotel is across from the Plaza where the conference is being held. We'll have no more on this tonight." With that Ivan dismissed the tall man and waved the waiter over. "Bring us a nice presentation of your best caviar and champagne, and be quick about it."

Schwartz lowered his voice and leaned in to his table companions, "I want you both to keep an eye on him. Low key, but watch him. He can be a hothead with a short fuse. I'll not put two thousand years of my plans at risk now, when it is all about to pay off."

Both men looked at each other, and Johann said, "2000 years? Isn't that a bit of an exaggeration?"

Schwartz was caught off guard, but grinned slightly and said, "I added too many zeros—of course I meant twenty years."

With that, the men resumed social conversation, focused on their caviar and what they were ordering for dinner.

The women stared at each other, seemingly with the same thought. Mac leaned across the table and whispered to Kate, "We have overheard something sinister, but I am not sure who it was they're talking about or what for that matter."

Mac continued in a whisper, "Kate, I don't know what you're hoping to do tomorrow, but I think we are on to something. My gut is telling me we should put on business suits and hit that conference at the Plaza Hotel. We want to be near these men; that means we need to separate. You dog the guy named Johann and I'll follow Ivan Schwartz. If we get there early and hang out around the entry we can make sure we are in the right rooms since we don't know anything about the format or layout. Since there are no accidents, I should tell you that I believe the conference is the same one my boss asked me to monitor."

Katherine smiled widely, "Oh I love a good mystery. But this is also a bit intimidating. Are you sure we should be doing this? After all, these men appear very stern, and seem rather dangerous, maybe even corrupt. What if we get caught? And anyway, what if this is not the meeting we were to attend? How could we possibly get in to the conference? John is going to be upset with me. He was not keen on my taking this trip, and if I get myself in trouble, he is going to be very peeved."

John and Kate had a happy solid marriage. To some extent they were rather independent of each other; and in many respects they did not have much in common. John was a man's man, totally into sports, rugged, handsome by most any standard, but without the attending ego one normally encounters. Kate could be bossy. No, let's make that Kate was bossy. She was bossy with her husband, children, friends and clients. She did not realize it, but she was. So John was pretty good about dealing with the bossiness. On the other hand, John was not Mr. Perfect; he had a temper, was reluctant to express feelings till they erupted in inappropriate ways, and could be childish with pouting and tantrums. Still, Kate ruled the roost. She could be warm and effusive, then quickly change to distant and aloof, or superficial; and at her core she was a Type A personality, and hyper, very very hyper.

Mackenzie thought back to the times she had traveled down from Seattle to stay with them. John was up early and out the door to golf all weekend. Once home he was in front of the big screen television watching whatever sports were being aired. Kate would do her own thing, and be quite happy. She worked incredibly long hours, went out with friends, went to church, visited family and friends and did not mind John not being around. But, Mackenzie knew that John had his limits on all things.

Mac had spent a lot of time with Kate and expected that John was less than happy about that. He wanted, nay needed, to be the center of attention at least part of the time. "Mac! Mac! Wake up. You are lost in thought? Back to our problem here," Kate demanded.

"Not to worry dear. I will check the information my friend sent, and if this is not the right gathering, he will get us in, and give us an idea that will also get us into that cocktail party at the Ritz. Let's enjoy this marvelous meal, go back to our hotel, have a night cap and work on a plan. If I am right, what we may discover could be of national importance that others may need to know about. But for now, can you believe these scallops?"

###

CHAPTER TWO

Passions spin the plot: We are betrayed by what is false within.

George Meredith
1828-1909, British Author

Once back in their suite, Katherine got out her laptop and tried to find out more on the identity of Johann Adler, while Mackenzie reviewed her files on Ivan Schwartz. Something about him was bugging Mac and so far she could not put her finger on it but felt she was getting closer. He had been her secret research project for some time and was like an enormous onion with layers of information, most of which could make any average person cry, just like the odorous onion.

Schwartz was a Hungarian Jew who had avoided concentration camps as a child, thanks to his father changing their name, and depositing Ivan with a Christian family for the duration of the war. Ivan apparently did not conduct himself with honor in those days. In fact he joined the man pretending to be his father, going from house to house in the Jewish ghetto to search for people, and to round up anything of value from each home—a job he relished and always recalled with fondness and pleasure. At the end of the war he was sent from the ghetto to Treblinka in Poland, where he was rescued by U.S. Marines in 1945. He was then sent to a youth home in Austria and from there he traveled to England to meet up with his family, and set out on a new life. Even though Ivan was one of the few Jews who survived without harm, and his family made it without serious harm, Ivan had a huge resentment toward the British, whom he felt owed him. He also held the belief that Jews were weak and pathetic and deserved their fate.

Thus as years passed, he denied his Jewish heritage and grew to despise Jews and all they stood for. By the time he arrived in the United States he was anti-Jew, anti-Christian and anti-American as well.

Mac's earlier research on Schwartz provided a reasonably comprehensive overview. She learned that his billions of dollars were made by often dubious, if not illegal means. He deserved recognition for having risen from a poor Jew out of war-torn Eastern Europe to a powerful billionaire, king maker and business man. But he was a man of seriously questionable character, with a belief system where the ends justified the means, always. He wanted what he wanted, and cost was never an obstacle, nor was resulting human misery, matters of ethics, or conscience.

There was always the matter of his personal agenda—what made this man tick? What drove him? What was his real objective besides amassing a vast fortune? Mackenzie had been studying him off and on for a long time, to determine just what he was working toward. He had long been in the background, rarely mentioned in all but exclusive financial circles. Few others had heard of him, except those on Wall Street who knew of his ferocious appetites and tactics; fewer still had seen much of him, and still fewer knew much of anything about him. A few years ago Schwartz could attend a meeting of most any organization or business, even those he owned, and be regarded as just some guy in the background.

Some people regarded him as an enigma, even though he seemed upfront about having an agenda. For Mac, the challenge was to connect the dots so she could see the big picture with him, in the hope of gleaning further insight into his purpose.

Schwartz had moved about the world, often interjecting himself into areas of political unrest, able to make huge sums of money out of each political crisis. But he had long been a man of mystery operating in the shadows, with some hefty connections including past presidents, Senators, Congressmen, and foreign leaders; as well as the heads of many major financial institutions, and stock markets in the U.S., Asia and Europe. He was also linked to the heads of governments and monarchies, such as the King of Saudi Arabia.

Mac discovered there were many alarming aspects of Schwartz's global alliances, not the least of which were links to several terrorist organizations and terrorist sympathizers. He was known to have financial and oversight ties to hundreds of organizations—think-tanks, non-profits and PACS, among others, geared to power plays and influence peddling within the body politic, mostly in the United States and the United Kingdom. Over time Mac came to realize that Schwartz had purposefully created a network of organizations involved in every aspect of society in both countries, providing an all-encompassing web of influence.

There was some indication of a dark alliance with one of the world's great mobster bosses, out of Russia. As the USSR broke apart it became a haven for thugs and criminals to run scams, but one stood out among the rest, Anatoli Mogilevich. Here was another Jew born during the war that grew up poor, but still managed to obtain a sterling education, so he was far smarter than the average Russian crook.

He began his dubious career by bribing police and those at airports to grease the machine that smuggled drugs and stolen gems into the country. Over time Anatoli amassed a fortune dealing in stolen art, prostitution, arms, drugs and financial scams. So it was no wonder that the paths of Anatoli, Schwartz and Madinski (another Jew from Eastern Europe) would cross, each working deals in the U.S. and Eastern Europe. With Madinski Schwartz did deals in South and Central America; Anatoli was Europe and the U.S.

Anatoli made an average man quake in his boots, despite his diminutive stature of 5'4", in part because of his enormous frame weighing in at about 300 pounds. His seriously pock-marked, square face was set off by intensely dark eyes that set their steady gaze on a person of interest without a blink or movement. People squirmed in his presence—but not Schwartz or Madinski. They were cut from the same evil cloth, a triumvirate of darkness, these three men.

Having spent a good deal of time digging into Schwartz's life, Mackenzie was by necessity led to his associations. As a woman with life-long interest in history and the human condition, Mac arrived at a conclusion about Schwartz that caused her great concern, and anguish.

She had not written of it in any report, nor discussed it with anyone, because in many ways it was just too shocking to mention.

Mac realized that some of history's most evil monsters, such as Hitler, Stalin, Mao, and many others, had committed mass slaughters and caused untold misery and pain to millions. Each may have had a different reason, from crushing their opposition to cleansing a race. But they were, albeit horrendous, still reasons. Historians and survivors could argue details and degree of evil, but there were reasons.

What Mac came to realize about Schwartz was that he too had created situations that ruined millions of lives, not with torture and mass killings, but destruction of whole economies. Where he stood alone among the many is that he had no motivation other than his personal pleasure for making money and wielding the control to bring down a government—not one moment of regret or concern for the lives ruined, businesses collapsed, suicides committed in hopelessness, or children left orphaned. If it served his purpose, he was fine with it.

One could imagine how horribly uncomfortable and intimidating it must have been to do a deal with those three men. Each man was below average in height, yet between them, they controlled the most ill-gotten money in the world and with sufficient power individually to tumble most economies on a whim. To sit across a table from any one of them would be traumatic, but all three? Shiver me timbers!

Apparently Anatoli and Madinski had an interest in money laundering for drug barons. Anatoli and Schwartz were involved in setting up banks and money deals in Eastern Europe. Anatoli alone had his hit squads scattered around the world; and in the U.S. combined them with specially outfitted torture chambers.

But on that day Schwartz had been meeting with other men of mystery, and was about to attend a clandestine conference, but to what end? Why the secrecy, urgency and anxiety? And who was the mystery person spoken of at dinner the previous night?

Mac shook her head to dispel the details and images of these dreadful men. She had the information with her sent by Jack, and was prepared for the conference.

"Kate, it took my pulling of some strings in Washington to gain access to this conference. It was all hush-hush, and essentially closed, by invitation only. I have a friend with the right pull who emailed me an invitation and information, which I printed out. I have their password-protected website, so am going to go online and get us pre-registered for the conference, which by the way is called "Progressive Global Economic Change," one of those fuzzy ill-defined, all-encompassing topics with a definite liberal slant."

The word 'progressive' seemed to be the born-again buzz word among European socialists, and the more radical liberals in the U.S. Why? Perhaps initially because it was a relatively innocuous word and did not create fear and distrust as much as the words 'socialist' and 'communist' inspired. Few people realized that 'progressive' was a word that was once associated with Communist-leaning and thinking groups here and abroad, back in the 1950's and 1960's. But the progressive movement and ideology existed long before, having taken form and substance during Woodrow Wilson's tenure as President.

Kate was pouring over the conference documents they received, and asked, "Mac, do you know any of these names? I am not familiar with any of them. This is an international gathering. There are people from Europe, Africa, the Middle East, Indonesia, and the U.S. Some of them list business connections to global financial groups, some seem to be banks, but there are organizations, investment houses, and government representatives. Hey, there are two guys listed here from Freddie Mac and Fannie Mae! So what is our story; how do we blend into such a group?" Katherine seemed at once curious, excited and worried.

"Kate, we are there as social entrepreneurs, but we need a better story than that. I did some digging online, and I think you will be a fund raiser and I'll be a community outreach professional. We are working on developing a new global non-profit geared to education of the impoverished in Third World countries. It is obscure enough that we should be able to blend in. It will be important for us to listen and take notes, and not talk much. We are out of our element so the less we say the better. But the key is that we are working on developing a global non-profit and are there to avail ourselves of every opportunity to participate in all global dialogue and problem solving, and to better understand the economic issues we'll face."

"So how do you plan on getting us into the cocktail party?" Katherine inquired.

"Um, well I've been thinking about that. First let me caution—this conference is no place for you to mention God, or spread the word. Pray if you need, but do it silently. We could get into quite a situation if Christian-based comments are overheard. As for the cocktail party, I think one or both of us need to sit at the same table as Johann. He seems somewhat approachable and knows information we need to learn about. Schwartz certainly is not approachable but I'm hoping to pick up something from him anyway."

Mac continued, "I thought we could strike up a conversation with Johann in the afternoon session and perhaps invite him to join us for a drink, suggesting we move across the street to the Ritz Carlton where it won't be quite so crowded. One of us can disappear to the ladies room and come back some time later with an enthusiastic report about a cocktail party at the Ritz to which we have been invited. With luck he will say he is going and suggest we join him. If that doesn't work, we will just try to crash it, indicating that we had been told about it by a conference member who was going to bring us, but who had an emergency, and suggested we just go on without him. That'll work right?" Mac asked.

"Mac that's brilliant. But tell me, what the heck exactly is social entrepreneurism?"

"It is a not for profit organization dedicated to creating some sort of business entity that is self-sustaining, and which serves the financial needs of the organization. As example, you have an organization that serves homeless youth. You create a business where the kids produce a product that can be sold throughout the community. The process teaches them skills and purpose, gives them pocket money, provides food and shelter, instills a sense of responsibility and self worth, all the while creating the product that keeps their program alive financially."

"That explains it perfectly," Kate replied enthusiastically. "I can relate that easily should someone question me tomorrow. Now let's get our beauty sleep. We need to be on our toes from the first thing in the morning. I just hope I can sleep, because this is like an exciting mystery novel. I do love a mystery," Kate said amid a yawn.

The next morning, dressed in dark business suits, briefcases in hand, they took a taxi to the Plaza in time to get a roll and coffee, checked in and mingled near the entrance to the main conference room. Sure enough, Johann arrived and checked in. A few minutes later the tall man from the restaurant arrived, equally as dreary and menacing as he had seemed the night before. Ten minutes after the doors closed, Ivan Schwartz showed up with two men and went straight into the main conference room, waving away an attendant that approached him.

The large gilded and gaudy ballroom reflected another era long past. A certain elegance and opulence seemed out of place in these days of uncertainty, political campaigning, and a stock market on edge with the status quo.

The women made their way through the crowd, Katherine seated at Johann's table, Mackenzie at the Schwartz table. Not long after getting seated and introducing herself to her table mates, Mac was sipping her cup of coffee when a dour woman approached and asked if she was Ms. Honor. Mac nodded and said yes. She asked Mac to step to the side of the room and talk to the gentleman, pointing to an equally dour man standing near a doorway, clipboard in hand.

Mac walked toward the man, held out her hand and introduced herself. He remained motionless and in a low tone asked "What is your purpose here? Are you in the media?"

"No, I am not media," Mackenzie replied. "However I do occasional research work for a publication that is focused on global news. My friend and I are in New York on a mini-vacation. But we are involved in starting a new nonprofit with global focus, so we try to get involved in every global gathering we encounter."

"I must insist that you take no notes and record no presentations. This conference is strictly off the record for you. If there is any reporting, be it online or in print, of the content of this conference, you will be held responsible and I don't think you will appreciate the fallout. Also, some of the sessions are closed to outsiders. You are not permitted

31

entrance. Are we clear? Please make sure your colleague knows too. Oh yes, one more thing. If you are spotted taking notes or recording anything, you will be immediately removed. This is non-negotiable. So you have a choice—abide by the rules or leave now. Also Ms. Honor, just how did you get an invitation? You were not on our list, but added at the last minute."

"I have a friend with the World Bank who thought I might be interested in the conference and offered his invitation since he was unable to attend. I will inform my associate of the rules, and we will abide by them," Mac responded without a trace of emotion. She turned and left the man, lest he decided to question her more.

Mackenzie went to the ladies room to compose herself, scribbled a quick note to Kate, and headed back to her table, dropping the note in Kate's lap on the way. She was shaking as she sat down. She tried to hide her anger, but her hand was shaking as she reached for her glass of water.

That man had truly intimidated and angered her. It was unnerving, and she felt that she had glimpsed inside a very foreboding door behind which was total darkness. Mackenzie suddenly realized that she was again seated at Ivan's table and that he was looking at her, as if to read her thoughts.

This was the first time Mac had gotten a good look at this man, up close and personal. Here sat one of the world's wealthiest, most powerful and evil men. He was dapper, yet conservatively attired; a short somewhat stocky man of about 5'6", give or take. His face was rather square with Germanic bone structure. He was in his 70s, evidenced by the deep creases on his face and wrinkles around his somewhat puffy eyes. His wavy gray hair was casually combed back, without much fuss or style, a bit too long to be fashionable. His hands were elegant, well manicured, refined—hands unaccustomed to anything more strenuous than wielding a pen or ice tongs.

He spoke with a heavy accent, "Young lady you look as if you have seen a ghost. Are you alright?" Ivan Schwartz sat there in his handmade sleek pin-striped suit, probably from one of the fashion houses in Paris or London. It was understated, but elegant and the cloth was utter perfection. The silk shirt in contrast was a bit rumpled, as if slept in, and stood out as terribly un-chic when paired with the fabulous suit. The tie was merely there, void of color, creativity, or flair, like an afterthought, or necessary evil.

"Yes, I am fine. I should not have called home," Mac answered. "I got distracted with some family drama. This is my vacation. And I am thrilled to be able to attend this conference. I am always looking for ways to learn more about the global condition. Where are you from?"

"America," Ivan responded dismissively, with his distinct Germanic accent. Though he did not invite further conversation, Mac thought it was a good time to display an ignorance that would put him off guard.

Mac pressed on, "I'm sorry, what was your name again? So you're American. What company do you work for?" He was obviously a man who did not engage in idle chat, or embrace discourse with any lesser beings.

Ivan pretended not to hear her; more likely he just blatantly ignored her questions, and said something to the man to his side. There was a brooding, mournful look on his face, which Mac expected was permanently etched there amid the deep wrinkles and sagging skin. He was as beguiling as a Cobra snake.

Mac imagined him to be extremely high maintenance, and wondered how he had ever found a woman who could put up with him, much less such a young one? The answer of course was money, which for so many women was the elixir that overshadowed flaws of personality, appearance and romance; even character. He seemed aloof, detached from his surroundings, very controlled but subject to fits of anger that bordered on the juvenile, at times even manic. This was a complex man who intentionally kept to himself, to remain under the radar, making his work much easier. It was not clear if he disliked women, or merely held them in low esteem, but there was an attitude of contempt I could sense, as well as one of acute arrogance.

Mackenzie recalled having read an article on Schwartz from many years ago where he'd discussed his hatred of his mother for what he perceived to be her weakness. She was ill and he thought she should die, but she fought on and he regarded that as her cowardly attempt to avoid death. Surely those feelings must have affected his general regard for women as a life-long pattern.

Mac glanced over to the table where Katherine sat. She was engaged in a conversation with Johann and another woman, and while they appeared serious, they were all smiling. Mac hoped Kate could carry off their game plan with no glitches.

The breakfast items were being cleared from the tables, so Mac excused herself to go to the ladies room, catching Katherine's eye as she got up. They met in the hallway and together they slipped into an empty meeting room.

"So what is going on?" Katherine asked with worry in her voice and eyes.

"We are being watched. A gruff and humorless man summoned me to the side of the room and told me that there would be no note taking, no tape recording and that if caught we'd be evicted. But he also said there'd be a price to pay and we'd not like it."

"Oh Mac, don't you think we should leave now? I feel like we are in some hot water here and I for one am pretty uncomfortable. I just don't get what is going on here," Katherine complained.

"No. We need to remain, and appear calm and somewhat disinterested. We just have to be smarter and more careful. I am convinced that there is something going on here that is somehow vital. What I suggest is that about once an hour we take turns going to the lady's room and write down what we have heard, both at our tables and from the presenters. Keep a pad and pen in your purse and leave your briefcase unopened and under your seat. Also, we need to find out just what sessions are closed and what rooms they are in. I need to hear what goes on in at least one of those sessions."

Kate was anxious. "You realize you are creeping me out don't you? But I don't think I have ever been in a situation so exhilarating. So I am all in, even if the situation is horrifying," Kate whispered with a weak grin.

"Great! I'll take the first restroom break in about 45 minutes. I am going to excuse myself to make phone calls about 20 minutes later, and will see if I can monitor a private session. If you find out where one is being held, come and whisper to me. You keep tabs on what is happening here and about 3:30 I'll come back in here and sit at your table. I'll announce the cocktail party. Now good luck and watch and listen."

They left the room separately and headed back to their tables. The presenter was just starting and the topic was World Banking reform. An economist from Harvard began addressing the group, talking about the movement of national and regional independence into integrated financial interdependence. He spent the next 20 minutes with a power point presentation of graphs and charts, showing the flow of cash, financial dominance, ebb and flow of financial markets, and recent movement of various currencies.

Mackenzie watched and wished she had paid more attention to her business finance courses, but she made mental notes to commit to paper shortly. One thing was clear, she was desperate to ask some questions, but knew she could not take the risk. Schwartz meanwhile, was scribbling some notes, leaning over talking to someone on his right, and motioned to someone in another part of the room. Mac had no doubt that Schwartz knew exactly what was being discussed.

To Mac's utter joy, a man to the front of the room stood and asked, "It's obvious from what you are saying that over the last fifteen years much of the wealth of the Western world has been shifted to other parts of the world by way of deposits into the IMF and World Bank. What I'd like to know is how can countries like America, the UK, Germany and Japan continue to allow their wealth to be moved and still maintain a level of balance and continuity in their individual economies? In addition, what possible benefit can be found in weakening these economies, when they use their resources to help the less fortunate around the world; to produce jobs and products for global sale, and that keep the cycle in a growth mode?"

The speaker responded, "For too long much of the world has been locked in poverty with no options, while the industrialized nations have achieved great wealth. We are dedicated to creating a broader degree of balance and opportunity for the less fortunate nations you mention. They…"

The man cut him off, "Excuse me, but if that is so, just who is going to pay for this so-called opportunity? How will those wealthy nations maintain their ability to keep their country and others solvent if there is an overt effort to siphon funds elsewhere?" the man in the audience probed.

"As I was about to explain, we work with leading financial institutions in combining funds to advance the quality of life elsewhere. The leading nations will continue to produce a GNP that can sustain this flow of capital, with only moderate impact to their existing quality of life," the speaker continued.

The man persisted, "I'm sorry, but it would seem to me that the countries making the money to support other countries will either run out of sufficient productivity, or will just stop producing, finding it pointless. Sir, your premise seems naïve and flawed. Actually your concepts are stupid and defy any basic economic model. There is a huge danger for most of the world's financial resources to be placed in the hands of a few monetary institutions."

The presenter was obviously annoyed (thank God I had kept my mouth shut, Mac thought), as he went on, "Sir, you clearly do not understand global finance, and can't absorb the complexities of these principles in a brief presentation. First of all, each country pledges to a long-range obligation. There will be one world order. There are consequences if countries don't maintain their level of contribution. Secondly, our objective over time is that the countries who receive this financial assistance will one day be able to produce a portion of their elevated economic needs, and help other countries coming along behind them. Now, moving along."

But the man in the audience, now himself angry, again persisted, "Sir, I'll have you know I have a Doctorate in economics; I have worked with a number of global banks. I understand very well what you are saying, and I am telling you straight out, your concept won't work, can't sustain itself, and will collapse, at the eventual cost of the countries that are being drained of capital. And What then? What countries will pick up the slack and tab? None sir. None. Now what possible good can come of such a twisted, foolish economic scheme? Enlighten me, us, with some reasonable objective. If this is what is being touted as world order and justified sharing of wealth, then I am saying your premise is utter crap; and I am saying this is subterfuge for control of the world's wealth. Is that clear enough for you?"

The speaker, red in the face, could have easily killed the audience member. Rather than give credence to the statements just made, the speaker opted to ignore the comments and move on. Meanwhile, someone tapped the audience member on the shoulder and motioned him to the back of the room. A soft buzz spread through the room.

The first session was brought to a close and people dispersed for a 15-minute break before the next session began. One could see from reaction and attitude those who were on the 'inside,' and those who were on the outside. Mackenzie thought those on the outside must be very uncomfortable with what they were hearing. She knew how upsetting it was to her. She decided to follow Schwartz, who was moving down the hall in intense conversation with another man. Lagging behind them were two men who were surely body guards, beefy bodies whose heads were turning constantly as they checked out each person moving through the area.

Schwartz and his companion entered a room at the end of the corridor, the body guards following behind them. Mackenzie hurried down the corridor and into the adjacent room. It was dark save for a shaft of light coming through draperies at the window. She decided to leave the lights off, but to pull the drapery slightly to the side. She checked the wall and realized it was a partition so was hoping the speaker would be using some amplification.

By now Kate was back into the main meeting room, having made her notes from the first session. The man who had asked the questions in the first session sat at her table and she could tell he was not happy.

Kate commented, "You were very brave to press that man for answers to your questions. I gather you're not happy with his answers?"

"That guy must think we are all idiots. He said a handful of key countries could maintain an indefinite transfer of wealth with only moderate impact to their citizens. Utter nonsense. What he is proposing will destroy at least this country. And when I say destroy, I mean literally, in ways you can't even imagine."

Kate sat there with her mouth open, eyes wide, not believing what she was hearing. She wished she could grasp what was being discussed, but she was hopeful she could learn a bit more here, so she pressed on. "I have to admit I'm woefully uninformed about financial matters. I was not very clear about his points, until he mentioned a transfer of wealth. That can't be a good thing. What did you get from his talk?"

"I am an international banker. I see warning signs of an economic meltdown. The U.S. has been shipping more jobs overseas, and a major percentage of our manufacturing. Economic factors within several countries show a slowing of GDP, tightening of financial markets, increased rates of unemployment, and declining values of some major corporations and currencies. Overall the signs are not good. Most industrialized countries are spending too much, and going into too much debt. Certainly we in the U.S. are, so I can see a few years out being in serious financial crisis. Imagine your own personal banking. You have income of say $50,000 a year, but you buy furniture, clothes, etc., and you spend $58,000 a year. Over time, the negative amount grows just as does your deficit, and you either have to borrow money to keep paying your bills and covering your expenses, or you have to revise your budget and stop spending."

He continued, "It's not the potential for an economic crisis that worries me as much as the concept of one-world order which is a code for big government and control. If you want to explore a frightening situation, look into that. And while at it, check out the World Bank. I think you will be shocked." With that, he stood and walked out of the room.

Kate sat there thinking about what had been said, and suddenly realized that there were comparisons between the concept of a world government and biblical prophecies, knowing something was very wrong and widespread. She turned her attention to the new speaker, wondering how Mackenzie was doing.

Mackenzie had managed to remain hidden in the dark room during what proved to be an explosive mind numbing, interactive presentation.

It was at times difficult to hear, often because some of the people speaking had thick foreign accents. Fortunately she had brought with her a funky lighted pen, a gizmo she'd had for years and never used. It proved its value in this one instance. Bless those long-life batteries!

Mac knew that what she had been listening to was shocking. She also knew that it would take her some time and research to fully grasp what was being said, much less the implications of it all. Her head was pounding and she actually felt sick to her stomach. The group was going to break shortly, from what she could hear, so she wanted to exit her hiding place and return to the main room. As she was about to open the door she heard two men talking on the other side.

"Listen, you are to be in Chicago fully prepared at 8 AM on Monday. No excuses, no delays, no glitches. If the weather is expected to be bad, then go a day early. He has been very clear about this. If you are not ready and present at 8AM you will be dismissed. Your counterpart from Geneva will arrive on Saturday, and trust me, he'll be there sharp as a knife. Once DN has been briefed, you come back and you'll await word from Mr. Schwartz. A messenger will be delivering some material to you tomorrow morning. You need to study it as it is background information for your next meeting with Mr. S. You got all that?"

"Yes. Is Schwartz sending me back to Eastern Europe or do I get Washington this time?"

"I don't know the schedule. Something is going on. You'll hear about it in Chicago anyway, and I'm not supposed to mention anything, but Mr. Schwartz has decided to drop his support, of, you know. He believes DN will go the distance and anyway, they have an understanding. It'll shake things up a good deal when she finds out, so be ready. I've got to get over to the cocktail party before Schwartz arrives. You coming?"

"No. I think I'll head home. I have a feeling I'm going to be on the road for awhile, and want to spend some time with the family. I'll be in touch over the weekend. Good night."

Mac slowly opened the door; the hallway was empty so she hurried down to the main ballroom, and slipped into the chair next to Katherine. They exchanged wide-eyed looks that all but shouted "OMG," but each resisted the urge to spill their guts right then and there.

Mac spoke to Kate so Johann could hear, "Well, I just sat in on a fascinating session about global trade. Oh, and a Mr. Grant invited us to a lovely cocktail party when this wraps up, across the street I think, at the Ritz Carlton. Sounds like fun. We should go don't you think?" Mac was trying to be upbeat and light, but her gut was in knots.

"I was just talking to Mr. Adler here, about joining us for a cocktail. Johann, my friend Mackenzie said we we're invited to a little get-together over at the Ritz. How about you join us?" Katherine inquired. "Oh, sorry Johann, this is Mackenzie Honor; Mac, this is Johann Adler."

"Nice to meet you, Ms. Honor. I am due at that party too I think. I have a business meeting as well, but I'll be happy to accompany you over there and have a quick drink. Ladies please excuse me a moment. I have to chat with a colleague. When I return, we can head over to the Ritz." Johann stood, bowed slightly, and departed the room.

Mac leaned over to Katherine and whispered, "We are in the middle of a hornet's nest. There is no way we can press to find out much information at this cocktail party. Our goal is to mingle quickly, to get business cards on the pretext of doing an informational interview at some point in the future. We'll need to move through the group rather quickly as I don't think we'll be given much time there."

"Kate, shall we freshen up? Let's go now while waiting for Mr. Adler." The two women headed toward the ladies room but Mac cautioned her to not discuss anything in the restroom.

Outside the restroom Mac grabbed Kate's arm and whispered, "We have much to discuss and figure out. I need to know what you have heard, and vice versa, and we have to do some major digging. If I am right, we are going to need some serious help too. We also need to check out the people at this cocktail party and try to figure out what their connection is, if any, to all of this. Keep it light and airy till we have gotten out of that hotel."

Not long after returning to their table an argument broke out between two men at a nearby table. It started off being merely a bit heated, but it did not take long before both men were embroiled in a loud shouting match that was joined by others at the table. It had something to do with comments made in a break-out session.

Mac was sure she had never attended a convention or conference where there was so much secrecy, hostility, and arguing, much less a foreboding air of danger. Within moments two men appeared out of nowhere at the table embattled in argument. One of them grabbed the shoulder of one of the men arguing, leaned down and said something in his ear. He went instantly silent. The other burly man made a brief comment to the table and then the two escorted out the man who had been enraged. The look on his face was somber, but Mac saw terror in his eyes as he looked at her when being shoved out to the hall. As the large double doors opened he was given a push and Mac could see him slightly lose his footing before he straightened up and left the area.

"Great, here is Johann!" exclaimed Katherine in a light and cheerful voice. "Johann, I think we are all ready for a cocktail. May we still accompany you to the little cocktail party?"

"Ladies, as I said earlier, I do have a business meeting, but plan on stopping by the gathering briefly. I'd be happy to accompany you. Please understand that I won't have time to visit or introduce you around. I'm afraid you will find it rather stuffy and not much fun. You're on your own once there. Okay?"

"Mr. Adler, thank you. We appreciate the escort and we won't be there long either. I don't know about Katherine, but I am exhausted, and hungry. So I think we'll be seeking out an early dinner and an early bedtime. I am curious if there are any special presentations tomorrow that we should plan on taking in?" Mac inquired.

Adler commented, "Ms. Honor, there will be a few sessions tomorrow, but I believe most if not all of them will be closed to invitees only. I don't think there will be anything you'd find interesting. It sort of boils down to high finance issues that few of us understand. Boring stuff you ladies should not be subjected to. Were I you, I'd just enjoy your vacation. Have you been to the Museum of History? Marvelous facility; highly recommend it."

They gathered up their belongings and headed through the hotel. Katherine did a sterling job at engaging Johann in chit-chat. He likely hated every minute of it, but at least he was off guard and no doubt regarding us as harmless if irritating. She probably invited him to church or a bible study, **Mac thought to** herself with a chuckle. They headed out the main entrance and across the plaza to the Ritz Hotel. Once inside, they went straight to the elevators, bypassing the lobby abuzz with guests checking in or heading out for the evening.

While waiting for the elevator, Kate said, "I had quite a good time today meeting a lot of strange and interesting people. I even had the opportunity to invite Johann to church," Katherine chided with a smile. "Oh just kidding." Johann stood in silence, ignoring us. **Mac sighed,** "Sometimes I think you can read my mind. It's remarkable and frankly unnerving."

####

CHAPTER THREE

Most of our obstacles would melt away if, instead of cowering before them, we should make up our minds to walk boldly through them.

Orison Swett Marden

The old world charm and ambiance extended to every nook and cranny of this elegant hotel. The threesome went to the eighteenth floor of the Ritz Carlton and was soon at the entrance to the designated party suite. It was huge and very tastefully appointed. Several large windows faced out over Central Park, with overstuffed furniture, appealing artwork; and subtle, indirect lighting created a warm and inviting room that was in contrast to the group of somber faces staring at them as they entered.

A butler took their coats and bags and pointed them to a bar in the corner. Off to the side was a large dining room with a huge spread of inviting food. To the other end of the living room was a large bedroom. A bar was set up in a corner adjacent to a powder room, and another door, perhaps leading to an adjoining suite. There were about twenty people in the living room, standing together in small groups, talking quietly. Johann nodded to a couple of people, but said nothing.

Drink in hand Mac nodded at Katherine, and steeling themselves for the upcoming challenge, they started working the room. Johann joined two other men in conversation, and then moved across the room to refresh his drink. Katherine and Mac wandered about the room introducing themselves, turning the conversation to their social entrepreneurial project. They voiced their desire to contact each person at a later time to conduct an informational interview regarding matters of concern to them and their venture. Most people were happy to hand over a card and be done with the two women. None of guests invited conversation, so the women took their cue and moved to the next group.

Mac's head was still pounding, so she decided to take a break and grab a bit of food from the buffet. While standing alone in the dining room she took the time to observe the people in the living room. This was not an American business group. It was somehow foreign, even though she did not hear that many accents; there was a look and attitude that seemed appropriate for a collection of foreigners. Even the clothes and shoes spoke of European design, not American. They could have been from most any country in Europe, or perhaps professors at various liberal colleges. No man or woman seemed any bit the warm and friendly American, as the world regards us.

She shook her head, thinking to herself, "You are being silly. You are seeing spies and conspiracy at every encounter. Your old life is getting the better of you. Get a grip old girl. These are probably just foreign bankers, bored with seminars, hungry like me, up to nothing more than sharing cocktails and minimal chat. Get a grip silly woman!"

Mackenzie was standing there lost in thought as Ivan Schwartz and two companions entered. She slipped further back into the room and out of sight, her antenna in full operational mode. It may have been some time since she was faced with demands of intrigue and secrecy, but one does not become inept due to passage of time.

Ivan Schwartz shook hands with a small group just beyond the entry, then introduced one of the men with him to the group. The other who entered with Schwartz held back just to the side, saying nothing. One of the men in the group, a short man with curly gray hair, bushy dark eyebrows, a somewhat bulbous nose framed by a pleasant round face and blank eyes, pulled Schwartz aside to a corner of the room by a window

They were engrossed in serious conversation, their voices barely audible. Mac moved across the room to a couple standing nearest Schwartz and his friend. After exchanging idle pleasantries, she pretended to be absorbed in the view, slipping closer to the window. She took out her cell phone and pretended to take photos, while trying to overhear their conversation.

The short man said, through clenched teeth and tightened jaw, "Ivan you bastard. I've funneled over $23 million into your organization. For my generosity you assured me you would get the hedge fund matter taken care of. You were to use that money as we'd agreed, not to fund your girl. I've got to turn around $150 million within sixty days; the market's down, and payouts are getting harder to process. I need you to keep your word, now."

Schwartz glared in silence at the little man as he spoke. When he finished, Schwartz lowered his voice, leaned in toward the man and said, "You ignorant putz. It's not my fault your business is in trouble. It's not my responsibility to bail you out. I don't give a damn that you're in trouble. I'll release your $23 million, but the rest is on you. Do you hear me putz? You disgust me. The only reason you are in the picture is because I can launder money through you and get it redirected without anyone knowing. That, and I can access your investor list, which has proven beneficial over the years. If you weren't my cousin I'd piss on you. Now keep your mouth shut. You'll get the $23 back. And I'll have about $300 that I need to move to Palestine in about two months. This time, I don't want my money bundled with anything else. You move it, get your fee and that's it. We are clear, right?"

Apparently the little man was not used to being pushed around or spoken to in that manner. He bristled to the point that you could almost sense hair on his neck standing up. He swung around emitting an audible hissing snarl, sputtering out his words, "You prick, don't mess with me, and don't threaten me. I can buy and sell you. I've done you favors because you're family. I won't be jerked around by you or anyone. You mess with me or even try to screw me, and I swear on the graves of your parents that I'll expose your game, your whole plan and you'll be run out of this country on a stake. You hear me prick?"

In a proverbial Mexican standoff, the two men stood, glaring at each other. It felt like the first one to blink or look away lost the game. These were two men of money, accustomed to getting their way, using people and power for their own purposes, and not backing down to anyone. So in a manner appropriate to such qualities, they both dismissed each other with a turn of the heel, each going a different direction.

⸝ man returned to the window, fresh drink in hand he stood
⸝g out across the Plaza as he took a sip of his drink, then
⸝ glass on the table. Mac heard him sigh as he took both hands
anu ⸝ ⸝thed his hair back, and then continued to gaze out the window.

She stood still, puzzled, trying to figure out exactly what they were talking about. First she needed to know who the little man was, so she could check him out. This whole thing was curiouser and curiouser.

Ivan returned from the hallway, likely having made a phone call. A woman came up and whispered into his ear, he nodded in acknowledgment, and then moved to the bar for another drink, followed by the two men who had entered with him. All three went behind the bar and through the door.

Another man moved past the bar and entered the same door; then another and another. Johann Adler was next to follow the group.

Mac heard her stomach growl, suddenly starving, so went back to the dining room. The butler came into the dining room and placed several plates of finger food on a large tray. She asked, "Are you clearing up the food so soon?"

"No," he replied. "I'm taking some food into a private meeting. They will need some food for their long meeting. Dinner will be served later." He left the room with a large tray and entered the same door.

The identity of the little man prompted Mac to go up to one of the few groups remaining, chatting with Kate. She introduced herself, and then asked, "I think I recognize the short man with the curly gray hair who was standing over by the window, but it's embarrassing, I can't recall it. Do you know him? I wanted to say hello but it would be bad form to not use his name."

The woman to my left nodded, responding "Oh you mean Barnard that just went to get a drink? Barney Madinski, or Mr. Wall Street as some call him. Do you know Barney? He's not very sociable unless with his close personal friends, or investors. If you aren't one or the other, he rarely speaks."

Mac shrugged, "Oh, no I guess I don't know him. He looks like an old acquaintance. It's a good thing I didn't go up and make a fool of myself. Kate dear, I'm going to have one short drink and then we should be on our way for our dinner reservation, don't you think?"

She went to the bar, which was now unattended, poured some scotch into a glass, then slipped past the bar and into the door that had swallowed quite a few people. Sure enough, there were ten people sitting at a round table and four others sitting in the background. In front of them was a television screen—they were listening to a man from China while a woman stood to the side of the room translating. The reaction to my barging in was instant and dire. One man took the screen to dark and muted the sound; another yelled at me "What the hell are you doing in here? Get out now. This is a private meeting you fool."

"I am so sorry. I thought this was the door into the restroom. I am not feeling well and was making a dash. Please forgive my intrusion," I stammered as I backed out of the room.

Katherine was now at Mac's side, helping her remove herself from the doorway before the door was slammed in her face. "What's happening for God's sake?" Kate questioned with real concern.

"Can you get me to the restroom please, now?" Mac quietly begged her. "Don't make a fuss, just act as if I am a bit faint." At that moment she thought she might really faint.

Fortunately people were not paying much attention as they squeezed into the powder room. Katherine stood there staring at Mac with her arms folded across her chest and Mac collapsed onto the toilet seat.

"What in the world is going on?" Kate pressed. "I am not sure I am cut out for this skull and crossbones life, much less that of an undercover spy. I don't know if my heart can take it. Perhaps this is God's way of telling us to butt out. Maybe?"

"Good grief I am too old for this assignment. I admit that we have bitten off a bit more than I originally expected," Mac responded. "But we have started the process, and now we owe it to ourselves at the very least, to sift through what we know or think we know, and whatever else we can find out. I realize this is not the restful fun vacation we bargained for, and that some of this has a sinister feel to it. What if, now hear me out, what if we have stumbled on to a plot of some sort, a plot to control international finance, or a plot to weaken America in some economic way, or even a plot to control the next Presidential campaign?" Mac held her head in her hands.

Kate turned quickly and asked, "What assignment? What are you talking about? What assignment?"

"Never mind for now. Let's get out of here and go get some dinner someplace quiet. I have a headache, my nerves are frayed, I am hungry, and I feel like I am going to throw up."

"Besides, we need to regroup and start to make sense out of all of this. If I can remember the location, I know a charming little place with terrific food in the upper East Side just a few blocks away. I'd suggest walking but I am a wreck. So Kate dear, let's cab it. You exit now and gather up your stuff. Give me a few minutes and I'll be right behind you." Mac waved Kate to leave so she could calm down.

She pulled herself together, dabbed some cold water on her face, applied some lipstick, and returned to the living room to gather her things. To her utter shock Ivan Schwartz was standing in the room off to the side, arms folded, looking, well, looking very threatening. He motioned Mac to come over to him.

"Why, hello there, Mr. Schwartz. I did not think I'd see you here. I wish you'd arrived sooner. My friend and I are so tired; we are getting ready to leave now. We won't be attending the conference tomorrow. We've fallen behind on our shopping and theatre."

Schwartz glared at Mac as he spoke, "Young lady, shut up. Do you know who I am? Hmmm? I don't know who you are, who you work for, or what you two are up to, and I don't really give a damn. You have barged in to areas that are none of your business, that do not concern you, and it stops, NOW! You and your friend go home. Trust me, matters of international banking and finance should not take up your time. I am a man of some considerable power. I doubt that you want to know just how much power I can wield if I need to. Go home. Do we understand each other? You go home and get your nose out of my business."

"Mr. Schwartz, are you threatening me? I mean, I'd not like to think that you are. That would not be good. I don't know who you are, and I admit that my friend and I are over our heads with global economic matters. But our lack of sophistication in that area is hardly cause for you to get huffy or threatening with me. We have shopping; dining, theatre and an hour of luxurious massage yet to do. Now if you will excuse me, we are off to dinner. I shall assume we'll not cross paths again. Enjoy your conference. Good night Mr. Schwartz."

They grabbed up their coats and briefcases and walked slowly out of the suite, feeling the burning eyes of Schwartz on their backs; then all but flew to the elevator. Mac could feel her heart pounding on the ride down to the lobby. She was sure as they exited the elevator they both looked like deer in the headlights. Silently they hurried to the exit and into the first taxi. Mac gave the driver general directions and while it took a few twists and turns, they ended up at the place she had recalled.

Seated, they both ordered a stiff drink and took deep breaths. Even Kate was ready for a wine. Mac on the other hand needed a straight shot of vodka. It was that kind of evening.

"Mackenzie, I heard what Schwartz was saying to you. It was as if he was going to set goons on us if we did not fold up our tent and sneak away in the night. I'm scared. I'm nervous. I think we should mind our own business. I mean, we are two private citizens, two middle-aged women from suburbia. What the heck can we do up against some billionaire and God knows who else? Its nuts to think that we can bring down any one of them, or do more than be irritating like a flea in their shorts!" Kate was clearly agitated.

Mac started laughing. God she needed a laugh. "I know I know. This is not what I expected either. I thought we'd get information or a great tidbit of news to leak to the media. It was a lark initially, but now, it is something quite different. I am unnerved too. That guy almost buckled my knees. Did you see his eyes? They were like the eyes of some beast—cold, dark and evil. This man is of course just a man, yet something about him sends chills down my spine. But, and this is a big but—we find ourselves unwittingly and unwillingly in possession of disparate bits of information that appear to hold as yet unknown common denominators. I feel that we have a puzzle here, missing pieces, but with enough of them in place that we can pull an image out of the fragments. I fear the resulting information or image will prove to be a warning to be shared."

Kate pressed Mac further, "OK so we pull this puzzle together enough to make some sense of it all. Then what? What are we to do with it? I mean, we live in Portland. Portland is hardly a news Mecca, hardly the center of the nation's political or economic pulse. And it's hardly at the center of the national Christian movement either. I don't understand what we can do, short of walking up to Schwartz and telling him what we know and that he'd better stop being a bad guy. And what warning do we give him? He'd laugh in our faces."

Mackenzie sat sipping her cocktail, then said "The way I see this situation, we have three choices. We can ignore it all and go back to our daily lives never knowing what we've let happen till after the fact. Or we can pull as much as possible together and see what the more obvious implications are, and then turn everything over to some reporter. Or we can pull it together, see what we have, and based on what shows up, decide who best to take it to that can do something with it. So here is what I think we should do. How about we just relax and enjoy our dinner. We'll go back to our suite and do some research, take some notes and get a good night's sleep. Tomorrow morning we'll order room service, spread out names, notes, comments and our research and start pulling pieces together, by topic and person. We'll spend the day at it. No later than 4PM we'll see what shows up and if there is a clear picture, decide with whom to discuss it."

"It's likely that the person or persons we would wish to talk with would be in either New York or Washington, in media or security. If we agree that this needs to see the light of day, and we can agree on someone to take it to, we'll see about getting an appointment for the following day. Can you give me one more day? Can we really dig into what we have and try to make sense of it? Will you give it your best shot tonight and tomorrow Kate?"

Kate was sitting perfectly still, listening, when she finally spoke, "Mac, I love and support you. You surely must know this is not the trip or vacation I had been expecting, wanting or needing, don't you? I am feeling, well, ignored, taken for granted? The tickets are mine and I could have brought John with me and done just as I want with no stress. Now, you want me to spend one entire day sitting in a stuffy hotel room?"

Mac was surprised at the degree of petulance and pouting coming from Kate. Mac sipped her vodka, looking out over the dining room. She did not feel comfortable in responding just then. "This fish is perfection, so light and moist and the sauce is heavenly. I am going to have to recreate this sauce. Have you decided on your main course yet?"

Silence continued, leaving Mackenzie's thoughts to wander. It is true that this trip had gotten out of hand and was far from what she had expected. She had to talk to Jack about this, and some changes needed to be made. Ten years ago she'd not have thought much about the risks. She thrived on the danger and excitement, which is why she got involved in the first place. But in recent years she longed for a more peaceful, normal life. She was estranged from her son, or at least their relationship seemed stiff, strained, and uncomfortable for them both. For some reason, her son was prominent in her thoughts now. Words could not convey how much she wished to spend a day with her son doing fun and goofy things, talking about anything, hanging out, getting reacquainted, just the two of them.

Mac realized that her work, and the need to keep it secret, had created a wasteland of relationships. Over the years none of them seemed as important as her work. Men came and went, and over the years none had stood out as a star, none but Wayne that is.

Every time Mac thought of Wayne she felt horribly sad and usually cried. She'd not allow herself to do that now, but the sadness came on anyway, enveloping her as if a tattered blanket.

Wayne was a man ideally suited to Mackenzie. He was an ex-military officer and pilot who had gone on to assume an important management role with a large mid-west company. The two met at a conference in Chicago a few years ago, a little over a year after his wife had died of cancer. Mac had long been without any meaningful relationship and assumed one was not in the cards for her.

Their brief meeting was of monumental impact to both of them. They had dinner a couple of times, spent an afternoon wandering a museum and then both returned to their respective cities, continuing to communicate by email and phone on a daily basis. It was not long before Wayne decided to fly out to Seattle to visit with Mac. During that week their relationship moved from joyful friendship to serious romance. They connected on so many levels, able to sit next to one another and feel a bond in total silence; or laughing and chatting about any topic. He gave her a sense of peace, security, happiness she had not known for a long time, if ever. She gave him a sense of fun, laughter, light-heartedness that lifted his spirits and made him feel whole again.

With all the good between them, it was still a surprise when some weeks later on his next visit, Wayne proposed. It took Mac less than a nanosecond to say yes, so positive she was that this was the best thing to ever happen to her since her son was born. The two set about making plans for an early January cruise, buying a new home in the Seattle area, getting his home sold and him relocated, and the wedding—a simple summer affair the next year.

During his two-week visit and shortly before he was to leave for a family gathering over Thanksgiving, he complained of flu symptoms. She dropped him at the airport, kissed him, and planned on seeing him in 3 weeks. On Thanksgiving Day he phoned, sounding terrible. He said he'd seen a doctor in an effort to feel better, and the doctor had urged him to return home immediately. He had cancer.

As quickly as Wayne declined, so too did Mac's mental and physical health. She made plans to spend the holidays with him, taking care of him but to her shock and disgust, his adult kids refused to let her come. One of his kids and family moved in with him and instantly began isolating him. Thereafter Mac and Wayne spoke only when his family was out for a time, but often enough that Mac knew he was declining rapidly, barely able to talk. Wayne eventually, much too late, had surgery. He'd lost almost half his body weight, was being fed by a tube, and was weak and in pain. Mac was beside herself, spending most nights crying tears of loss and misery.

After several weeks of silence where Mac had been unable to reach anyone by phone, she phoned Wayne's home and to her shock was told most matter-of-factly that Wayne had died. Thinking of him now her heart ached, still missing and longing for him after such a long time. She knew that a huge piece of her heart had died with him as had her dreams.

At the time and since, she had harbored end of life thoughts, not wanting to go on. She was not one to 'share', and kept most of her personal life private. So no surprise that her friends had no idea of how bereft she was after Wayne's death. Even now she felt such a void in her life. Ah, but, she must shake these thoughts off and return to matters at hand.

Mac brought her focus back to the table and Kate, sitting across from her. She did not realize she was crying, until Kate said, "Mac what's wrong? I did not mean to hurt your feelings. I don't want you to fret. We are in this together. Of course I'll stick by you tomorrow and see what you come up with, okay? So please don't cry. Things will work out."

"But I have a question. I have been observing you during this conference. You seem a bit edgy, but strangely composed and confident. So how come? What is in your past that enables you to deal with such evil without peeing your pants? You have me bursting at the seams with curiosity! No fair. As for your request, sure, no sweat, we can cram in some other stuff in a couple of days. As long as I get lunch at Tavern on the Green, get to see a play, and can wander the hallowed halls of Bloomies, I'm good. Waiter—another round for her and tea for me please. You have my undivided attention back at the hotel. Right now I want to enjoy this lovely little place and have a good meal. No more spy stuff till later, OK? Except for one thing, you should answer my question girlfriend."

Mac chuckled, "Great! I need to relax too. You know, I ate here with Andre a few years ago and I recall the food was fabulous. I think I am going to have the duck, and the special salad. The fish course was wonderful. And I already know I am having a Grand Marnier soufflé for dessert. Lunch at Tavern on the Green eh? Gosh, I've not been there in years. In fact the night Andre brought me here we were going to dine at the Tavern but it was closed for a private party."

Kate persisted, "Mac! Come on, tell me. Tell me why you were crying and tell me what warning you see out of all this."

Mac smiled and said, "You know what they say, if I tell you I'll have to kill you. Honestly I did not know I was crying. I was thinking about Wayne and darn but I can't seem to avoid crying each time he enters my mind. My heart still aches over his loss. As for warnings, just relax. There is nothing all that special really. I just have a gut feeling about all of this. I suppose it is being exposed to a lot of powerful people. Remember, I worked on the Hill. Actually they don't scare or impress me. But, this guy is different. There is something rather 'other-worldly' about him. I can't put my finger on it, but he is not your average evil dude."

They chatted, laughed, sighed over the wonderful food, sipped a glass of wine, devoured their superbly fluffy soufflés with the equally delectable Crème Anglaise sauce, and managed to avoid any mention of their last 2 days. After a leisurely dinner, they hailed a taxi and headed back to their hotel, just too full to walk a minute much less a mile.

Once in their room, they kicked off their shoes, put on their robes, and settled down with their laptops. They divided up Kate's business cards, the roster of those at the conference, the additional names they picked up, and started digging, without any idea where they were headed from this exercise.

Since Mac had already been digging up information on Schwartz, she wanted to see what connections, if any, existed between the people she had identified and Schwartz. Various names started to pop up in conjunction with one of Schwartz's activist groups. Mac had looked at it before, but brought it up again. As she went down the list of board members she noticed names that appeared in other radical groups' list of donors. To her surprise the petite Barney Madinski appeared on the board of Schwartz's favorite organization. Mac wondered what Ivan got out of that association. He was obviously wealthy beyond most, and well known. It's time to check Madinski out, Mackenzie thought.

She poured over various websites to learn about the Madinski operation, which consisted of investment banking, asset management where he handled stock portfolios, some hedge fund activity on his own and with Schwartz. He was a big deal on Wall Street, revered for his extraordinary success in building fortunes.

"Oh my God!" Mac shouted. "You remember that little man with the curly gray hair at the party? Guess who he is related to? None other than Ivan Schwartz! They are cousins. Their families are both from Eastern Europe, though Barney's apparently left before the War. I tell you Kate, this is remarkable in its complexity. We need a full CIA team to identify all the players and how they are all connected. One thing we need to do to help us pull the pieces together—as we come up with a name that appears more than twice, let's make up slips of paper with the person's name on it so as we assemble the bits and pieces we can keep track of the web of connections. We'll surely need dozens for Schwartz, Madinski, and others."

Kate, absorbed in her reading, just mumbled and carried on, essentially ignoring Mac. Mackenzie had found several articles on Ivan and his wife Irma, reflecting a man of extreme privacy, an active and generous philanthropist (with caveats), a man who lived a life of the mega-rich with homes in various places in the U.S. and abroad, and a family with whom he did not seem especially close, based on the articles. One tabloid showed a photo of Ivan with a woman who claimed to be his mistress.

Ivan was besieged by requests from wealthy people to take over their portfolios or give advice. He would refer them to Madinski, not wanting to tie up his time or resources. Besides, he really didn't want social ties. For him it was all about business, and social connections were an interference, a waste of his time.

It was very curious to Mac that two men of the same generation and background, the same Jewish family, who each had amassed an enormous multi-billion dollar fortune, and both were anti-social, anti-Jew and ruthless. Neither man had a close relationship with his children either. Mac wondered if Madinski was as vile, evil and vicious as his cousin Schwartz? She'd have to see about that.

###

CHAPTER FOUR

A good puzzle, it's a fair thing. Nobody is lying. It's very clear, and the problem depends just on you.

Erno Rubik
Hungarian Inventor

Before they realized it, the clock read 2:30 AM. They shut down their laptops and with bleary eyes trundled off to bed. They were too tired to comment or analyze.

The wakeup call came at 8:30, in time for them each to grab a quick shower before their breakfast arrived. They pulled the table and chairs closer to the window for light and view, sat quietly sipping the first cup of coffee and staring out the window. Their minds were on overload and still groggy.

Kate let out a loud sigh, "At least the weather is not terrific, so we won't feel quite so bad being cooped up today. Does that work for a rosy spin so early in the morning?"

"Honey, the day will pass and I am guessing quickly. We have lots of work to do. I suggest we get started, and take a break every couple of hours for a walk around the block and some fresh air. I feel sort of overwhelmed with all the information we have to explore, but what do you think about finishing what we were doing last night? Then we'll look up organizations and start doing a comparison. The trail will either be clear or require more digging. I was thinking just now that if we don't have a clearly defined point to all of this, we take it all home and continue to probe and investigate till we do."

"But if we have that ah-hah moment we then set about getting out information to the right persons. Does that sound like a plan?" Mac asked.

"Okay, let's get on with it!" Kate encouraged.

Over the next two hours they both zipped about the Internet, and at the end of that time they had gone through all the business cards and the roster of conference attendees. They printed out one sheet per person with the various notes, and then started with the first organization that appeared more than once and went from there. At the end of that process, it was break time.

A brisk 4-block walk and they were ready to get back to their work. Thankfully the maid service had done their room, so they had the rest of the day to work without interruption.

They next took the organizations whose names appeared multiple times and did a search on each. This proved to be a huge challenge because many organizations were fronts for others, or part of a network of allied groups. But they persevered at their task and in a couple more hours they had amassed quite a load of notes.

They stopped and ordered some lunch and tea, and then sifted through the organizations and stacked up those that had a common connection, either with another group, or company or person they had not yet investigated. But they were far from done—remaining were companies, foreign countries, and key people.

The suite was covered with sheets of paper spread on the floor and both beds, and on the furniture—mostly 1-4 pages in a stack, but there were a few that had several sheets of paper. Slips of paper with individual names were appearing on several stacks.

"Mac, take a look at this...you see this list of names? I have not checked the whole list, but so far out of a list of 87 people, 23 of them appear on our group of names we have been tracking. That's one in four. How about you check out this group? I am betting it shows up as part of a network and is linked to many other organizations," urged Kate.

"Kate, I am almost done with my lists. I'll do this group, then I want to dig some more into Schwartz and Adler. Then it's time to figure out what we have here." There was a knock at the door, with delivery of their tea and chicken sandwiches.

"Yes please! I am starving. I'll be done here within the hour," Kate responded. "If we are going to decide to get in contact with someone, we had probably better keep at this so we have some idea of where things stand by 4PM," Kate responded, her voice trailing off as she returned her focus to her computer.

"Mac, I started a search on an organization that appears on your list, *Socialist World Integration of Neo Environments*, and it shows numerous connections and sub-sets of other groups. I don't know where the basic common link is, but look at the names of these groups—*United Nationalists for International Taxation, Coalition of Hegemonic Agents for Neoliberal Global Economy,* and the list goes on. I swear this looks like a bunch of Communist groups; or at the very least, Socialist. Who thinks up these ridiculous names? What do you think?"

Mac looked down the list and was struck by how leftist they appeared. "I see what you mean. I wonder where they get their money. I wonder who is behind them, and what they really do. The names mean nothing really. They are signs of purpose, but could as easily be diversionary. This is looking more like a snake pit, isn't it? But there are a couple of innocuous names that stand out for their simplicity compared to the others. I have not heard of either, which means I need to investigate them. Have you heard of Apollo, or Tides?"

"I've not heard of any of these groups! But I agree, with such long leftist names, a one-word title is so obvious. I wonder what they are about? Hey let's take a break and have our tea and sandwiches before we resume this work. I'm starving."

After their lunch break the two women went back to their research and about an hour later decided that they had accumulated enough information to mull over and arrive at some sort of an interim conclusion.

Meanwhile, in a luxury condo on the upper East Side, a meeting was taking place to discuss the resolution of a problem. Seated in his lavishly decorated living room was Ivan Schwartz and his close-knit circle of goons who handled his 'special' situations. Ivan sat glumly staring out the window, swirling his 100-year old whisky absent-mindedly. Silence, but for a few nervous moves on the sofa.

Schwartz stood and walked to the sliding door to the large verandah, started to open the door, but changed his mind and turned to face the small group of men. "Okay. This is a thorn in my side. This is a nuisance that threatens to become far worse. I want you to keep them tailed at all times. I want to know exactly where they go, who they see, when they eat and where, I want to know everything. I want to know who they are calling, what they are saying, and most of all I want to know what they are working on."

"In addition, I want them scared, so scared they can't function; so scared they'll leave here immediately. Then when they leave here, I want them followed," Schwartz fumed.

A burly man with long blonde hair asked, "If they leave how are we going to follow them?"

"You damn fool, you'll follow them to where they live, Oregon I think it was. You will keep scaring them, keep following them, keep the pressure on till they cave and stop. You got that you putz?"

"Yes sir. Do you want them eliminated? Wouldn't that be easier and more reliable?"

"No No! You can't kill them. That would draw attention to me. That would create a need for an investigation. No killing. I want those two so frightened they are afraid to leave their pathetic little houses. So to start with, break into their room and take the computers and papers. Then some roughing up, especially that tall one, Mackenzie. An attempted kidnapping would be good; and making one of them sick enough to go to the hospital—good. I want a full report with and their work on my desk by 7 P.M; the day after tomorrow. And I'd better have news they have left town too."

"Now, about them leaving, George you pick someone to go with you. I want you on their plane, and I want that Mackenzie woman to have some sort of injury that has keeps her down. You stick to her like glue, hear me? Those silly women will not continue this exposure of me; they'll be too scared. Make sure of it. Now all of you get out of here."

Mac had a sudden chill rush over her body. She wondered if she might be catching a cold, since the room was plenty warm. No time for colds, too much work to do, she thought.

The stacks of papers had deepened as they shuffled pages into an existing group. It was stunning what a complex network this was, and while they did not yet understand how intricately it was entwined, it was easy to tell that this was a web that spread far and wide through many countries.

"Kate, let's divide up these stacks; then highlight connections and common denominators that exist in people, organizations, or their purpose. Once we have finished that we'll see what we have."

They slogged forward, growing ever more weary, and mystified. Mac suggested they take a short break and go for a walk around the block, so they grabbed up their coats and made their way to the street. It was good to move, to get some fresh air. By the time they got back to the room their heads were clear and they were somewhat revived.

The organizations they were studying had names that seemed trite, or some secret code known by a handful of insiders. In looking over the boards, employees and major donors, they discovered several names were on several boards, and of them, all had been working in a high level position with one of three previous White House Administrations. An additional group of about 30 people who were staff in these organizations had been on Committees or Congressional staff within the same three previous Administrations. Mac recognized some of the names, and knew personally a couple of people, such knowledge sufficient to give her grave concern.

The political ideologies of these groups were aligned based on the mission statements of the various organizations. And it was especially interesting to see that some private foundations were backing a number of these groups; foundations thought to be Conservative, but yet fully engaged with radicals and far left Liberals. Now that was confounding, and worrisome.

They switched their attention to foundations and companies, and their boards. It took a while, but they soon realized that this was so inbred, so incestuous a web of connection, one was struck by how few people were controlling so much—be it money, attitude, actions, or influence. This was the pinnacle of power.

The list of people read like a "Who's Who" from Wall Street, New York Society and Corporate America—the wealthy elite, supporting left-wing ideology? Could this be? How did this happen? Why? And how could they donate money without being connected to these radical groups? Mac continued through the papers, hoping that one name would stand out as the key link, the money guy, the inspiration; the glue that was holding all of these groups together.

Engrossed in their papers, they both were startled by a knock at the door. Neither of them had ordered anything and there was no maid's announcement. Kate gave a shudder as she slowly stood and went to the door, putting her finger over her lips to hush Mac. She looked through the peephole and the color drained from her face. Mac got up and moved quickly to the door to view who was there. Just as she leaned toward the peephole there was another knock, causing her to leap backwards. As she looked through the hole she recognized the face of the man who had been with Schwartz, as a body guard. Then another knock!

Kate whispered, "shhh, be quiet and he'll go away."

Instead, Mac responded behind the closed door, as she bolted it, "Yes? What is it?"

The man said, "I have a package for Ms. Justice, and it needs to be signed for."

"I'm sorry but Ms. Justice is not here. You can leave the package outside the door. I can't open the door as I am not dressed."

The man was agitated and said again, "I need to have a signature for this package. Look lady, you can sign, and sign you must. I can't leave the package without a signature."

"Just where is this package from," Mac asked. "I need to know who sent the package and what it is, since we are not expecting any package."

"I don't know lady. I was hired to deliver it. It's none of my business who or what. My service just assigned me to deliver it. I can't stand here all day schmoozing, I need to get a signature and get on with my schedule. You gonna sign or what?" he demanded.

"Like I said, I am not opening the door. Ms. Justice is not here. So either leave the package, or return it. I don't really care." Mac was getting irritated when she heard another voice in the hallway.

"Hey buddy, what's going on here? You bothering one of our guests? Well, you're outta here, either you leave freely now, or I'll be escorting you to a police car. What'll it be dude?"

The security officer from the hotel was on his rounds, thank goodness—more divine intervention!

Mac left the chain on the door and cracked it open to see both men standing there. "Sir, this man has been pounding on my door demanding to leave a package. We are not expecting anything, and I am not comfortable in accepting the package. Would you see that he leaves with it now," I pleaded.

"Yes ma'am, right away. Sorry he was bothering you. Okay dude, let's go. I wanna make sure you make it to the street without any detours, and with that package in hand. Now let's go."

The man swung around to leave, but before he left he slammed his fist into their door. The guard grabbed him by the neck and shoved him down the hallway. The two women stared at each other, both shaking. They now realized that someone knew where they were, and was trying to frighten them; and doing a dandy job of it too. Kate took my hands and started to say a prayer, asking for protection and their safety as they embark on this dark journey. AMEN!

Both women collapsed on the sofa in silence, still shaking and pale. After some time Kate spoke, "Mac, this is Schwartz, you know that. This is not just a warning. Oh he means to scare us, but I have a feeling there is more. In fact, I have a feeling there will be more. He wants us gone, one way or another. You realize that right?"

Mackenzie sat there, her mind reeling. Images, words, vignettes having to do with Schwartz were flashing through her mind like puzzle pieces—an endless array of random images and thoughts. She knew the answers were there but where?

Mac finally spoke, "Katherine I am so sorry. This is my fault. I knew Schwartz was dangerous, but honestly I did not expect any of this. I did not think we'd encounter him, much less incur his wrath. I am not used to being so rattled, and I admit I am unnerved. Still, I know we are sitting on some big answer to this puzzle. It is within our grasp and it's explosive. My gut is in overdrive now. I know a great deal about this guy but its all bits and pieces. What I must do and do fast, is to pull them together into some sort of plausible story."

Mac continued, "Listen Kate, I don't want to get either of us in any deeper. I'd like to pull all this information together in some sensible format, and deliver it to a key media person who will run with it. At that point we can wash our hands of it all, and resume our lives. Yes, I know, this is far and away just too much. What has me so stunned is this—with all the power mongers in the world, those who can make or break Ivan Schwartz, why would two women from Oregon upset him or cause him any awareness at all? Makes no sense. Something is wrong here, very wrong. I think we are sitting on a time bomb and I think he knows we are almost on to him."

Kate had walked over to their bar, pulled out some bottles, poured them straight into glasses and handed one to Mac. They drank in silence, their nerves starting to calm. Kate said she needed to call her husband, so she went into the bedroom and shut the door. Mac sat there sipping her drink, staring out the window, wishing all of this would go away. This was the first time she had been threatened and physically confronted and she did not like it one bit.

In the other room Kate reached John, "Johnny! Hi. I miss you. Oh nothing is wrong. Just feeling a bit homesick I guess. I am not a big city girl and this is one big city. Overwhelming ya know? No, I'm okay. It's just, well, just needed to hear your voice." With that Kate started to cry. John was initially irritated, but then he felt concern and demanded to know what was going on.

"Johnny, I have been helping Mackenzie. We went to a conference. It was sort of boring, but she needed to gather information. We met some really horrible people, and things have gotten a bit scary. I wish you were here."

John was obviously talking a lot, so after a long pause, Kate responded, "John stop! I will be okay. I am being a bit of a ninny, so alright I am. But I am not going to leave and come home tonight. I am not leaving Mac here. I am going to stay and we are doing our spa day. Tomorrow will be a better day. Now I am sorry I called because you are all upset. Listen, we will be okay. Mac is no fool, and we will hand over our information to someone tomorrow and then we have one day to play. Yes, I will be careful. Do not ask me about money again either. Is Mikey okay? How are the grandkids? Tell them I miss them and nana will see them soon. Are you doing alright on your own? Okay, I love you too. I'll give you a call tomorrow. Bye."

Kate came back into the living room and tossed back the rest of her drink. "Alright, let's get this crap job done. I am about to overdose on all this intrigue and mystery. The booze helped me get a grip, now I just want done."

They returned to their reading in silence, making occasional notes, trying to balance the unnerving experience with the stranger at the door and with all this information. Mac had four pieces of paper in her hands, looking back and forth between them, and then it hit her!

"Holy crap! I've just had an AH-HAH moment. I see the light! I was hoping for one name to stand out, but there are four—so far. Take a stab—who do you think they are? I was sure it would be the former President, but it isn't. Go on, guess," I urged Kate.

"Mackenzie, you know I can't guess and by the way there is no such thing as holy crap. God is the only one that's holy. I likely wouldn't know the names anyway. Just tell me," Kate insisted.

"Okay. The big kahuna on the list is none other than our Mr. Schwartz; the same Schwartz whose goon was just at our door. It seems he is intricately involved in a number of these organizations and groups. His primary organization, The International Shadow Coalition, claims to provide global consulting in matters of political unrest, governmental reorganization, strategic planning, and economic recovery. It sounds like a think tank that aids countries into or out of revolution. Schwartz has created a giant spider web that spreads far and wide," I told Kate.

"There are other names, but only one of them is totally familiar to me. She is a woman who was with a previous Administration. Since she left government she has been quite controversial, taking a leadership role in a very active, strident socialist group that is part of Schwartz's network. Another name is a Member of Congress and regarded as an up and comer, Damon Nadir. I don't know much about him, but he just announced a run for the Presidency. What is both startling and interesting is that he is clearly aligned with Schwartz but he has no experience, none, zip, nada. Wait a minute, Damon Nadir, DN, what do you want to bet he's the one we heard those men referring to? Perhaps Schwartz is looking for more power? Or he wishes to influence our Government? Schwartz also seems to be involved with more than one would-be presidential candidate, but it seems he's picked Nadir as his access to the golden ring," Mac related to Kate.

"So our list of organizations is tied together through Schwartz, and these other few people. It would also appear that some of the presidential potentials are involved too. They have some pretty far—out sounding entities that include New America Vision, Arab American Alliance, Progressive Coalition, Progress in Government, Dialogue for Change, Global Arab Alliance, Muslims for Change, United Nationalists for International Taxation, and that one you mentioned, Socialist World Integration of Neo Environments. What the heck is that? I've never heard of so many alliances, and call me suspicious, but this looks like a collection of groups that are not especially pro-American," Mac said shaking her head.

Kate responded, "This sounds like Jesus looking down on the last generation, seeing the world involved in a massive deception similar to what caused the destruction of Jerusalem. Hey, that Socialist World group, its acronym is SWINE! Is that not hilarious? I wonder who thought up that name, and don't you know they did not think of the Swine factor." She giggled.

"What the heck are you talking about?" Mac asked Kate.

She smiled knowingly and said "Never mind, we'll address the heavy stuff later."

Over the next hour they determined there were specific corporations, foundations, wealthy patrons, political figures and nonprofit organizations uniquely aligned at various levels, from boards of directors to employees, advisors to backers, and special interest.

Of the names that appeared over and over within the various organizations, the women tracked their backgrounds and found many of them to be foreign born, or with family ties abroad in countries not regarded as allies of America. They found men and women with expertise in banking, foreign relations, corporate espionage, opinion research, finance, fundraising, communications, terrorism, and a few with clandestine backgrounds.

One could argue that any one entity or individual was of a particular ideological persuasion, but at a high altitude overview (which was their perspective at that time), all players had a far left, even socialist agenda, from communist to extreme radical to very liberal.

Numerous platitudes and old sayings were rushing through Mac's mind, from "divide and conquer" and "strength in numbers" to "power corrupts absolutely" and "there are no accidents." No indeed, this collection of people was no accident. Their mentor did not accidentally select them based on their degree or former employers. They all had an agenda, a purpose and a shared ideology. The question was, to what end?

Standing out among the network of groups and individuals, aside from Ivan Schwartz and his cronies, were 3 entities, ACORN, Tides, and Apollo Alliance. Mackenzie had stumbled on Tides and from there the trail expanded. She now knew a good deal, but realized these groups deserved their own in-depth investigation. Still, at the surface it was clear how these three groups served a bigger picture.

Apollo's board was telling in and of itself. One man was head of the primary Schwartz organization; another, a 'green' communist with activism and radical ideas who is associated with various people in the Nadir camp; another the founder of ACORN; among others.

The organization was formed in 2001 but in 2004 revised their mission to support elections, and is closely aligned with Tides. Ah yes, Tides—this radically liberal, leftist group, which itself supports over 200 other leftist organizations and groups. It very cleverly has created a way for anyone to donate to liberal causes while maintaining their anonymity, via an online grant program.

Mackenzie was truly agitated, and said, "Kate listen to this. Tides Center and Tides Foundation are spread out nationwide among most if not all leftist groups. It funds environmental groups and causes, incubates newly formed groups, launders money for other organizations like PEW (thus putting up barriers to those who might wish to follow the money trail), manages PEW's three major projects such as journalism initiatives where reporters are trained in the proper PEW 'techniques', for planting stories and propaganda; and forming a clearing house of propaganda for leftist groups who engage in anti-war protests, slave reparations, earth liberation front, violent animal rights activists, black anarchists, and anti-American activists. Good God, this is appalling! And it does not stop there. They own and operate a network of credit card companies, mutual funds and phone service companies that attract investors. The money gets funneled into Tides and back out to support their activities."

Kate looked over the names of the groups, and what each implied. Mac could tell she was having a revelation, when she said, "You know, if these groups are working in some way against the United States, under the support and guidance of Ivan Schwartz, and there are one or more potential presidential candidates involved, this is like a Trojan horse arriving as a marvelous gift, but hiding a sinister plot".

Kate went on, "You and I come at things from different directions, you being influenced by political experience and knowledge and me by my relationship with God and the Bible. So what if I told you that some of the concerns you have voiced, some of the things that are starting to happen in this country and around the world, are actually talked about in the Bible? You may think this is far-fetched, given that the Bible was created over a period of 1600 years by many people, from long before Christ's birth to a century after his death."

"Each book from Genesis in the Old Testament, to Revelations in the New Testament, relates stories about the work of God, the birth, life and resurrection of his son Jesus; stories collected over time, and witnessed by Arabs and Christians. In addition, there are prophecies that stem from the word of God, carried forth by men of faith and godly wisdom. For those of us who are believers, we trust the word of God in the Bible. We believe without doubt or reservation how the story of mankind plays out. We know too that mankind has been given many warnings, many chances, to get it right, and in many instances has failed. It does not matter how or why, merely that we did not learn from earlier mistakes and repent, therefore have contributed to the downfall of our once-great civilizations."

"In ancient history there are events from the Bible that correlate to more recent events in medieval and modern times. In Chapter 11 of the Book of Revelations, the events that are man's eventual undoing are revealed. As a Christian I can look at those events and have a pretty good idea of how the coming years will play out. Based on some early predictors, many say we are soon to enter the period of Tribulation (if we have not already), when the world will be overcome with chaos, crisis, catastrophic events, unrest, and serious pain and peril to mankind," Kate stated with conviction.

Mac looked at Kate's frown and as her words sank in, she felt a sense of foreboding and anxiety come over her. Returning to their papers and lists Mac decided it was time to figure out whom to go to with all this information. Who could quickly grasp the unholy alliance of the SEIU, ACORN, Tides, PEW, Americorp, Apollo, and Ivan Schwartz? Who could regard the Bilderberg group and the Illuminati with serious concern?

Mackenzie was not what most would call a religious person. She had chats with God, prayed on occasion and believed in God. She thought of herself as a spiritual person. Being a student of history, she also believed that most of the most atrocious actions of man against man have been done in the name of one religion or another, and she found that an odd and unacceptable contradiction. She wished to be a good person, with a good heart; sincere, trustworthy, caring, but in a direct way with God, not filtered through a church. She had read bits of the Bible but admitted to being woefully lacking in knowledge and understanding of its contents.

But Mac realized that there was something ominous in the comparisons of events recounted in scripture with events of current times. Even though she had dismissed comparisons as coincidence, there was mounting evidence that made Mac question her thinking. She vowed to pay more attention to Kate's observations, but also to do more digging on her own.

"Kate within the media who would you suggest that would know about biblical prophecies and political events, excluding ministers and religious leaders? We need two reporter-types who have a following; a bully pulpit for spreading the word. Based on what you are saying, we should have two people who are supportive of both Christian and Jewish perspectives, each with national following and broad name recognition. Ideally they are here in New York and accessible. One man comes to my mind, *Eli Gabriel*. Do you know of him? He has written some best seller books, he has a talk show on radio, and an evening news commentary on the cable network IWN. He is also on the lecture circuit now and then. I don't know where he does his radio show, but it has to be here in New York, since his evening cable show is here. I'll check while you think about this."

Kate responded matter-of-factly, "Oh there is no need to think about it. I had the perfect person immediately. It could be no one else but Patrick Hennessy. He is on radio each morning and nationally syndicated. He was fired from one network for being too conservative, and now has a new television program where he interviews and comments on politics and events of the day. He is huge. Many believe he is the perfect combination of thoughtful Christian and hard-hitting political analyst. He is also here in the great city of New York, also on IWN."

"Yes, I know of him. I like him also. I only recently discovered his evening television broadcast on IWN. He is earnest, honest, straight talking and hard working. Good choice. You realize we have little chance of getting in on such short notice. But okay, get us in to see him tomorrow afternoon while I track down *Eli Gabriel*," Mac responded as she returned to her laptop.

She could hear Kate chatting with someone on the phone, so pressed on and managed to get a lead on Gabriel. It did not take long to learn that he was with a New York radio station, KTNY—talk radio. She grabbed her cell phone and went into the bedroom and called KTNY, only to learn that he had just finished his broadcast (Divine intervention?). After a bit of subterfuge and name dropping, she was able to speak with him directly.

Eli was pleasant but did not seem pleased to have an interruption from a fan, thinking it was a business call. Mac quickly explained that it was a matter of vital importance, national security and the future of our nation and she begged for a meeting the following afternoon. Eli seemed at once intrigued yet reticent, but ultimately did agree to a meeting, indicating it would have to be brief, as his schedule was slammed all day. He then joked by adding, "Hey, if you bring a big bag of M&M's I might be able to give you more time. They have removed all my candy from the set." Mac laughed and promised to have plenty of candy with her.

Moments later Kate was jumping around the living room, clearly excited. Mac joined her in the moment, since both had gotten appointments. It was as if they were guided in the process—nary a glitch in schedule or logistics.

Kate was exuberant as she reported on her conversation with Patrick Hennessy and Mac briefed Kate on what she had found on the web about Gabriel, as well as more about Schwartz and the network of evil surrounding him.

Kate said, "Let's celebrate and go have a nice dinner and a brisk walk, then we can come back here and get each other up to speed in preparation for our meetings. We should be prepared to discuss both in our meetings tomorrow. I'll handle scripture, you the politics and news aspects."

"Kate I agree totally," Mac told her. "Let's freshen up and go get a good meal. I hate to be paranoid, but I am thinking we need to protect all this work and not just leave it lying about. What if we load documents into a briefcase, and take it with our laptops to the front desk to put in the safe? After that goon coming to our room, I am wondering just how much at risk we are now. I think we need to be very careful and very observant of our surroundings."

They changed clothes, cleaned up, gathered everything up and headed to the elevators. A man was seated in a chair near the window reading a newspaper. It was like a movie scene with an actor spying behind a paper, so Mac decided to take no chances.

She turned to Kate and said just a bit too loudly, "I want to drop by the drugstore off the lobby and pick up a couple of things. Then let's get a taxi and go straight to Tavern on the Green. We'll be a little early for our reservation, but we can have a drink if we have to wait."

Kate was about to question Mac's comment, but Mac nudged her and they proceeded into the elevator talking about how hungry they were. In the lobby they moved down the corridor toward the drugstore, stopping to look in a window and see if the man was following them. They did not see him, but another man was leaning against a column thumbing through a magazine.

Their radar was on high alert so they took nothing at face value. Mac handed Kate her briefcase with laptop in it and Kate headed to the front desk while Mac went to the drugstore. She went out the side door and down a different corridor to meet up with Kate. They dashed out a side door of the hotel nabbing a taxi immediately. As they pulled away they saw the man with the magazine hurrying out the door.

"Driver please run the upcoming light and take a fast right and then a fast left and then head down to Broadway and turn right and back to the upper East side."

He seemed puzzled, asking "you running from someone?" They shouted in unison, "YES, please hurry."

Hanging on, the driver darted between cars and without colliding with anything, got them to Midtown and back up the East side. They got out in an area loaded with restaurants and decided to walk and pick something that appealed to them.

They felt safe at this point, so walked comfortably along the street till they found a delightful Italian restaurant and settled in for a delicious meal with some wonderful Borolo wine. It was a lovely meal and a welcome respite from the intensity of their research and the resulting cloak and dagger events.

After dinner they took a taxi back to their hotel, stopping at the front desk to collect their things from the safe. No man with a magazine, no man seated by the window in the elevator lobby, so they headed to their room to await their order of tea and cookies to accompany a long chat.

Kate opened the door to their room and let out a scream. They went in to the room to find someone had broken in and torn through their belongings. Everything was tossed all over the place, beds torn apart—the place was a mess. Kate was in tears and Mac felt her heart pounding with anxiety.

She immediately called the front desk and told the manager their room had been broken into and was a total mess. He said he'd be right up with security. Within moments the two men arrived. The security officer said he wanted to bring in the police and the manager said they'd move us to another room. He called a porter to bring up a new key, and maid service to bring all on duty to move their things.

"I am so sorry for this trouble," the manager said. We will make it up to you. I am upgrading your room, and the rest of your stay will be as our guests. The police are going to want to talk to you I'd expect. So please remain here till the porter arrives. Joe here will remain with you. The porter will take your bags to the new suite, and the maids should have your personal items moved over within the hour. If there are certain items you need with you now, please gather them up so the porter can take them for you."

"Joe, you wait here for the police. I want a report, either from them or you, as soon as one is available. Other than the ladies' belongings, don't touch anything. You too ladies, don't move anything. And if you need anything, call me or the night manager. We'll get to the bottom of this, don't fear." With that the manager left and they gathered up their cosmetics, lingerie, items in their safe, and were ready, but still shaken when the bellman arrived.

He took them up a few floors to a concierge floor where a concierge desk was manned 24/7. That alone made them feel better. Their room was an elegant and spacious suite with view, large terrace, living room with fireplace, and large bedroom with two queen beds. The bathroom was a dream of superb lighting, double vanities, an enormous sunken Jacuzzi tub and separate walk in shower.

"Can you believe this?" Kate exclaimed. They dashed between rooms, taking in the luxury and ambiance, more than satisfied with their new digs. They put their toiletries and clothing away in drawers and stepped out on the terrace to enjoy a mild evening breeze, still shaken.

A knock at the door brought them back to the issues at hand. Three maids entered the room with all of their clothes, shoes etc., and within minutes had things hung up and tucked away. Mac called the concierge to reorder their tea and cookies which came with amazing speed.

They were sitting on the overstuffed sofa sipping tea when the police and security officer arrived.

"I'm Detective Burke. Have you figured out what if anything is missing? I'll need a list, and an estimated value. They'll be fingerprinting your room to see if we can get a lead on this."

Mac nodded to the Detective and said, "We have not found anything missing. We don't think it was a break-in to take personal items."

"OH?" The detective seemed a tad annoyed. "And what do you think was going on? And if nothing was taken, then we don't have a case that needs to be pursued now do we?" The security officer interjected, "Yes we do have a case. Any time a guest's room is broken into, that is a case and in this case we will work to identify all details, for the protection of these women and the rest of our guests. Period."

"Actually, we had a fear of our work being taken, so we took our laptops and research work to the manager's safe when we went to dinner. On our way out a couple of hours ago, a man was seated by the window near the elevator and in the lobby another man was standing thumbing through a magazine. It is quite possible the man by the elevator on our floor was the one who broke in. The man downstairs was seen leaping into a taxi to follow us as we fled out a side door," Mac explained.

"And what are you ladies working on that has people chasing you and breaking into your room?"

"Well, I don't want to make too big a thing," Mac told him, "but we have been doing research on some organizations with ties to a very bad man."

"Who is the bad man?" asked the detective. "And why would he care what sort of research you are doing? And for that matter, how would he know? It says here you two are from Oregon. Your premise seems a bit far fetched."

Kate was agitated, and said "You might think so, but we have had other encounters with various goons who are working for this man. They apparently know we have research and they don't know what we are going to do with it. We have been threatened already, and now our room? Don't you find all of this a bit odd, and worthy of serious investigation? And if you check with the manager, you'll learn that one of the man's goons was banging on our door earlier, and was removed by security."

The detective was growing irritated, "Now I don't mean to be rude to you, but perhaps you just pissed off an ordinary guy and his friends. Maybe an online blind date gone bad? Maybe you decided to check him out and he found out? Maybe he is getting even? Maybe he is trying to scare you to leave him alone?"

"Look officer, I know you are trying to do your job. But you are way off base here, and frankly you are being disrespectful," Mac declared. "Schwartz is a man in his 70s; he is a billionaire. He is evil, and is working against America. He operates in the shadows and I believe he is worried about having his hand tipped, of being exposed for who and what he is. Now you can make jokes and trivialize this all you like, but we know what is going on here. Officer Burke I think you can leave now. This line of questioning is pointless, and frankly an insult."

The security officer interjected, "We'll be going along now miss. Just so you know, no one is allowed on this floor without a key and a double check by the concierge. Also, if you are missing something, your old room is locked and won't be reassigned. Call me and I can look for whatever is missing. Now you ladies relax and have a good evening. You are safe here. Maybe a nice brandy would soothe your nerves. I'll have some sent to the room. Goodnight."

The men left. Mackenzie and Kate looked at each other and then hugged, knowing they were in a precarious situation, rife with some level of danger, perhaps making them more determined. Mac was somewhat used to this sort of thing, and felt badly that she had dragged Kate into such a mess.

They settled back on the sofa, tea in hand, and began what proved to be a discussion that was mysterious, confounding, maddening, and illuminating.

####

CHAPTER FIVE

Only the unknown frightens man. But once a man has faced the unknown, that terror becomes the known.

Antoine de Saint Exupery 1900-1940

It must have been the heart-pumping room incident, or the meal, or that they had spent a long day in their room and in front of their laptops, but sinking into the overstuffed sofa with tea in hand, Mac felt she could have fallen asleep within moments. She suggested to Kate that they take a walk. The air was cool and clear, trees lighted with twinkling lights, and since it was still early, they could afford a thirty-minute walk to get the blood flowing and refresh the mind.

They both felt a need to stretch and move, so they headed out. Neither of them was thinking about any evil lurking about. They believed that they had been hounded enough; that their tormentors were trying to frighten them, felt they had done a good job and they'd be good girls and disappear. Anyway, they were both tired, numb and needed to breathe some crisp fresh air.

Outside the front lobby on the street they paused, Kate wanting to take a different route. So they went left toward the Upper East Side and decided to stay on that street and head toward the park. Their pace was steady, but not so fast that they couldn't pay attention to the shop windows they passed, the tiny bars and restaurants, apartment lobbies, and occasional brownstones.

People were out and about, headed to dinner, walking their dogs, laughing with friends—it felt good to be alive and on the streets of this great city. A mother approached them with a baby carriage and from behind them came a man walking his gigantic Newfoundland dog. Mackenzie was an animal lover, some might say she was nuts about all animals, so when this huge fluffy black dog appeared, she had to stop and pet it. The man was not particularly friendly, but he encouraged the two women to pet and interact with the dog. As they oo'ed and ahhed over the dog the man ignored them, looking up and down the street and keeping track of his time.

Kate pulled on my arm and urged, "Let's get going. We have more walk and lots more work to do. "Thanks for letting us pet your dog. Bye," they said in unison.

They took off. They were far enough north to be in a mostly residential area, with much less foot traffic, despite the vast array of high priced apartments and town houses. They made it about five more blocks when they decided to cross the street and return down the other side.

Kate strode into the intersection and began across the street, hollering at Mac to hurry up. Mac stepped off the curb, preoccupied with her coat which she was trying to button up, when she heard a car. She had not looked up, but began to quicken her pace a bit, still wrestling with the buttons. When she looked up a car had spun into the street from a nearby alley, and sped up. She instantly had a sense of fear and danger.

Just as she made it midway across the wide city street, the black car screeched to a stop, the door opened and a burly man grabbed her arm, pulling her to the car. She screamed bloody murder and Kate, a couple of feet from her, ran to her, grabbing her other arm. There was a tug of war and Mac knew that for their side to win, she had to kick like crazy and fight to remove his iron clutch on her arm. Two passers-by, hearing the screaming and seeing what was going on, rushed to their aid. The woman began hitting the man hanging out of the car in the head with her purse and her husband punched the guy in the nose. At that point Mac fell to the ground and must have blacked out as she hit the pavement, because she did not hear the car roar off down the street.

Moments later she came to with Kate kneeling beside her and the couple talking about what happened as he called 911.

Mac moaned, feeling the pain in her hip and arm, "What happened? I saw a black SUV pull out of an alley a few cars back and then it sped toward me, as if it did not see me. Oh…my leg is hurting."

No sooner than she had spoken than the ambulance came up the street. She was put on a gurney, placed in the ambulance and given the once over by the two EMT's. "Miss, nothing seems to be broken but we will get you to the emergency room to be checked out."

"NO! I don't want to go to the hospital. If you can just patch up the banged up elbow, wrap my ankle, and cover up any minor cuts, I'll be fine. I really want to go back to my hotel room. I am sure about this, so please don't argue. No hospital."

The EMTs and Kate objected, but Mac said she'd be fine. So the EMT got some bandages out and started taking care of the abrasions, at which point the police arrived. The policeman took a report from Mac and the witnesses, asking for a description of the driver, if there were passengers, make of car and license plate number.

The man who had called for emergency help told the police, "I saw the car move quickly out of the alley and it sped up. I'd swear it was trying to hit this woman, but instead it stopped beside her and two men were trying to pull her into the car. There were two men in the front seat, the car was a late model Lexus SUV, not the sort of car driven by reckless kids. The windows were tinted so it was not possible to get much of a look, but the driver was a big man. The guy hanging out the rear door pulling on her had long blonde hair pulled into a ponytail, and was built like a wrestler. I'd take him to be in his early 40s, though can't be sure in this light. As soon as he freed his grip on her arm we grabbed her and they sped off, turning up the next street."

The officer came back to the ambulance. By now Mac was bandaged, and trying to put some weight on her foot. "Ladies, what do you think is going on here? This is a clear case of attempted abduction. Do you have any idea who is behind this?"

Kate spoke first, "Mac, we need to be honest about what is going on here. You know there is a connection with what's been happening. Tell him!"

"NO!" Mac groaned. "Look, this is no big deal. We encountered a couple of men who seemed most unsavory, and who could not take no for an answer. They had been drinking, and apparently decided to get even. There is no need for anyone to get overly excited. I am sure these jerks have gone away, after their silly attempt to frighten us."

Kate continued, "But Mac, you know there is something going on. It's pretty frightening for us." She looked at Mac with a look of concern and pleading.

"Ladies, you seem to be involved in some sort of intense situation. I'd suggest that you focus on your vacation, and leave these big boys alone. There can be no good to come of your involvement. Now, let's get you back to your hotel; that is if you're sure you are not going to need attention at the emergency room?"

Mac nodded no and they climbed into the patrol car for the short ride back to the hotel. The policeman again cautioned the women to leave well enough alone and go shopping tomorrow, but said to call him if they had any more trouble. He handed them his card and bid them goodnight.

Kate took Mac's arm and helped her to the elevator and on to the room. She called room service and ordered a brandy, and a large pot of coffee. At this point they just looked at one another knowingly, afraid to break the silence that embraced them. Kate silently left the room and went to put on her robe, bringing Mac's to her. "Mac I think you should call your son and tell him what has happened."

Mac shook her head and vehemently said "NO. Why worry him when there is nothing he can do. NO."

Their room service arrived, and they sat a few more minutes sipping their coffee, each lost in thought about the events of the day. Both women were shaken, and frightened. Kate interrupted the silence, "I've been thinking about what is going on here. I may not grasp just what it is we know or think we know, and two days ago I would have said to forget the whole thing, hit the spa and take in a Broadway show. But now I'm mad. I am scared spit less, but I'm damn mad. We need to hang in, and take this wherever it is going. Now I know that you have been the target of threats and attacks. I know you are pretty beaten down now and you have every right to be. Still, I can't imagine you wanting to give up, to roll up our tent and sneak away. So honey, let's get busy. We have work to do and an important day tomorrow."

Mac smiled weakly, "Katherine, I am not going to quit, nor fold up my tent. This is probably the worst experience of my life and I have to be honest, it has me really anxious and fearful. I don't like these feelings, but like you I am damn mad. Schwartz can go to hell, and I hope we can speed his trip. I need more brandy."

They got out their laptops and notes and set things out on the table. Mac put her foot on a chair with a pillow and leaned back in chair, feeling drained.

Kate looked over at Mac and wondered if she dare ask, then decided she would. "Mac, I have to share something with you that I've not wanted to mention, and because we have those meetings tomorrow, it seems like I need to speak up now. I have managed to keep up with political events thanks to you and our conversations. What I am woefully lacking in is our history or history in general. I hated it in school, and have avoided it all my life. I am worried that I will not be able to understand what is going on and I really don't have much idea of why things are as they are. Are you too tired to give me a crash course in American history? We don't need to start with the Mayflower or General Washington, so if you are tired, well we can do it another time."

"Kate I did not realize you were not up on our history. I am tired, but I think I can give you a thirty-minute overview that should put your mind at ease and hopefully shed light on why things are as they are."

She continued, "I see five or six key issues affecting America now, issues that seemingly involve Schwartz and others of his ilk. These issues include the European Union, the whole global warming issue, anti-Americanism abroad, Iraqi war and other related problems of the Middle East, and then within our country we are being torn down by a moral decay of our society, as well as an environment of greed that fosters corruption in business and government. We may be headed for some economic problems too, since Bush is not keeping a tight hand on spending."

"How about we take each one, I'll address it on a basic level from my political and historic perspective. Perhaps you will find similarities from Bible stories we can talk about another time. Does that work for you?" Mac asked.

"Absolutely! Carry on," Kate said with enthusiasm.

"Okay, here goes. The matter of anti-Americanism has been a reality for a long time. I know that Bush gets blamed for most if not all of it, but it has been around, probably since not long after the Second World War.

"I believe that America is respected for what we are and have accomplished, but that respect also fosters resentment and envy. Then add to that our 'youthfulness' as compared to the rest of the industrialized world, and we are regarded as upstarts. There is also a psychological aspect to negative feelings toward the U.S., derived from our long history of foreign aid, where we send out billions of dollars around the globe to help people in a time of crisis, or to rebuild a country after war, or in humanitarian aid. Of course the money is taken eagerly and with appreciation. But it is human nature to harbor resentment and anger toward the benevolent donor. People resent being needy, having to ask for help, having to receive help, and even in having strings attached to that help (such as, how the help is to be used). In our case, it is a matter of the world biting the hand that feeds it."

"They take with one hand and slap us with the other. And it seems that they resort to passive aggressive ways to get back at us. They say thank you for being their friend, for helping them. Behind our back they say we are too rich, too powerful, too successful, and they will 'show' us by not supporting us in the UN, or any global alliance in which we might seek their vote, or other support.

"Our foreign policy has been costly beyond belief, and yet has not earned us the type of strong alliances we no doubt thought we would gain.

"Add to that the growing Liberal attitude in the U.S. Our own, our fellow citizens, now find it popular and trendy to slam our country, and to display a disrespect and internal anti-Americanism that is driving a wedge of separation throughout the country. I believe that wedge comes in various forms, including the modern trend of identifying first in a racial, or ethnic identify, not as Americans; or our hyphenated society.

"This has grown since the days of the Civil Rights movement, and with the flow of immigrants to our shores that have opted to hold their culture as more important than assimilating into American culture.

We have grown more divided, and citizens feel justified in expressing anti-American sentiments. So does this wide-spread negative regard of a country and its actions align with a similar condition in the Bible?"

Kate thought for a moment, then responded "Mac, history was never my best subject. I guess I have never paid much attention to historical issues, so I have not compared such things in the Bible. I'll have to think on this."

Mac was puzzled but asked "Do you want me to continue with this historical perspective or should we wait on it? If need be, I can relate some of this tomorrow, though I don't think I will have to."

Kate said, "No, please continue. It is interesting. You bring up things I did not know, so it helps understand a bit about what is going on now. Just keep it tight so I can absorb this stuff."

Mac agreed, and continued.

"In keeping with the foreign view of America, there is the European Union, which takes its roots in the 1950s when some European countries formed an alliance over coal production. Then in 1993 the European Union was formalized and now has 27 member countries, referred to as states. This organization of states has common laws, objectives, pooled resources such as imports and exports, and developed policies on trade, foreign relations, and providing the freedom for citizens to move freely between all member states. Of the 27 members, 16 use the Euro as their common currency. These countries, while with different heritage, some differences in culture, and natural resources, none the less have certain aspects of history in common, and some common experience. So it made sense for them to merge in a way that gave them clout within the global marketplace. That clout continues to grow and is nearing one third of the world's gross product production.

"As far as I can recall, few if any of these 27 countries are without debt and significant obligation to America. Most still believe that their freedom is a result of America's entry into the Wars I and II, and realize, if begrudgingly, that they'd be living under Nazi Germany's dictatorship had America not stepped up.

"But here again, there is little respect and appreciation, and still that underlying resentment. At various times our government, however, has forgiven significant portions of debt owed us by most of those countries, to help them through difficult times.

"So I guess the bottom line is that a large number of diverse countries created a strong alliance supported by laws and policies, to advance their economic position globally. And of course, I am curious as to whether this scenario strikes a Biblical cord with you."

Kate rolled her eyes and said, "Well you are keeping me on my toes at least. Mac, I am not an expert in the Bible. There are scholars who spend a lifetime studying the Bible to seek truth, and yet there are so many different interpretations. I understand the parts that relate to me, family, how to live a virtuous life, how to parent, to serve my church and community. I feel inadequate to this truly. I don't wish to mislead you. I mean, in this example, we talk about countries coming together to expand their power, and America giving and forgiving assistance. Well, America has long offered assistance to those countries in need, which is serving God's will. God blesses those who work in his name for those less fortunate. So I am thinking that God showered good fortune on America in praise and blessing for all we have done for others, and in that way America quickly grew to become the greatest success story in history."

"Honestly Mackenzie, this is a lot of pressure for me. I am being forced to take something very private and expose it, for evaluation. No Mac, I don't want to do this."

Mackenzie was speechless. She had spent the last several years listening to Kate espouse endless scriptural references, as lessons she felt Mac needed to learn. Now when asked to contribute comparisons, she dries up? "Kate, I just don't know what to say here. If there was anyone who seemed comfortable discussing the Bible, it would be you. For years you have been relating scripture to me. How can it be that you now find it too much pressure, too uncomfortable?" Did not you tell me at the onset that we needed to balance the political with biblical?"

Kate seemed suddenly awkward, and as she fidgeted, she said, "Mac I know you are upset with me, that you don't understand. Frankly I am not sure I do either. All I know is that I have gone from something very personal and private, to having to delve into areas of history and the Bible that I am not familiar with. The Bible gives me peace, this is not peaceful, but a huge stress for me. I may not be able to explain it well, but I am very sure about this. I do not want you to pressure me. I'll help you find someone, or perhaps dig up some more information, but I personally do not want to be pressured into giving scriptural commentary to balance your other stuff."

It was as if Kate had dug in her heels and dismissed the topic totally. She resumed sipping a cup of coffee, silent and distant. Mac stood there, not knowing what to do so she collapsed into a chair and sighed.

An uncomfortable silence filled the room, neither woman wanting to break it. Mac, finding the coffee too cold, opted for a shot of brandy to warm her. She limped back to her chair and sat there. Kate eventually broke the silence and urged her to continue.

"Of course Kate, if you wish. Well, history is heavily laden with wars in all corners of the globe. They were waged initially over land acquisition, money and power; then religion; and later over a combination of factors. Few wars are good, many are not even necessary; but some are good, and carried out for all the right reasons, such as WWII.

"Looking at the period since WWII, the world has undergone vast changes, both in emerging countries and those relinquishing colonial controls.

"Religion is still a factor, as exhaustively reflected in the Middle East, and the relationship with Israel; or the string of ethnic wars in Eastern Europe, and the decades-long war in Ireland.

"The stakes, however, continue to elevate to alarming degrees. Now we have renegades and rabble-rousers, nut cases and loons with nuclear bombs. Any one of them could at any time launch a killer attack. Their erratic behavior and penchant for forming alliances with each other only enhances the tensions and anxiety, and the collective threat.

"With the terrorist attack of 2001, our entry into Iraq initially seemed appropriate. But it did not take long for it to wear thin on most Americans, partly due to the expense, partly due to the death toll, and the seeming inability to gain the upper hand there. It was much like

Vietnam, in that we sent in too few troops to get the job done, until the enemy had gained some level of advantage.

"Israel has long been our ally, one that America has vowed to protect and support. But through the years most of the Middle East, under one leader or another, has turned its back on Israel, often with violent outcome. You know better than I the historic issues Jews have battled for centuries, from accounts in the Bible.

"To maintain our support for Israel we are up against most of the Arab world and their supporters; and against the many terrorist groups around the world. Our troops are subjected to the most horrendous conditions likely ever experienced by ground troops anywhere. They are exhausted, their equipment is tired and worn, and they suffer from PTSD. Their families are under tremendous stress and strife too.

"The end result is that they are spread too thin, and to their own peril. We have disbursed troops around the globe in response to crisis, in addition to maintaining a military presence in key locations such as the DMZ that separates Korea. We have been engaged in the Middle East for years, and no end is in sight.

"These men and women are the force behind our freedom and protection, yet it is a struggle to get Congress to give them what they need, favoring instead their endless ear marks for wasteful unnecessary projects. God help us if we are attacked in any significant way. Now we have politicians making outrageous comments about the soldiers and their work, serving to demoralize the troops.

"So the Iraq war has an economic impact, an influence on our political climate as we near the presidential campaign; and morale issues among the military, plus a huge vitriolic division among Americans. All this, as we move into campaign season. It is going to be ugly, and mark my words, it is going to overshadow other issues and be used to cloud a number of them."

Kate sighed. "You make it sound so bleak, and yet I can see that your points are valid. I can also see that with an all-volunteer military serving global needs, we have troops that are just exhausted, and suffering emotional trauma. We won't go into it now, but based on the Books of Daniel and Revelations, this is the sort of environment and political climate that fosters the End Times and period of Tribulation. As you can imagine, this is something being discussed in churches across the country. Experts are weighing in on the topic, and believers are preparing. Most people believe that this is just the earliest of stages; that it is not something that will happen in a year or two. At some point we can talk more about this. I do have notes I have made, and have read some about what is expected to happen and why. But for now, back to my history lesson, okay?"

"This is good Kate. I have been doing some reading too and it's a bit unnerving, so a future discussion would be good," Mac replied. "Another area of huge impact on the country is the moral decay that has been eroding the fiber of our culture for a long time. I am sure there are conflicting opinions on when this started—some believe it began after WWII, many others believe it was during the Vietnam War and thereafter. I tend to agree with the latter. I'm not sure it matters what contributed or when, merely that it exists and has a negative influence on most of society."

Kate continued, "We now turn to violence to resolve neighborhood conflict. We are so used to seeing violence in the media that it is generally accepted as part of daily life. We have witnessed criminals get away with murder, literally. News reports are filled with drive-by shootings, gang warfare in the streets, road rage, mass murders, and worse."

Mac continued, "People cheat on their taxes; contracts are broken; too many corporate leaders pull every imaginable or unimaginable trick and maneuver to cheat investors and employees, to fill their own pockets. Our government leaders, especially Congress, have for eons been short on ethics, long on self-service. Major corporations have pulled horrendous scams on citizens and state or city governments. I mean, there is a long list of major companies that have committed crimes, be it stock, various swindles, trashing environment—billions of dollars up in smoke from foul play. But I believe we have seen nothing yet. It will eventually be an issue that explodes like an atom bomb."

"And speaking of scams, I saw a documentary a few months ago about global warming. It was produced abroad and featured many leading global scientists. I can't recall all the technical information, but it seemed totally clear that the warming is a repetitive cycle of ebb and flow over time. What is alarming is that a handful of people are promoting the notion that warming is man-made from carbon emissions. The documentary showed valid scientific data pointing to ocean currents, tides, and the solar system as the cause, nothing that man affects or can alter. So this means that a few people will soak the rest of us and acquire enormous wealth. A real scam perpetrated on all of America, at enormous cost to us all, for the benefit of a few, and sanctioned by our government.

"So now we have a citizenry that is jaded, far too accepting, and oblivious to what goes on. If Americans look to Congress, government, and corporate leaders as examples of acceptable behavior, then there is nearly no one to stand out as an exemplary model. We have dumbed down our expectations, oversight, morals, and ethical standards. At the same time there has been an effort to secularize everything and to remove God and Judeo Christian values from our lives, in government, the workplace, schools, even churches.

"With criminal and unethical behavior as a standard, secularism suppressing God and moral values, we have a society that is essentially out of control. Some seek meaning in all this chaos, but little makes sense. People can turn to God and find solace, but it does not diminish the chaos and the environment that fosters (and protects) the bad guys when doing their bad deeds.

Katherine sat there looking out the window then back at Mac, saying, "You know this hits a cord with me. It is a topic of major importance. Not that I don't believe in the separation of church and state, because I do. But people have sunk so far in their beliefs, in their adherence to our founders' beliefs and values that served us well for over 200 years. I am sad. I am dismayed to see our fall from greatness. Two hundred years to greatness, but only forty years to failure, in part from excessive immorality, but also over-taxation, growth of government and uncontrolled spending."

Mackenzie nodded in agreement. "Do you realize that back in the 1950s we were a nation of adventurers, risk-takers, innovators and pioneers in so many fields? We believed we were the best, and we behaved accordingly. We rose to meet any challenge, and set the bar high for success and achievement, meeting and exceeding it with ease. We produced the best products in the world, products made by skilled craftsmen, of the best materials and design. In that era we had the most efficient and dedicated workforce; and geniuses in the design, engineering and development arenas. Moms did not have to work for families to live well and kids were safe to play in their neighborhoods and yards, to bicycle to activities; and knew they could do whatever they wanted when they grew up. Why, we produced the world's most advanced airplane in those days or since—a plane that protected us from up in the atmosphere for decades and nothing has ever been produced since to equal her brilliance. But I digress."

Kate interrupted, "So, the Bible says that man's cold hearts, blind eyes and deaf ears will lead them to their own demise. The prevailing liberal thinking imposes a separation from God and emphasizes self-empowerment rather than serving God. Time and again Biblical history shows countries fall under duress when forced into self-serving policies and actions. Yes we must take care of our environment, but the Bible tells us we are in the world, not of it. Believers know that God is in control over all, and through him they can do all things. Too many people in this world are lead by their own will, and fixated on condemning or finding fault with those who follow God's word."

Mackenzie was struck by the calm that Kate exhibited when referencing the Bible, so it was all the more strange that she did not want to draw comparisons. "Kate I am far from a place of peace or the belief that all of this is pre-ordained and as a child of God I will be fine. I am damn worried. Now this is probably a matter of belief and faith, maybe even a lack of knowledge of the Bible."

"It's bad enough that Congress is a mess, corporations have run amuck, and Wall Street is in an ethical vacuum. But we have this messy and unpopular war, and a president that seems to be shooting himself in the foot at every turn, plus is making decisions that go against principles of capitalism. I believe we have a deep shakeup coming.

I sense rumbles and have a feeling that we are on the precipice of something dire," Mac continued.

"Well sweetie, I think we have covered the main talking points, have sufficient notes, and we're ready to set a fire under the seats of our two media titans tomorrow. Let's call it a night and try to get some sleep. I feel exhausted. Plus my body is bloody sore. I'm going to get some bags of ice sent to the room to pack around the sore spots."

Kate yawned as she put her papers neatly in the briefcase. Amid yawns, she said, "From now on, let's refer to our media titans as what they are going to be, based on similar roles in the Bible. They are our "Witnesses" who will carry the word to the people. Okay?"

Laughing, Mac said, "You got it babe. Witnesses it is!"

###

CHAPTER SIX

He who passively accepts evil is as much involved in it as he who helps perpetrate it. He who accepts evil without protesting against it is really cooperating with it.

Martin Luther King Jr.

Morning came too quickly, and while the pain in her leg had improved, Mackenzie felt like she had been hit by a Mack Truck. Bruises and sore spots dotted her body, such that she suddenly realized what old age was going to feel like.

Showers, coffee and muffins, and they were ready to hail a cab for a ride to KTNY on Avenue of the Americas, where they were to meet with Patrick Hennessy. Later they'd be meeting with Eli Gabriel at IWN.

Patrick Hennessy was perched on a stool outside his radio broadcast studio, talking to his producer. He was animated; pen in hand, waving his arms about. He was an attractive man, sleek and well groomed, but with a friendly, casual air about him. He had piercing eyes, thick hair, well tended hands that showed some signs of an earlier life of hard labor. There was nothing effete about him, appearing more the common man than a media darling.

He was as warm and welcoming as the women had imagined, but they were both nervous, since their mission was to present some belief-shattering and mind-bending information, and they were worried he'd think them a couple of nut case crackpots and dismiss them quickly. There was nothing to do but dive in, first with introductions all around.

Mac started off by saying, "Patrick, we both have been familiar with your work on your syndicated talk show, as well as on IWN. It seemed obvious to us both that we had to meet with you to share information that we accidently fell into, and that we find alarming, but which should be right up your alley.

Patrick nodded, and asked "How did you fall into alarming information, and how do you see me involved?"

Kate leapt in, "We came here on an innocent vacation and found ourselves at the right places and right times so that we overhead things they should not have. Being curious, we started digging around, and the more we learned the more we knew we had hit the mother lode of darkness."

"Go on," he said.

Mac spoke, "We first sat at a dinner table next to Ivan Schwartz and some dangerous-looking associates; and just prior to that he had been in a private chat with Cora Lamia. The men next to us were talking about a mystery man, referenced only by initials, as well as a closed conference they were attending the following day."

"Well, we were very curious. I have some useful DC connections, so I managed to get us an invitation to this conference, where we pretended to be social entrepreneurs seeking a breadth of information that might be useful in our development plans. Ivan Schwartz was there and I managed to be seated at his table, while Kate was seated with one of his so-called associates, Johann Adler."

"During the conference I positioned myself to overhear a private session discussing the matter of One World Community and global economic maneuvering that seemed counter-productive to the U.S. Other open sessions were talking about global finance and alliance-building with other foreign entities. I am not really sure of just what we heard, but my instincts tell me this group is conspiratorial and evil. There was discussion of the World Bank, which frankly I found disgusting."

Patrick smiled as if a cat having caught a mouse, when he interjected, "So you two are seeing conspiracies galore and we are in jeopardy? Is that it? Can hardly wait for Eli to hear this."

Kate had an odd look on her face, so I poked her. She said, "Patrick, I am surprised you are taking this all with such levity and lightness. Don't you think this is serious? My gut is telling me that you are pulling our leg, that you know more than you are letting on. Right?"

Pat smiled broadly, gave her a wink, and moved right along as if he did not hear her.

Given his silence, Mac continued, "That afternoon we managed to score an invitation to a private cocktail party to which Schwartz was going, in the company of many dubious people. I've no idea who many of them were, but most were from other countries. There was a private meeting going on behind closed doors in that suite, which I stumbled into by mistake, intentionally. I was about blown out of the room by unified outrage. I heard nothing, but saw a couple of familiar faces and most interesting of all, a video conference set-up where these people were talking with someone from Asia. I don't know if China or exactly where. But there was a tone of deference from this group to that man, and to Schwartz."

Pat interrupted, his penetrating eyes gleaming, by asking, "So what do you two ladies think is going on here? What do you want from me?"

Mackenzie replied, "Patrick it is not that simplistic or easy to answer. First of all, we learned that Schwartz is a Jew-hating Jew with tremendous anger toward the U.S. He is aligned with a vast number of very questionable organizations here and abroad. He's been instrumental in government overthrows and their replacements, and in the mix, made himself a vast multi-billion dollar fortune. He uses his money to promote his ideology whatever that is, in government, politics, socially, in the media, and in business. There is essentially no arena in which he is not playing, even though he remains in the shadows, pulling the strings without visibility."

"He seems an avid follower of sociologists Cloward and Piven, who supported radical socialism, and promoted the belief that one could bring down a government and its economy by placing enormous demands on government that could not be met, while attempting to support the needs of the poor. According to Cloward and Piven, such actions result in a class warfare, leading to the collapse of the economy, then the government. I believe we are headed in that direction now."

"He works fast and furious in this regard. It seems he has at least two presidential candidates in his pocket, plus he is working to support several others running for Congress, and even within state governments.

He is in cahoots with some outfit called ACORN which we are just digging into but they operate community outreach programs and appear to be crooked, yet well connected in political circles. I have a great deal more information on Schwartz."

"Needless to say, he seems the cornerstone of what we have discovered. He could be the Number One guy overseeing some pretty dark stuff. But beyond him, there is a network of social, political and economic groups, think tanks, fund raising organizations and activism groups that he supports and/or controls in one way or another."

"He worked in the background for an earlier administration, spending time abroad when governments toppled. He was known to have created what was called "shadow" governments, waiting in the wings to take over once the overthrow had happened. Some say he has such a group here in the U.S. now, which gives me a chill from the implications."

Patrick interjected, "Whoa! You are making my head swim. I am aware of much of what you are telling me, but you have found out even more than most with whom we associate. I have formed an opinion based on what I have learned over time. Have you an opinion about what you know? Listening to you, I'd swear you were talking about the Devil himself. Next you'll have me convinced that I need to get my affairs in order as the end is near."

Kate, a look of disbelief on her face, prodded me, "Go on Mac, and tell him."

"Well," Mac said, "I hate to sound like a doomsday merchant, or conspiracy theorist, but there is a pattern of behavior, and an intricate web of connections. They serve various vertical and horizontal radical elements in this country, such that all aspects of our society are touched in some way. They all have at their core a social re-engineering of this country away from capitalism to some new form of socialism that is off the charts. I have a feeling Schwartz will make every effort to buy the presidency, and thereafter, begin tearing down most of what we stand for. Now that may be too wide in scope, too over the top, but there is something foreboding about what he is doing and every one of my antennas is on alert. There is much more to tell you, which I believe will solidify what I have been saying. What do you think Patrick?"

He nodded, "Very good ladies; you may have stumbled on to the essence of what it all means collectively—buying the presidency. I've know this information over time, but to hear it all laid out at once, well it is stunning. Mackenzie, I am curious, what is it you do for a living? How have you managed to unearth such complex information on this guy? The question remains, why? Why go to all the expense and trouble? What's in it for him? And Kate, I'm also curious as to what your role is in this?"

Mac responded, "Ahh, well, I am just, well, just a marketing professional. Kate as my friend is along for the unexpected and unplanned adventure, far more than she bargained for. In reality we are stumbling along not really knowing just what we are doing, but we felt a huge urgency to make contact with you and share what we have learned."

"As for Schwartz, here is an interesting part of his past. He hates America and Americans with a driving passion and obsession. He has made his vast wealth by wiping out national economies and banking systems, while working the stock markets and hedge funds to his advantage. His private fund is located offshore in the Netherlands Antilles, a federation of five self-governing Caribbean islands, regarded as a primary drug-shipping area to the rest of South and North America. It's the same area where the Russian mafia commands their drug operation under the command of Mogelevich."

Mac continued, "It's long been rumored that Schwartz and his cousin have been laundering drug money for the Russians, despite their denials. Both have been found to have large sums of money sitting offshore, unable to be tied to their investment funds and portfolios."

There simply is no bigger fish for Schwartz to fry than the U.S., and the economic gain for him, if it were to play out as in other countries, would be beyond belief and comprehension. He is, I believe, driven to that accomplishment. As a lay person unfamiliar with the details of the Bible, I have read passages concerning Lucifer or the Devil, and the Anti-Christ, all pure evil. Schwartz is no less so, and from my perspective, could be any of those entities."

Kate could contain herself no longer, "Now, take all of that and look at scripture, which I know you are versed in Patrick. Take a look at prophecies, both in the Bible and in the Catholic Church, and you'll see that what may be about to happen has been spelled out in scripture. There are so many comparisons to make that I could keep you busy for weeks reviewing them all. I am a Christian and a strong believer in the Word of God. Mac here is coming along, but not there totally," as she reached over and patted **Mac's** arm with a smile. Mac looked over at her and could do no more than roll her eyes. Here we go again, she thought.

Mackenzie told Patrick, mid eye-roll, "Good grief. Every weekend she invites me to church. Every weekend!" He grinned in Mac's direction and she got a little tingle—he has a great grin she was thinking to herself. Geez, could he be single? He seems quite flirtatious. Oh stop. He's too young anyway. Back to business here.

Kate unaware of that little 'moment' said, "A man like Schwartz accomplishes many things by working to somehow bring down the U.S. He achieves the culmination of a life-long hatred; he enriches himself beyond anyone's imagination; he brings destruction to the Judeo-Christian values of America, and to both religions; he wipes out the most important currency in the World; and no doubt there is much more I don't understand or know about. I believe that he is likely, knowingly or not, working to fulfill many of God's prophecies. At least that is my take on things based on my knowledge of the Bible."

Kate continued, "We were doing some research last night and found an interview he did, in which he said something to the affect that he had messianic feelings since childhood, but now that he was living the life, he was very comfortable being God. Blasphemy!"

Mackenzie, watching Patrick deep in thought and silence for what seemed like an eternity, said "So Patrick, as you can see, we are grounded in some measure of reality, but swayed by fabulous implications of infinite what-if's and possibilities. We need to lessen the what-if's and more resolutely cling to reality."

Patrick smiled at Mac's comment, and then broke the silence by saying, "I have to say very seriously that his comment is offensive, since there is only one God, the God of Abraham. Who else have you told about all of this? Have you met with anyone else? Does anyone know of your work?"

Mac sighed as she answered, "Actually we think that Schwartz knows. There have been some very upsetting events in the last couple of days. Our hotel room was ransacked. We saw one of Schwartz's goons outside our room one evening. And I was almost abducted last night when we took a walk—a black SUV sped up alongside me, the door opened and a big dude tried to pull me into the vehicle. Kate was tugging on me, and soon was helped by a Good Samaritan couple. She hit the man with her purse and her husband socked him in the face. The creep let go of my arm and the van sped away. So yes I think he has some idea of what we are up to. But in addition to contacting you, we made contact with your cohort at IWN, Eli Gabriel. We are to meet with him when we leave here."

Kate interjected, "We knew we needed two people who would understand the implications, and who have a bully pulpit from which to spread the word and warn people. And frankly it is a relief and comfort to be able to share this information with you both, since we have felt the heavy weight of it."

Pat smiled, "Well, we do have a world audience and are not shy about spreading the word. It's unfortunate that so many don't hear us, or can't seem to grasp our purpose. I am headed to IWN shortly for my evening show. Let me give Eli a call and let him know I am on my way over there with you two, and see if we can have a joint meeting before he leaves and I go on air."

He got off the phone laughing, "Eli is a funny guy. He can take the bleakest bit of news and give a humorous twist. His humor may come in very handy in the coming months and years, especially since we are in the early weeks of the next presidential campaign. OK ladies, let's go see Eli. I have a driver waiting to take us over to IWN."

It was not long before they arrived at the towering IWN complex—a mass of offices, studios, green rooms, staff, and huge rooms filled with computers receiving direct feeds from around the world. They were on top of the news, for sure.

They met Eli Gabriel in his office. He had just come off the air, and was comfortably seated with his sneaker-clad feet on his desk, his hands behind his head and an enormous grin on his round cheery face. Eli was known as a candy freak, so there were bowls of candy sitting on tables around the room. The office was a bit messy, loaded with stacks of papers, and reading material. The walls were lined with photos of him on stage with famous people, receiving an award, and many of his wife and kids. He was a warm and affable guy, lacking in hubris, and very down to earth; refreshing for a media/news personality.

It was clear that these two men were close friends, enjoying each other's company and sharing a basic grounding in news, ideology, and religious beliefs. Rumors of rifts and jealousies to the contrary, they warmly received each other. They were like the boys next door—down to earth, warm, compassionate and totally real. Eli was no push-over, and was known as something of a fire-breathing dragon if attacked. He called things as he saw them, and he did his homework. He was a bit on the stocky side, with medium blonde short hair, graying at the temples, rosy round cheeks, a huge disarming smile, and friendly yet no-nonsense eyes.

Patrick on the other hand was tall and fit, striking good looks, dark intense shining eyes, and wavy dark hair flecked with touches of silver. He smiled a lot, exposing brilliant white teeth that you could imagine giving off that sparkly glint on a tooth paste commercial. While calm and composed most of the time, he was also known to get fired up.

Both men were prone to wearing dark jeans and tennis shoes, usually dressing them up with a blazer or sport coat and tie. They were average Joes in most respects, but they wielded a great deal of power and influence to an ever-growing audience of fans of all political persuasions.

Eli waved us into the room and to comfortable chairs adjoining a sofa, saying to us, "Hey Pat, welcome ladies. Pat, I heard that bit on your show today. My secretary taped it. You sure stirred up Cora Lamia. I could see some pretty nasty thoughts going through her head, and almost hear her teeth clench behind that taught mask of hers, as well as her knuckles hit the desk. There is one vein that really pulses when she is hot and it was really pumping! Had to laugh. Good work buddy."

"So what's the mystery about ladies? Why Pat and me here, now?"

Patrick interjected, "I thought you'd get a kick out of Princess Cora's tight-lipped reply. You should have been there. Her face was immovable, her eyes glaring. Oh that's right, her face doesn't move anyway. But there was a moment when I thought she'd levitate right out of her chair. For some reason I do get a kick out of lighting her fire."

"Now Eli, I want you to give Kate Justice and Mackenzie Honor your undivided attention. Ladies I want you to tell Eli pretty much what you told me, and if you have more information, now's the time to spill it. We need to know it all, and we need to know you both."

Eli added, "And you do understand that Pat and I have to handle this in our own way, decided between us. You have no say over that, right?"

The two women nodded in affirmation but looked at each other with curiosity, almost as if he knows already why they're there.

"Okay good. Eli you should also know that Kate and Mackenzie have decided that we are the ones in media to spread the word; the similarities between what is happening in the world today and what the Scripture says are very close in the future."

"OK Mackenzie, you're on."

They repeated their story for Eli's benefit, embellishing here and there from their notes, providing more names and details than when talking with Patrick. Midway in their presentation, Eli held up his hand to silence them as he called his secretary and asked her to bring in a tray of drinks and snacks, since they were going to be a while. Kate and Mackenzie continued to elaborate on their findings, the events of their time spent in New York, and of their beliefs based on all that they had discovered.

The four sat in silence, sipping their drinks and nibbling on tea-sized sandwiches. The women were nervous and Mac was wondering if both men were going to burst out laughing and then show the women the door.

To the contrary, both men had serious looks on their faces. Eli broke the silence saying, "I need jelly bellies. Pass me that bowl please." He scooped up a handful, tossed a few into his mouth, and started laughing. Not what Mac had hoped for. Kate, smiling, raised her hand and begged for chocolate, now in need of some comfort food too!

"Well I'll be! Eli laughed. "I do believe that you two women have just popped the lid off Pandora's Box. A round of chocolate for us all! All hell is gonna break lose, you know that don't you? And I think you have acquired a life-long enemy. May God bless you both with long and healthy lives! Okay Pat, what's on your mind? I want to hear if you and I are seeing this in the same way."

Pat threw up his arms, moaned slightly, and replied, "I'm struck by how two private citizens, in a matter of a few days, unearthed so much information, first of all. Secondly, I am overwhelmed by the implications, and a sense that we are all staring at the tip of the iceberg. I am thinking we need to create a damn good plan, and hold our cards tight to our chest. And I'm thinking this is explosive and heads are going to roll, somewhere, somehow. Just hope it's not any of ours. And you Eli?"

"Oh I agree. I totally agree," Eli said between bites of jelly bellies. "Listen, you and I know about what has been going on and will be going on. We probably are pretty pragmatic about culpability, and just how widespread some of these problems are. We know what's going on in Washington and we've not really talked about that yet. Yes, we have quite a situation here. If, as we all seem to believe, most of this is true, and then some, we do need to educate voters and warn people. But we'll need to deliver something more than innuendo without giving too much information. Subtleties don't play well in Seattle or Sioux City. It's risky business dude. You know that. And Ivan? Now he is a really spooky dude!"

Patrick was lost in thought, then leapt out of his seat and said, "We've got to get The Arab in here, now. He can fill in some gaps, and he needs to hear some of this information provided by the ladies. I'll call him. I spoke with him this morning, and I know he was having lunch with Geoff. He can be here in 30 minutes or less. Ladies, can you two wait here? I can give another forty-five minutes before I have to get to my office and prepare."

He did not wait for an answer as he took his cell and called The Arab, whoever that was. The women nodded yes. Mac looked over at Kate who was so wide-eyed and still, Mac could not even see her breathe. Mac nudged her and she jerked around, looking at Mac, who motioned Kate to follow; they moved to the doorway and Mac whispered to her.

"We've hit a nerve. They are digging in deeper. Are you okay? I mean are you okay with this, with getting further involved, with staying around to meet that Arab guy?"

"Oh Mac, this is like a dream and nightmare all at once. I love the intrigue and possibilities, but the bad guys are scary people. I should be talking to my hubby about this. He's gonna kill me, but I need to think on this for a bit. God help us both. I mean, you can't get into a big mystery novel and put it down half way through, never knowing how it is going to end, or what the clues are along the way. I have a feeling the outcome is preordained, but getting there is a huge part of the intrigue. I am going to call John. I can't do this without checking in with him. Say, Eli, do you have an empty office where I can make a private call?"

They moved back to their chairs as Eli said that The Arab would be joining them shortly. He told Patrick that he wanted to talk with him in private, and directed Kate to his secretary's office. The men were going to chat in the hallway, so Mac excused herself and went to the ladies room. Once there she decided to use that free moment to place an urgent call of her own.

"Hey, this is Mackenzie. Is he there? Great, I need a minute of his time; put me through please. Hi Jack. Yes I'm fine. I am in New York still. Well, the vacation part never got much of a start. Things have been happening. Actually it's what I am calling about. I need to talk with you, but not on the phone. Can you catch a plane or train up here? Can you come up for lunch tomorrow? Great! Don't tell anyone we are getting together—no one. In fact, make your own reservation. Don't run this through your secretary. Yes, I know but trust me this is important, and you need to keep this totally MUM. Let's meet at the OB restaurant, our usual place. Easy for you to get to; busy with people; but safe for us. One o'clock, I'll be toward the back with a table. Bring paper and pen too, and your little black book. Bye."

Kate returned to Eli's office, feeling uncomfortable for interrupting the men and their conversation. The men waved her in the room and ended their conversation. As silence took over, Kate gathered up courage and said, "I feel a bit silly even bringing this up, but I also feel a compulsion to tell you about a dream I had about you both. I dreamt you are the Witnesses in Chapter 11 in the Book of Revelations, from the Bible. In my dream you're wailing to the world, warning them of pending disasters and evil events to come. I have not said anything to Mackenzie because I feel silly, and she'd just roll her eyes at me anyway."

Patrick and Eli looked at each other in silence. "Well now, Eli said, "we are left speechless, and that is rare. I'm not sure how you have come to your dream, but, well, right you are in knowing, and yes you'd be correct in your dream's vision. We seem to have been called into action. Just as you two have. There are no accidents."

Kate blurted out, "Mackenzie is never going to believe this! She'll think I'm a—"

Both men started laughing, "a *loon?*"

"Yes, that's it! She calls me a loon on occasion. She is not really a full believer and struggles with my preachy talk."

"Kate, you should know that Mac will believe, and very soon now. Also, she has a deep secret she's wanted to tell you but has so far resisted because she is not sure she can trust you. She will tell you soon. That is how much change she will go through immediately."

Kate being much too curious asks, "What is the secret? I need to know now."

Again both men chuckled but told her she'd have to wait because Mackenzie would need to tell her. "By letting her tell you, you both will learn greater trust of each other. Remember fear is what separates people from God," Pat told Kate.

Still curious, Kate asked both men, "Why us? Why are Mac and I here and why has God chosen us, now?" Eli responded, "It is because you have a heart for God, and soon so too will Mackenzie. And God has a mission for you, of which you'll learn shortly."

Kate nodded knowingly and excused herself and went into the corridor to wait for Mac. Mac approached her prepared to return to the room, but Kate stopped her.

"Mac, I have something important to tell you. Eli and Pat aren't who you think they are," Kate told her.

"So, who are they, if not the two media power houses that so many know and love?" Mac prodded with a grin.

"Mac, this is going to sound off the wall. You may want to polish off your favorite word, LOON; but I have been talking with Eli and Pat. They shared with me that they are the Witnesses in Chapter 11 of the Book of Revelations, in the Bible; that they have been called into action. And they have told me that they knew we were coming to see them; oh heck, they know everything about everything. Because they knew you'd not believe me, they told me that you have a secret you have wanted to tell me. Now's the time girlfriend."

"Are you nuts? You are a loon! What have you three been smoking while I was in the ladies room? I mean, come on, this is just too far out there even for you," Mac said in utter frustration and disbelief.

"They knew you'd say this and even call me a loon. But listen up. I am very serious. I had a dream about all of this last night, so I confronted them with the information just now."

"Ah, you had a dream! Well now, that explains everything," Mac huffed.

Kate responded with somber conviction, "The Witnesses told me, "right you are in knowing," so you just need to accept this. Now, about that secret. You are not going to put me off again."

"Good grief. See what happens when I leave to take a phone call. Okay, I am working on my incredulousness but how did they know I have a secret? And as for that secret, I've been delaying because I was not convinced I could trust you. I am prepared to take that leap now, at your insistence," she said with bemused resignation.

Kate jumped up and down and blurted out, "They said you'd say that. See? They know everything."

"I'm giving the abridged version due to our time constraints. I've been working undercover within a secret government department off and on for some time. Not continuous, but on special assignments. My most recent assignment has been to investigate Ivan Schwartz. For that job, I needed a so-called decoy, or loon in your case. So our interaction with Schwartz was planned and you were part of the plan. But of course, the plan was not to include all the drama we've had."

Kate looked forlorn and betrayed as tears welled up in her eyes, "Mackenzie, we've been friends for years now. I can't believe you still do not trust me. How can that be? I feel really hurt."

Seeing and hearing her reaction, Mackenzie felt terrible. She hated to see loons cry. But being moved, she threw her arms around her dear friend and told her how sorry she was to have misjudged her, and gotten her into this mess.

Mac felt terrible, "Clearly there are no accidents. We are together for many reasons; some only now becoming known to each other. But together we are. And I believe what you say about the two men, regardless of how crazy it sounds. We are all in this together. But what do they want from us?" The two women hugged and cried together. Mackenzie was not accustomed to such emotions, but her heart was open and she sensed this new bond between them would surely be stronger than in the past. Mac sensed she was joined in kinship with Katherine for eternity.

Noses running, eyes weeping, Kate took Mac's hand and said, "Oh Mac I forgive you. We can't be mad at each other. God has a mission for us and we need to stick together."

"You are right Kate. Somehow I realize that this is preordained, and that we are together in this, and whatever else comes our way."

Kate said a little prayer of wisdom and protection for them both then said it was time to rejoin the men and find out what was in the plan, so they returned to the office.

Pat broke the silence, "Ladies, we know you are curious and want to know what is in store for you. We see that you are both on the same page now and that is both good and essential. We appreciate your candor, and courage. Your willingness to put yourselves out there in a way that poses danger for you is admirable. Eli and I believe all you have told us, and we strongly believe this is but a small part of the big picture. We were talking about what will need to be done, who we can bring in as more feet on the ground to help us, and a sense of responsibility to you both henceforth. Also you should understand that we know everything, but knowing and proving are two different things. If we are going to gain trust and belief from our listeners, we must have proof. That is where you and others can help. Eli, would you tell them about The Arab?"

Eli took a seat and began, "We both have useful contacts. Those contacts come from various places, in background, work, or areas of expertise and knowledge. So it is with the man who for now shall be known as The Arab. We both rely on him, and we both know him well. He has been reliable and very helpful. However, his circumstance is very sensitive. You can't know those circumstances, nor are you to ever ask him about them. Accept that he can be trusted and is honorable and loyal to this country and to us. In addition, you can know that he is powerful in his own way, and he has helped convert several Jihadists to Christianity. When the time is right, he'll be instrumental in bringing many more Muslims to Christ. He is their brother.

"He'll be here momentarily. You'll hear things, today or in the future, that may shock or surprise you. Regardless, you are to keep silent, and share information with no one. Mackenzie, you seem to somehow know a bit about the back end of what goes on so you may not be surprised, and it's not marketing that got you to this point now is it? Anyway, we are going to set up a game plan here and now and you two are an essential part of that plan. If for whatever reason either of you wish to back out of this, now is the time. And I mean now. You can't be privy to the information we will discuss, for your own safety and ours. And let me be clear, you are at risk. We can assist somewhat in that, and your being in Oregon does help, since it is hardly the Mecca of international intrigue. But make no mistake; this is dangerous business amid dangerous people."

His words were appropriately sobering. Mac looked over at Kate and could see the wheels turning and a look of both concern and intrigue on her face. They were all silent for what seemed a long time when Kate requested a few minutes to speak in private with Mackenzie. The two headed out the door into the hallway.

Kate stood silently looking down the hall, and then she turned, "Mac, I spoke with John a bit ago. I related a few basics to him, but did not give him any details. I did tell him about your encounters though spared him most of those details too. Mac, he is pretty upset with me and you for that matter. He is angry that you got me into such a mess, that I have gone along with it, that I did not get on a plane and leave. He is very upset, and worried, as he should be. Mac, he wants me to leave here today, and he wants me to end our friendship. He believes that you are going to bring harm to me and our family."

Mac stood looking at Kate, feeling remorseful and understanding John's position fully. She asked, "So what did you tell him?"

"Oh I let him rant and rave for a few minutes and I thought about what he was saying. I agree with him on some of what he said. But in all honesty, his demand to leave now, and to end our friendship; and other things were, well, they made me mad. I don't take well to anyone ordering me around, least of all John, and he knows that. So I told him how I felt, and that I could not leave today, and could not abandon our friendship." She smiled rather weakly at Mackenzie, they hugged each other and quietly returned to the office.

Momentarily there was a knock on the door that brought them up short and the secretary announced the arrival of The Arab. Eli told her to have him wait a minute.

Eli continued, "So Kate, Mackenzie, what will it be? I worry about you the most Kate, since you have a family. You need to be sure."

Kate cleared her throat, took a drink of water, looked at everyone, started to say something, cleared her throat again, and finally said, "I am a simple person from a simple background; a life-long resident of Oregon and not yet corrupted by this world. My family ties are close and important to me, as is my relationship with God. So it is with conviction and faith that I know without reservation this is what I must do."

"That said, the primary purpose is to serve God, and thereafter my country. My honor to God and my family would not be worth much if I knew I could contribute in some small way to keeping America safe, and did nothing. And for that matter, if I did nothing, what am I subjecting my whole family to eventually anyway? I can't back out now. I know enough to sense the danger and urgency, and I am in. God protect us all and light the way through this darkness. But I am in."

"Good girl and well said," Eli commented, as he reached for the phone to have his secretary bring in The Arab.

The door opened and a man of considerable stature entered. He had on dark sunglasses, shortly cut black hair that was very thick and wavy. He was well attired in a sport coat and slacks. Nothing extraordinary stood out about him. However, when he took off his sunglasses and extended his hand to Eli and Pat, his eyes were striking. They were an odd shade of blue green, and piercing. His lips were defined by sharp edges and medium in color, while his nose was long and angular, set off by high cheek bones and long chin.

Eli welcomed him, "Man, glad you could make it so quickly. I'd like to introduce you to these two women, and we'll use first names only. This is Kate, and standing behind her is Mackenzie. The women are visiting New York from the Western U.S. Ladies this is our friend, Al."

The Arab faced us, bowed in acknowledgement, then turned to the men and in a thick Arab accent, said "What is the urgency? I had to leave my lunch appointment early. Nice to meet you both. Alright gentlemen, what's up?"

Patrick jumped in, "These women have brought us information they stumbled upon by accident. In the ensuing days they've dug up yet more information, and experienced some threatening situations. Eli will give you the overview and pay attention, as you are going to hear a name or two you know."

Eli proceeded to tell the story again, glossing over a few things, placing emphasis on others. When he was done, he said, "There you have it. Interesting isn't it? So here is the deal. We have been clear with the women that this is a dangerous situation, their services are needed, your identification and associations are off limits, and for the purpose of this and future communication, you'll be referred to as Al, so as to avoid "The Arab" moniker. Further, the information we discuss today or at any time in the future is to remain between the five of us. However, we know already that we each will have to make contact with others, some vital to our investigation, and they will be told only what is relevant to them. We will deal only in first names. Agreed?"

They each nodded in agreement.

Patrick added, "I want us to come up with a game plan now. We each have work to do and I am almost out of time as I go on in an hour and have work to do first. Timing is an issue, because there is a presidential election season upon us. And Schwartz, well, he's a huge issue. I knew he'd be a key player eventually, but it seems he's gotten an early start. Al, you have access to information about Schwartz and can get access to information about all the candidates. We need to know who Schwartz is turning to abroad, what sort of deals he's making for money and support in this election, and especially anything reflecting an anti-American agenda. Mackenzie, would I be correct in assuming that you have government experience or some sort of political background?"

She smiled and responded, "I do have a background that had me on the Hill, and otherwise involved in government. I am not at liberty to give details, but have been involved in some rather secretive projects from time to time, but that is all I can say. I have some contacts that remain active in Washington. In fact, I'll be meeting with one tomorrow to enlist his assistance and input."

Eli nodded, "Okay, fair enough. I hope that we have different contacts and different areas of expertise to draw from. We need to cast a wide net on this and fairly quickly. Pat, you've been exploring some economic issues for an upcoming program. Can you and your staff dig deeper and take a global view, staying at maybe the 5000 foot level for now, but look for commonality in purpose and association? I am also going to look at Schwartz. I interviewed him last year on a hedge fund matter and found him difficult, arrogant, and closed. So I'm happy to dig deeper. That said, Mackenzie would you be able to tackle the issue of the many organizations you have mentioned, but get deeper and go wider. Finally Kate, I'd like you to look at ACORN, plus two organizations that need some in-depth probing. One of them is the Tides Foundation and the other is the Apollo Group. In that regard, their involvement in the last couple of elections, their leadership, and what is rumored to be dozens of 'front' organizations. And if you can, get anything on their involvement with Congress and the U.S. government."

They all were taking notes, and all agreed to their assignments. Kate, prompted by curiosity, asked, "Since you both know all that is going on and will go on, why do we need to do research?"

Eli smiled as he answered, "That's a good question Kate. The fact is that we do know in a general sense. But as we said before, if we are going to gain the acceptance of the public, we need to provide details. Knowing generally and disclosing specifically are two different things. We want to give examples, details, and sources."

Eli continued, "We have our assignments. Please put down your first name with a cell phone number and email address on this sheet of paper. When you have found out something you think is critical, or have completed your assignment, please share with us your findings, by encrypted email. If you need help, call either Patrick or me. Keep a low profile, and use an academic research project as your cover. I'd like us to get together here in New York in about forty-five days, give or take, sometime after the first of the year anyway. Mackenzie, Patrick and I will cover your travel, right Pat?

"Ladies, if you have any threats or situations that appear to be associated with your project, you must call the police immediately. Then call Pat and me. I am hoping that once you leave New York, any threat to you will evaporate. But Schwartz is an evil dude and must be regarded as dangerous no matter what. One more thing I should emphasize to you. You will find that information comes to you in unexpected ways and timing. Do not be skeptical, alarmed or put off. Just accept that what you are discovering is based in truth.

"Now, Al, you have heard some of their information, and experiences with Schwartz. Do you have any thoughts at this point?"

Al twisted around in his chair before speaking, "I'm intrigued that he 'hired' a large number of first and second string members of the last Administration. Their cover is that of a think tank, but one of my contacts indicates they are essentially doing nothing except feeding misinformation to the media. I find that odd, but indicative of an agenda.

I might add that Schwartz has gathered together people who serve his needs and wishes when he's aided in the overthrow of a government, and replaced it with his own government. Also, a contact tells me that Schwartz has been traveling frequently to China, and The Hague, with his interests being focused on the American dollar.

"I recall how he brought down the Bank of England, almost with child-like glee. He's a hater, who takes pride and joy in the destruction he induces. I believe him more dangerous as any man on earth; a man who does not give up, and is used to getting his way."

Eli stood up and they assumed that was the end of their meeting. He motioned Kate and Mac to remain seated. The two men bid goodbye to Al, then returned their attention to the women.

"There is one more thing. Kate, you have accurately determined that Patrick and I are the Witnesses, as in the Bible. It is our destiny, we have been chosen and this is something we have to do; no, are called to do—to wail and warn people, and to bring some balance to the inaccuracies presented by the world-wide media. As is oft stated in the Bible, media gives power to the beast, and we need to weaken that power. It is our calling and we will give it our all over the coming years. We have been called to do no less."

"But, there is more to this. I expect that Kate sees it now. Mackenzie, you don't. You think your encounter and subsequent involvement with Schwartz was by accident. There are no accidents. In fact you two have been called here for your own mission. It is not to tell us what we already know, but to write a book about what we all know, to warn America and the world, and expose those who would do this great country harm."

Mac sat there, with a desire to object, to stand and refute, and to say something, anything. But she was immobile, as if paralyzed; her head was spinning with this latest announcement. Kate touched Mac's arm with concern.

Mac managed to mumble, "I feel like I am in the twilight zone. Is this a dream? Surely this is a dream. Things like this don't happen in real life. Besides, I am one who functions in the gray areas. You are asking me to accept things as black and white. And one question begs to be answered—after your three or four years, what then?"

Pat nodded with understanding as he said, "At the end of that time, with people resistant to repenting, there will be massive disasters that create havoc and crisis far and wide from coast to coast, and around the world. It is determined that these things will, and must happen."

Eli interjected, "Mackenzie you will be safe, and taken care of. Trust. Believe. Have faith."

Kate said softly, "Mac, this is no dream. What you have just heard is real—we all believe it—they know it. Well, perhaps not Al, but the rest of us. I did not know what our mission would be, but I felt there was one. It all makes sense now. We can do this. You can do this. We just need to go home and get organized, and stay focused."

Using a soft quiet voice, Eli said, "We are in this together. We have our work cut out for us. There are risks, but this is important, and my sense is that one year from now we will be far more aware of how critical our work is. Are there any questions? Are we all clear now? If so then I suggest we go our separate ways and remain in touch. Pat will arrange to get you two back here, but when is not yet clear. Please do your research, and get busy on the book Mackenzie. It will come to you as if with no effort, trust me."

Patrick asked for their attention, and continued, "People here and elsewhere in the world are uncomfortable, confused, searching for they know not what. I want to relate to you a brief piece from Scripture that speaks to this situation well."

"The Pharisees and Sadducees (in the Book of Matthew), came to Jesus and tested him by asking him to show them a sign from heaven. He replied, 'When evening comes you say, It will be fair weather, for the sky is red,' and in the morning, 'Today it will be stormy, for the sky is red and overcast.' You know how to interpret the appearance of the sky, but you cannot interpret the signs of the times. A wicked and adulterous generation looks for a miraculous sign, but none will be given it except the sign of Jonah."

"The sign of The Time is taken from Jonah 3:10, 'But the Lord said, 'You have been concerned about this vine, though you did not tend it, or make it grow. It sprang up overnight and died overnight. But Nineveh has more than 120,000 people who cannot tell their right hand from their left and many cattle as well. Should I not be concerned about that great city?'

Patrick continued, "People are so confused, and it is in this confusion that evil can thrive. Essentially, if people don't believe, they leave themselves open to having their souls taken over by evil. But if they fill themselves with the word of God, they are protected from such evil."

"We all are here to help people find their way, and to successfully battle against evil with the full armor of God. It is our mission and calling, to do this now. We know that they will all be tested in the not too distant future, which according to the Bible is from election-day 2008 a total of forty-two months, and we will be given power for the same period of time, and they will have power to devour their enemies."

Eli said, "When we have finished our wailing the beast will rise up against us, out of the darkness, and attack us, and kill our broadcasts."

They were solemn in their acknowledgement of the tasks before them. They stood, shook hands, took their contact sheets and departed the building. Once at the street Mac told Kate she needed a drink, so they headed off to a hotel bar. They decided the next day would be their spa time, and they'd head home the day after.

Once tucked away in a cozy booth in a pleasant bar with fireplace and warm décor, they sipped their drinks in silence; so much to absorb, so much to understand. Both of them were lost in thought, putting their personal involvement into perspective. Finally Kate broke the silence when she asked, "Shall we go out to dinner or order room service?"

"I am definitely in favor of room service and a quiet evening to talk and reflect," Mac responded. They ordered another drink before heading to their hotel. Kate said, "You were going to tell me about that phone call of yours. How about now?"

"Oh Kate, it is complicated. I can't tell you the whole story. But you recall I did legislative work on the Hill years ago? Well, I met a man who was involved in a very secretive project and he recruited me to do some research for him. One thing led to another and over the years I have been recruited to work on, well, various undercover assignments.

I have made some valuable and creepy connections over the years. My involvement, while infrequent, includes relatively current activity, as of two years ago. Don't ask for details or I'll have to kill you," Mac smiled and laughed.

"Funny, but I am actually not surprised," Kate commented. "Okay, I'll leave the topic alone, though I might die anyway from curiosity."

With that, they stood and headed out to nab a taxi, both lost in thought, but eager to kick off their shoes and relax with a good meal, in anticipation of a luxurious spa day.

###

CHAPTER SEVEN

A crisis is an opportunity riding the dangerous wind.
Chinese proverb

The following morning Kate and Mac had a light breakfast in their room. Kate had forgotten that Mac had a luncheon appointment, so she decided to hit the spa immediately, and then take in a matinee theatrical production. They agreed to meet back at their suite by 5 o'clock.

Mackenzie stood in the street, the cold winds blowing between the giant concrete monoliths of business. Though dressed warmly, her body was chilled to the bone and she began an involuntary shivering. She had a sudden urge to release a primal scream, but opted to contain herself till a more appropriate time and place. She had plenty of time so she decided to walk a few blocks. She walked slowly, taking in the sights, sounds and smells of this city she loved and as she walked she was struck with an eerie feeling that she'd never return here to have things be the same. It felt like a huge loss that left Mac almost in tears.

A man hurried past her, bumping into her shoulder, jarring her out of her morose thoughts. She stepped to the curb and hailed a taxi for the ride to Grand Central and the Oyster Bar; arriving a bit early and able to get a table at the back of the room with a clear view of the hostess desk. Jack was on time, bless him. He came dashing into the restaurant, breathlessly looking around as he stripped off his top coat. Mackenzie waved and caught his attention. He made his way across the black and white tile floor with mass of tables abuzz with chatter and clinking glasses.

"Mac girl! It's been too damn long. I was getting ready to call you back here anyway, so it's good that we are having this meeting. I know something is on your mind, so we both have stuff to discuss. But before that, let's spend a few minutes getting caught up. You first."

They spent about twenty minutes updating each other on what had been going on in their lives. They had been friends and co-workers for years, so conversation passed easily between them. Mackenzie knew Jack's family, spent time out at their house in the North Virginia suburbs on occasion, and felt that Jack had her back. She felt safe and secure in Jack's company. So it was quite natural for them to huddle closely over a cocktail, engrossed in conversation and laughter. She felt immensely better after spending time with Jack. Finally, Jack held up his hand and said it was time to get down to business and order lunch. He was starving.

"Mac I read your last report. You have dug up quite a bit. We still have a hole of information regarding the Middle East. Now I could get it quite easily, but as you know, this project involves very few people and must stay that way. Do you have any current contacts over there?"

"Jack, most of my contacts there have retired or been reassigned. But someone new has popped up and I think he will be helpful. I'll fill you in on him shortly. All I can say about the report now is that this guy has been very cautious, and he's been at the planning for many years—at least twenty from what I can tell. His power base is enormous and global. I just don't know how we can get him. It seems to me that he is getting a bit more open, a bit more exposed and I think that's so because he is very confident, so he can afford to be more brazen. Frankly I don't see us implicating him in much of anything. He has covered his trail well, and he has hordes of minions watching his back. The question is—would any one of them be willing to insert a knife in it?"

"That said, I have been pulling together different pieces into various scenarios, in an effort to glean just what is his ultimate objective. There are a number of options, none of them good, but the worst-case scenario is just too extreme for me to wrap my mind around. Frankly I am worried, that we can't stop him, and that he will succeed at any level."

"Yeah, I read the reports and I agree. We had stuff on him from back in the Clinton days. He turned into a hot potato then, as you know, and was dumped for fear of drawing attention to what he was doing. But he kept doing it, just outside the administration, and went further underground, but no less successful.

"You have a right to be worried. Until your reports I believed his main agenda was the take-over of the World Bank. Now I believe it is a much bigger plan and far more insidious. So listen Mac, the pressure is on to wrap up this investigation. I don't think I can give you more than two, possibly three weeks at the most. Can you finish in that time? So who's the new contact for the Middle East?"

"Jack, I'll focus on this project and get it done, hopefully in less than three weeks. As for the new contact, I don't know anything about him except that he was educated in England, is an Arab, has a mysterious background and a broad pipeline of contacts in the Middle East. That brings me to my update."

Mac proceeded to relate the details of her experiences while in New York, from encounters with various people, the conference, and the attacks. She handed Jack an envelope containing notes from the conference then leaned toward him to speak quietly.

"Jack, did you know what this conference was about? Did you know who would be there? We were not allowed to attend some breakout sessions, but I managed to listen in on one of them. I had a hard time hearing through a wall, but what I did hear was at once confusing, and chilling. It seemed to me that there was a core group there whose primary interest is to bring down the dollar, take control of the Federal Reserve, and move it into a One World Bank, with control over multi-national economies. If this is so, then it would seem the International Monetary Fund plays right into the plan. I can well imagine this plan has been many years in the making, and as far as I know there is no oversight of either the IMF or World Bank. I have been trying to find out where the controls are over the World Bank and it's as if it is some underground top secret facility devoid of any transparency at all. How the hell can this be? It's OUR money!"

Jack grimaced with understanding as he began speaking, "I knew about the conference, but not who would be there, nor about the private sessions, but I am not surprised. The IMF was set up as a bank to handle U.S. money after the war and to work with foreign countries to make loans to rebuild. There should have been massive hearings on what is going on there, but like all the hot potatoes, this one remains tucked away and out of sight in the darkness. But worse than that, the organization is being protected by the Fed Chairman, the President, and numerous Senators, among others.

"Did you find out what they are doing over there at the World Bank?" Mac nodded in the affirmative. "So what have you found out?" Jack prodded.

She lowered her voice, "Jack, I don't know where I got the idea that there were controls over the IMF and World Bank. But what I have found out is that no one is charged with oversight, at least anyone who holds U.S. interests as primary. These groups are not accountable to our government or any other. As if that's not bad enough, their history is deplorable and outrageous. It seems that the organizations that control the ebb and flow of money do so in the dark of night. You can't even get freedom of information action there. But, over many decades the World Bank has used its money (from whatever source) to make loans to poor countries. Generally those loans have been forced on the countries to be used for infrastructure projects. You know, bridges, dams, hydro-electric projects, highways and airports, stuff like that."

"And who uses those facilities? Next to no one since most people in these countries don't have vehicles, plumbing or electricity. So essentially only a handful of wealthy people benefit in each country; add to that, the money ends up in the hands of some giant U.S. companies that do these projects. There are apparently only a handful of engineering companies who are financially and legally authorized to handle such huge projects; so the same ones come up time and again."

"Those companies and executives are enriched, the leaders of these poor countries are enriched and the poor people remain poor. Then it comes to paying back the World Bank. When each country can't (and almost none can), a deal is orchestrated whereby the country's government signs over to the World Bank its natural resources throughout the entire country, as a means of paying down the debt, or as collateral for the loan. The World Bank then leases those assets to companies that go in and suck each country dry, making it all the more poor, and with no options."

"Now I don't know how this goes on without being uncovered and investigated. The whole thing is crazy. Can't you get access to records through your department? I simply do not understand how we have allowed Congress to abdicate their oversight, to turn our money over to this institution, and then let them dictate how our economy goes. And essentially that is what is happening. How the dollar goes affects other currencies; and the boys who head up the WB and IMF can hedge their bets and manipulate currencies to work for them, without concern about negative impact elsewhere. This is NUTS! Plus there is a question of legality. I mean, the WB and IMF are using taxpayer money. They are investing that money and gaining enormous enrichment from commodities being sucked out of various countries. Yet, that money is not used to pay down our debt, lower our deficit, or get returned to the taxpayers in any form. What the hell is going on? Where is all that money going?"

Jack sat contemplating what Mac had told him, sipping his cup of coffee before he spoke. "I have tried to access documents before to no avail. But you're right, they long ago moved beyond a point where these institutions should be guarding our money; much less have free rein on how it is used. It seems like the fox guarding the hens. I am going to do some digging on this one. It is not clear just who is responsible for the pillaging and diverted profit."

"When are you going back to Oregon? You seem out of sorts, nervous, something going on. What's this about? Have you found out other information you're not sharing? Mac, I've known you a long time; we trust each other and have covered each other's backs. Is there something wrong, something I need to know?" Jack pressed.

Mac looked across the table at him, wishing she could tell him everything, but she knew she had to keep much of what was going on to herself. She replied, "Oh Jack, I guess I am just tired. This has been far too eventful a trip. I am worn down by the work on Schwartz and in many respects I feel like I am mired in a stench-filled slimy pit. It's beyond unpleasant, and like an onion, layer upon layer discloses more stench and evil. I'll be okay. I need some rest. We are heading back to Oregon tomorrow, barring further crisis."

Jack nodded knowingly, but still puzzled. He said, "I'd like you to promise to keep me posted on any further problems, and if there is another incident of assault or threat, I am going to put a team with you. You have my permission to put them to work gardening or whatever you need done. They need to earn their keep and not just sit on the porch hiding behind sunglasses."

Mac laughed, "Now a couple of beefy boys doing my gardening and chores. What an image. What a concept! Okay I promise. But really, Oregon is just too far removed from the action here in the East for those creeps to bother with little old me. For that matter, I still don't understand why Kate and I have attracted any attention or interest from Schwartz. That has been the most unnerving part—why me, and how many things have happened here. I've thought about it and now have no doubt that we'll be on our own and without incident back at home. I do want to complete your project so I can get on with another one. As for those boys? It might be kinda fun to have them wandering around in shorts, shorts and aprons."

Jack winked and gave a low hoot. "Mac, I'll hand pick 'em just for you. Now I need to get going. If you want to talk, about anything, I am but a cell phone call away (the quiet one). My train leaves in thirty minutes. Get that report in and I promise to keep you off the charts and calendar. I know you want no more assignments. But you have to admit, this one fits well with your writing project, right? I am dead serious about you being alert once back home. The man has tentacles around the world, and he will stop at nothing to get his way."

Jack paid the bill, gave Mac a hug and hurried out of the restaurant to his train heading south back to DC. Mac sat there staring blankly at the crowd in the restaurant, still busy at 3 PM. Each time she is in a group of people, she can't help but wonder if any of them have any idea of what is going on in Washington or in this world. She figured that most people are wrapped up in their lives, business appointments, family, and social activities; and take for granted the life they have. She thought they must feel secure in their belief that it will always be like this. But she knew it would never be the same again. She wanted to stand and scream out to them to wake up, to do what they needed to do.

She thought, "call me crazy, but I sense this finite undercurrent, barely evident. I'm not sure what it bodes, but something is afoot and Ivan Schwartz is I believe, at the core of it." She shuddered again.

She drank her tea lost in thought when her cell phone jarred her back to the moment. Kate was calling wondering where she was and to announce that she had tickets for an evening theatre performance. Mac said she'd be back shortly, then hurried out to the street, grabbed a cab and returned to the hotel. Kate was there all smiles, having had a good day at the spa. Mac was jealous and exhausted.

"How long do we have before the show? Can we grab a snack and then have dinner after? The reason I ask is that I'd like to run over to the spa and get a massage and that sea salt scrub. Two hours? I am sure I can get back by then, and one hour to get ready. It's 4 o'clock now, so I can be back and ready to roll at 7. That would give us time to grab a snack before the 8 o'clock curtain."

The spa treatment was most welcome, the scrub heavenly, offering much needed relaxation. She needed this respite and relaxation. She hurried back to the hotel to dress and they dashed off. They saw a terrific play, followed by a good meal and back to the hotel to pack and get ready for their flight. It was a pleasant and relaxing way to end what had been a hellacious week. Mac wanted to remember New York this way. She wanted to think back to this evening, to earlier visits with Andre and for it to remain a happy image, especially in light of what Eli and Patrick had told them.

Kate and Mac returned to Oregon, filled with enthusiasm for their project, anxious about the possible unknowns, and eager to get to work, but also relieved to be home and back to normal lives. However, after a few days at home they realized that they felt an emotional let-down after all the excitement in New York, which offered them the sort of big-city energy and sophistication that was energizing. Plus, their involvement in uncovering the mysteries of all those experiences while in New York served to heighten their curiosity.

They concluded their research and forwarded the results to both Patrick and Eli. Mac was urged to begin the writing project, so they started gathering information as Mackenzie worked on an outline for the book.

Even with the holidays of 2007 in full swing, the news was filled with reports on the many candidates running in both parties. Most people thought we'd elect the first woman to the office of President but we had gained insights in our research that showed us that would not likely happen. A strange man rose up from the sea of people, grabbing media attention; his name—Damon H. Nadir. He was tall, attractive, had an appealing family-man image and seemed gifted at public speaking. He held even greater appeal because he was of mixed race, and if elected, would be the first minority President. We already knew that he was Schwartz's 'chosen one,' but now he was out there in a big way.

Certainly the media had found its new political darling, fairly clucking along behind him like faithful little chicks; or drooling with adoration like pups. One pompous, ridiculous guy in the media even raved about feeling tingles up and down his leg whenever he heard Nadir speak. But then, he was a fool. It seemed of no consequence that Nadir had no experience in business or management, or that he was a junior Congressman with minimal government experience. Why, he'd not even run a hot dog stand or delivered pizzas! Many were impressed by his presentation, but some questioned the lack of substance, and of them a few started questioning his background, which was vague at best.

Some people felt that he was likely a solid candidate at some point in the future, but could not imagine him being taken seriously now. Mac tended to that belief, for a time anyway.

2007 seemed to fly by. They were busy with their lives and Mac with the writing project. News was dominated by all things politic, especially when a group of celebrities came out with an endorsement for Nadir. The media responded with increased adoration and a virtual coronation, of sorts. Still, there was the matter of lack of experience, which would assuredly be cause for alarm, if not the void in his background. Besides, there was a wide open field of state and national politicians, ex military, business leaders, members of the legal profession, and of them, more than a couple of highly qualified people.

As political 'seasons' go, this one got underway far too early, and was wearing thin far too soon. Lost amid the miniscule reporting of candidate activities and statements was an overview of what was going on in the world.

The last half of 2007 saw millions of recalls of Chinese-made products; massive winter storms with flooding, landslides, earthquakes, and record snow falls in various places. There were bridges that collapsed killing many; fires ravaged Greece; anti-government protests in Guinea that resulted in martial law. Chavez expanded his control within Venezuela and his powers elsewhere; and suicide bombings dotted the global landscape. Masses of people sought out drugs to calm their fears and gnawing unease.

Tony Blair decided he'd had enough as British PM and resigned. Ireland finally signed a peace agreement and formed a coalition government. Nigeria's elections were held amid outcry of rigging; and Hamas and Fatah eased stress in Palestine by forming their own coalition government.

The United States, rife with its own natural disasters, also saw the horrifying massacre of 32 students at Virginia Tech; the first woman, Cora Lamia, elected as Speaker of the House; and the first woman was elected President of Harvard in its 371 year history. We were bombarded with information from the UN and a government panel that indicated global warming was a result of gas emissions at about the same time President Bush was at the G8 conference where all countries vowed to lower their gas emissions; and Al Gore was awarded the Nobel Prize for his work on global warming. Questions galore dogged the global warming issue as thousands of global scientists produced a document stating it was a false claim intended to create fear and to get people to go along with drastic and costly measures to lower emissions in the U.S. Follow the money; yes that was an especially valid call in this instance. There were billions to be made by the few (Gore and his cronies), such that there was enormous motivation to fudge if not outright rig the data.

Meanwhile the first signs of economic unrest began to emerge, initially with a downslide of the stock market in response to the 9%

drop in China. The mortgage crisis was just starting, though the CBO announced the third year drop in our national deficit, down to $200 billion. The Immigration Bill hit the wall, with public outcries and outrage against it. The nation was on edge, and the war in Iraq was a central theme of dissent and disgust. People wanted the war to end and were vocal in the extreme, to which most candidates directed their rhetoric, supporting immediate withdrawal, generally against the surge of which General Petraeus was put in charge.

Americans seemed in a state of anxiety and angst. They were dissatisfied with status quo, but not really aware of just what it was, or what alternatives might be better. The country was divided on so many issues, not the least of which was politics, and the war. Oh they were really up in arms over the war. Hearings, finger pointing, accusations, debates, costs of money and lives—Americans were for the most part against the war, and against the President.

We had become a hyphenated society and the national spirit of unity we experienced on and after 9/11, that joined us all together as one, was no longer. Mac sensed a level of racial rift that was not unlike what she had witnessed long ago as a child, only now there were many races involved.

Far worse was the prevalent attitude of entitlement, and blame. It was not 'my' fault, but 'theirs.' We had become a nation of victims, looking for an easy mark, a way to get even, a scheme that would bring us fast and easy money. As a society we had become highly litigious, and juries were eager and delighted to punish whatever evil business in favor of the 'victim.'

Hot buttons that prompted one group or another to speak out or silently rumble, but what was evident was that we were divided on most topics, and a level of dissatisfaction permeated the various campaigns going on around the country.

Mac figured it was no wonder that a dashing multi-racial candidate was able to make endless promises—of peace, easier days ahead, freebies and programs to make life easier, and all the while, to be believed. It's called wishful thinking—hope and change. And if one wants to believe, one will believe, no matter how many contradictions or facts are proffered to dispel the dreams.

Americans had become so apathetic with such cold hearts, they did not see; could not see the truth. Some people cared not that Nadir had no experience while others believed there was no free lunch and experience and substance were king.

Kate was balancing her extremely busy schedule with doing some research for the book. Having more free time, Mac devoted a great deal of her time to research as well as starting the writing. Mac wanted to know about the backgrounds of some of the candidates, and the many issues being raised on the campaign trail.

Now, Mac was an experienced researcher, having done years of special assignments within her secret past, as well as marketing projects. So she knew the process—one starts with a name or concept, and in the digging, goes deep and wide in multiple layers. Mac expected as much, as she dug into four key candidates. What she did not expect was the scope, depth, complexity and curiousness of what she discovered when digging into Nadir.

Frankly the details were overwhelming, even astonishing; and she could not understand why there was no mention of this information in the media. Certainly if she, as a savvy but private citizen, could find the myriad of information she had uncovered, anyone could. She did not impose any freedom of information requests; though felt someone should be demanding documents that were not readily available, even though they were standard fare offered by every Presidential candidate. Her findings were causing her sleepless nights and she was beginning to doubt her findings, so outrageous and disconcerting were they.

Several days of digging and Mac needed to unload, in an effort to make sense of it all, so she called Kate. "Kate, have you got a free evening this week? I really need to talk about what I have uncovered. I'm beginning to doubt myself, you, these two witnesses, and how I am assessing it all. Let's do dinner and chat. How about coming over here and I'll fix us some comfort food. Besides, we've not had more than phone visits in weeks!"

"Mac sweetie, I'd love to come over. I have been working too much. How about tomorrow? I can cut the day short and be over there about 5. Does that work? Can I bring something? I have lots to share with you too, notes for the book, and notes from my own research. Ya know, something in all of this is bothering me too. Something is looking fishy. I can't put my finger on it yet, but I have this icky feeling, so the timing is perfect for us to share and spend time together. And comfort food! YUM. With a touch of snow in the forecast, comfort food sounds perfect."

"Gee, icky feelings, snow, notes, and my own angst—me thinks you should bring luggage and stay a few days! Okay dear, see you tomorrow about 5:30. No need to bring anything, just your notes and laptop. I'll have a delicious meal prepared. Am in the mood to cook—it's therapy for me. Night."

The need to buy groceries and prepare a meal was all the excuse Mac needed to distance herself from her research. She needed a break. She realized she had not left the house in several days. The weather was getting colder, the sky gray, but Mac felt energized by the cold brisk air as she left the house to drive to her favorite specialty market, even though it was a bit of a schlep. She stood in the driveway breathing deeply, tempted to let out a bearish growl, like a bear that had been in hibernation. The smells of winter, the barren trees' limbs waving timidly in the chilly breeze all served to lift her spirits.

Once in her car she headed out to the main road south, picking up a winding country road that took her to the market. She was admiring the woodsy scenery, her window cracked with cold fresh air blowing in, oblivious but to her thoughts about the meal she was going to prepare on her return home, and a sense of peace.

It was especially startling when a small sporty car darted out from a side road, squealing as it corrected direction, pulling up behind her. Mac thought it was an over-eager kid in his parent's car, who would have hell to pay if that expensive auto got dented. She resumed her thoughts about groceries when her car was hit from the rear, and she suddenly realized the kid in the fancy car had rammed her bumper. Could he be any worse a driver? Mac was looking for a place to pull over to check her car and hopefully wring this kid's neck. The road was very narrow, with a steep rocky cliff on one side, ditch and dense trees on the other. She saw a driveway ahead and motioned to the kid to pull over up ahead. As she slowed to pull off the road the sports car pulled up alongside her car, so close she could have touched the sleek shiny mirror on the passenger side. Mac lowered her window when suddenly the other car swerved in her direction, forcing her off the road and into the ditch. The airbags went off, the car rolled down the embankment, coming to rest in the ditch.

Mackenzie lost consciousness briefly somewhere in the roll, and while she had no sense of where she was, she could distinctly see a thin man dressed in a dark topcoat standing above the wreckage of her car. He looked down at the wreck, then turned and walked back to his car and drove off.

Her body was dangling from the seatbelt, her head bleeding, she hurt everywhere! Fortunately her cell phone was still in her pant pocket. She was able, after painfully maneuvers, to retrieve it, and place a call to 911. She hung there, waiting, in and out of awareness, except that she knew there would be no gourmet comfort food tonight. She must remember to call Kate. Oh, are there people up there? "Hello? I am cold. Can you help?" She really wanted to fix Beef **Bourguignon**. Where is that emergency crew? Oh God, my head is aching, and I am so cold, she thought. Her mind raced through random thoughts, scrambled and disjointed.

She awoke in the emergency room, having momentarily forgotten what had transpired. A sheriff entered her ER room and began asking questions. Images of the crash came back, as she tried to relate the events, from when that stupid kid in the sport car skidded into the road behind her, and then hit her car.

"Officer, I am not sure just what happened. I don't know if it was an accident, or if I was run off the road. I think it was a prank from some stupid kid. Except, there was a man there."

The officer was making some notes in a pad when he said, "Ma'am, you were very fortunate to get only bruises and a cut on your forehead. This was a pretty serious crash. Did you know the man in that car?

Have you ever seen him before? Do you know the make and color of the car? I also need a description of the man if you can recall?"

Mackenzie stared at the officer, and suddenly she felt sick in the pit of her stomach.

"Oh no. Not again! I have got to call my friend right away."

The nurse handed her purse to her, and she hurriedly called Kate.

"Kate I've been in an accident. Can you get over here and pick me up? This is important, be very careful to be sure you are not being followed. I am over on Sunnyside. Come as soon as you can. I'll explain everything when you get here. For God's sake, be careful. He's at it again."

The sheriff was peeved. "Miss, I need you to focus, and provide the information requested. We'd like to find this guy, as I am sure you'd want as well. Now, if you don't mind, back to the questions."

"I am sorry for the call. I needed to get a ride home, and to alert my friend. Things are a bit fuzzy, but it was a new sports car, dark, blue I think. I thought the driver was a kid, but apparently not. He hit the back of my car, and then swung up alongside me. I thought he was playing around, but he quickly maneuvered my car to the ditch. I rolled over and as I was dangling there, but before I lost consciousness, I saw a man in an overcoat standing at the top of the ditch, looking down on me. He was the driver and I believe he thought I was dead. In any event, he turned and went back to that sports car and then drove off. That is about all I remember."

The sheriff pressed on, "What did the man look like. How tall, color of hair, clothing, or anything unusual about him? And first, tell me what you meant by your comment Oh No, not again."

"Officer, I am very tired. I hurt everywhere. I am not sure what I said before. I may have been talking about another accident, or another neck injury. Both are relevant now. I was upright and at an angle so I could see his full body. He was very thin, to the point of being gaunt. His eyes were very dark and sunken; and it looked like he had circles under his eyes. He had short black hair. He was wearing a dark topcoat, dark gray perhaps. Aside from how overall dark he was, and he had on strange boots, with his pants tucked inside them. The boots had heels and pointy toes, but not like a woman's. I have seen similar boots abroad. He was void of expression. I was struck by the circles under his eyes. He could have been sleep deprived, or had on makeup, or perhaps was Middle Eastern. I just don't know any more."

The sheriff said he'd be in touch later, and asked Mac to come in to the office and work with a police artist to get a rendering done of the man, as soon as she felt up to it. She nodded in agreement, and then sank back into her pillows in an effort to block out everything around her. She suddenly felt very tired and just wanted out of there, but she had yet to see the doctor and apparently needed stitches.

By the time the doctor had administered to her lacerations and abrasions, Kate breathlessly flew into the room, highly agitated.

"What is going on? What has happened? Are you alright? Oh please, tell me what is going on. You look a fright honey. Tell me this is not New York redux? Well, are you alright?"

"I am banged up as you can see. I hurt almost everywhere. But it is cuts and bruises, so I'll live. And that my dear, is going to be the fly in someone's ointment—me living. Yes, redux indeed! They are at it again, and it is pretty obvious they'd like us, or me anyway, to disappear, permanently. Get me the hell out of here—we need to regroup. I was headed to New Seasons to get some fabulous meat and other goodies, lost in thoughts of a grand meal, when the bastard ran me off the road. Okay, let's get out of here."

The ride to Mac's house was mostly in silence, both women lost in thought. They each knew they were not safe and that they had to do something about that. Kate interjected at one point, "Mac you really must call Jamie and let him know what has happened. I insist this time. He has no idea what you are involved in. You must promise me." Mac just nodded in silence.

Once inside Mackenzie's home Kate went about fixing them something to drink—vodka for Mac, wine for Kate. They sat in the living room sipping their drinks still pondering the implications of today's events.

Mac broke the silence, "Kate, today was pretty overt. When the guy tried to kidnap me in New York I could dismiss it since I knew we were in their hair, and we were leaving. But with things heating up here I am now worried. I think we need to give a call to Patrick and Eli first thing in the morning. Now I know you are not going to like this, but I think we need a safe house, someplace where no one knows where we are. We need to stop using our cell phones immediately, or any GPS devices. And we need to keep our location secret from everyone.

"I'm thinking we should get far from Portland, either to another state or we could go to Central Oregon out in the country. Wherever we go we'll need to rent a house, and not in either of our names. You can tell your husband, but no kids or friends should know. We'll get one pay as you go cell phone for communication.

"Now I know this is going to create havoc and hell for your work. It presents a hardship. We need to talk to Pat and Eli about that, and you have to talk to John about it too. I'm thinking we need to stay hidden until we have the book finished and everything is turned over to the publisher. It will be a couple of months at least. I can tell by the look on your face that you are not keen on this and I don't blame you. I can drag my dogs with me and not disrupt anything. But for you it's a different matter. Thoughts?"

"WHOA there girl. Yikes! Mac, this is huge. This would throw my life into a hard core spin cycle! Isn't there some other way? What about you going into seclusion and I can come on weekends or one week a month? There must be another option," Kate moaned but with humor in her voice. "Mac I just can't do this. It's just too much."

"Kate I know how difficult this would be. But really, our lives are in danger. I can get us some protection, and I can get us a safe house where I know we can be secure. I can even get us on site protection through my sources, but I can't guarantee us both safe haven if we stay here. Nor can I get a team to protect us in two different locations. I guess it boils down to how driven we both are in getting this book done and out, and how committed we are to supporting Eli and Patrick."

"You know they pressured us to be sure that we could handle the stresses and were committed to being involved. Maybe it's time for you to sit with your family and take some time to pray about all of this. It's not too late to back out you know," Mac stressed.

"STOP!" Kate was clearly agitated. "First of all, I do not feel that I am in danger. Why? Because all the actions have been directed toward you; and my belief in God keeps me safe and secure. But what kind of patriot or friend would I be if I bailed out? Look, I have gone from average Susie Q citizen, to being involved with Biblical witnesses, gangsters, evil people, and a newly discovered clandestine friend. It's rather a lot to hoist aboard. I think I have good reason to fret. However, look at what so many before us have sacrificed! Can we do no less? We are at a pivotal point in our relationship with the Witnesses, and from all indicators, we have been called to write this book. If either of us turns away from this, we are essentially turning our back on God and country, our friendship, and promises to Eli and Patrick. I won't do that. I don't think you will either. My sacrifice and that of my family is a small price to pay to succeed in helping these two men in their mission."

"I don't know how my John is going to react, but he understands the importance of all of this. He knows now what you have been through, except for today. So while it creates some hardship, he'd want us both to be safe. Listen, it is my faith that keeps me going. I know what is going to happen so I don't worry. You still believe that there is a way for you, me, mankind to somehow impact the inevitable. It is all in God's plan and hands. Our role is to help spread the word and in so doing, bring more people to Jesus. It is time now. I know you see that. I know you believe in God. You just need to go the final step to bring Jesus into your heart and have faith that he'll take care of you."

"But Mac, all that said and aside, I am not going to abandon my business and family. I do not feel the need. But I strongly urge you to make such arrangements for yourself, to find a remote place, a guard, and get some rest. I can't do that to John. I won't do it to my family. I need you to understand. You are fancy free to come and go as you wish but I can't. I have obligations. And John is correct in feeling ignored. We don't need to spend weeks together in hiding. We can talk on the phone and by online chat."

"Oh Kate, it's hard for someone like me who is in their head all the time; who tends to take charge. Remember I don't do well with black and white options. Plus I love my country and am filled with pride over our history and accomplishments. I am so outraged that anyone would seek to destroy what we have, and have accomplished. I feel driven to contribute in any way I can to protect America. But let me say this to you Kate, God helps those who help themselves. I do not believe his intent is for us to have faith and then sit on our butts and wait. I do not believe that all events are inevitable and that we as individuals are powerless over our life's events."

"But I digress. What has me so upset is that I have been doing research on this Nadir fellow. I've made a point of listening to some of his speeches, broadcast on TV or on YouTube. If I just watch and listen to his words he seems a fine fellow of moderate thinking and beliefs, one who genuinely desires to protect what we have. When he was first introduced on a TV talk show with the hint of him running for President, I thought, gee, this is a guy I can get behind," Mac said.

"But the problem is that I have dug deeply into his life and his associations, and have a far different picture now. He seems to be regarded as some sort of savior, or a prophet to guide us to a better place. His words and his life don't match up. He has been and is surrounded with the most evil people, those who really hate America and all we stand for; people who have some sort of agenda that does not bode well for this country."

"At first I thought it was a coincidence that he had relationships with so many people of dubious repute and background, but once I started digging I realized there were just too many of them to be accidental. In fact I've not been able to identify any normal God-fearing, tax-paying regular person in his background. I mean, how many Communists do you know? I know none."

"I've got to recover from this accident and get back to my work. The book must contain all of these characters, and details about most of them. The problem of course is that each time I start delving into one, another springs up, which takes me in yet another direction. But there is commonality amongst most of them, which in itself is really creepy."

Mac continued, "Listen Kate, I understand that you can't just walk away from your life and all your responsibilities. I am just rattled. So disregard the panic plan. I'll work something out.

"Anyway, I have gathered together a lot of information and have much yet to find. For now I am going to take a pain pill and sleep. Oh, I guess we should call Pat and Eli and let them know what has happened. I'm also going to call my friend in DC before I crash, but we should call the guys while you are here."

Kate had been listening intently, but Mac could sense she was lost in thought. She sort of snapped to attention and asked, "Honey have you ever been baptized? You are the primary target of these thugs. And that makes me think there is something more to all of this. Have you told me everything, at least all you can? I think it is time to have you baptized, as soon as you can work it out. It might be a good idea for you to spend a couple of weeks out at the coast, perhaps even longer. My family has a cabin that should be safe. You can take the dogs and the atmosphere will be restful while you work. I'll come out on the weekends to visit. But I'd like you to think about being baptized. If you would like to do this, I'll get information for you. It is something you can do in a few weeks, when you are ready."

"Gee, have you had a vision that I am going to kick the bucket soon? If so, to heck with the beach, I have a long bucket list I'll need to be working on," Mac chided Kate.

"Hey you noticed that I'm the one getting banged up, over and over! May I point out that I am much too old for all this physical stuff? Besides, I am not getting hazard duty pay, and my Hollywood stunt performer card expired a long time ago!" Mac managed a weak laugh.

"Okay, I jest; sort of. But you are right, I have been the target, or else I am not positioning myself very well when we are out and about. Henceforth, each time we hit the sidewalk, you are on the curb and I am on the inside. Now let's call the guys so I can get to bed. These meds are making me goofy."

Kate put through the call, first to Eli. He came on the line with his usual jovial upbeat merriment that filled Mac's living room via the speaker phone. He really was a joy. In his voice you could see his smiling face and bright mischievous eyes.

"Eli, Kate here and Mac is here too. We've had another situation. Well no, Mac has. I think she had best tell you herself, but before she does, I wanted to let you know that I am going to send her to the beach to hole up for a few weeks. She could use the R&R and it will be a quiet environment for her to resume her work."

Eli sounded concerned as he spoke, "Mackenzie, are you alright? I am starting to believe that you should not be out and about anywhere. Someone is sticking to you like glue. So tell me, what happened?"

"Eli, Hi. I am okay, but sore, very sore. Well, I was going along a back road to a specialty store a few miles away, lost in thought about a fabulous meal I was going to prepare. A sports car swerved onto the road from a side road and sped up behind me. I thought it was a kid fooling around, but before long that car rammed the back of my car, then came up beside me and edged me off the road into a ditch. I rolled and ended up upside down looking up the embankment, where I saw a thin man in dark coat, with odd looking boots, standing there looking down at the wreck. He must have thought I was dead. Anyway, he went to his car and drove off. He was, hmmm, well I think he was Middle Eastern, though I told the police he could also have been sleep deprived because he had very dark circles under his eyes."

"I was taken to the hospital and released. I'll be okay, but it will take some time to get healed. Now I thought Kate and I should both go away for a while to a safe house I can get arranged. I am not sure I want to go away alone. I feel I need a bulky guy to guard me. If I am going to the beach, then I am going to get a friend of mine to get me some hefty hunk to come along," I told Eli.

The women could hear Eli pounding his fist on his desk and gnashing his teeth, as he strained to reply. "This bloody business gets to me sometimes. It is frustrating; Pat and I have responsibility for us, our families and now you both. I'd not blame you if both of you wanted to bail out. That said, Mac you have been attacked far too many times. I think it's time for you to get baptized. You know that faith is what keeps me going, and I know it's that way with Kate and Patrick. We all need to keep God in our hearts as we set about doing his work, and Mac, you are a special case that needs some urgent attention. Please go along with Kate, and say your prayers my dear. That beefy guard is a good idea too."

"Have you tried to reach Pat yet? He's off for a couple of days, so I'll get to him upon his return. We'll be in touch next week, and Mac would you please get a temporary cell phone for your time at the beach and make sure Pat and I have the number? We're going to work on getting you two back here in, oh, probably about six weeks or so, but it could be longer. We are a bit behind schedule. Just keep it in mind as you work your calendars," Eli urged.

"Now ladies, please take care of yourselves; Mac, especially you. If you need anything let me know. No more attacks. I've been getting threats too. All of this has me rattled. I feel like we all are in a very bad movie. Goodnight ladies. God bless."

Kate gathered up their glasses and straightened up, then ushered Mac to her bedroom. Next thing she knew she was in bed amid fluffed pillows, ice water on the table next to her bed, phone in hand, heating pad for back, ice bag for bruises, dogs hovering nearby. Kate gave Mac a kiss on the forehead and bid her goodnight. "Sweet dreams dear. I'll stop by in the morning. Call me if you need anything. I'll turn out the lights and lock up as I leave, so don't get up."

Mac laid there in a daze, feeling every inch of soreness and decided she had to put in a call to Jack. She knew he would be asleep so not too happy to hear from her, but it was necessary.

"Jack, it's Mac. I am so sorry to wake you but this is important. There's been another incident. I think I need one of those beefy guys now. I am actually getting pretty scared."

Jack's voice was hoarse from being in deep sleep, but he snapped to quickly, as he shouted in disbelief, "What? Are you kidding me? There? Good grief. Damnit! Dare I remind you I told you that bastard would stop at nothing to have his way. Okay, I'll custom pick a beefy guy and he'll be on his way hopefully tomorrow, but day after at the latest. He'll rent a car and come straight to your house. I'd like you to have someone with you in the interim. Can your friend hang out there?"

"Tomorrow, beefy, good. Kate picked me up at the hospital and I just sent her home. I don't want to call her to come back. The dogs are here with me. I am sure one night will be okay. I took a sleeping pill and am not long for this world anyway."

"You were in the hospital? What the hell happened? Mac, what happened?" Jack seemed as if he'd slide right through the phone.

"Jack, I'll be okay. I was run off the road into a ditch. The car's totaled, but other than bruises and some abrasions, I'll be fine. Sore though. So Jack, can we talk tomorrow? How about you calling me once you have someone lined up to come out, so you can tell me who, when, and a bit about him. Kate locked up the house, and I'll be fine tonight. Don't call before 10 my time though. Night Jack and thanks for your help."

She slept fitfully, periodically awakening to some distant sound, as the dogs slept soundly. Kate showed up just after 9 AM with a latte, even though she shunned coffee and scolded Mac when she ordered one. It was a very welcome addition to this morning.

Kate fed the dogs; fixed some tea and they settled down in the living room. She said, "Mac, have you called Jamie? I thought a lot about things last night. So here is what I am thinking. You need to go to the house at the beach for a few weeks, or longer. We'll work on getting someone to visit or stay out there with you. You'll need to rent a car, which I'll drive out to the coast, John will follow and drive me back after we get you all settled in. Then one of us will come out each weekend to visit too. If you are comfortable out there you can stay for a month or two, and when you are feeling better, walks and drives will do you good. I don't think you should come into Portland unless for an emergency or doctor appointment, and if you do, you'll stay the night at our house."

Mackenzie was warm and cozy on her sofa and the thought of pulling herself together for a few weeks at the beach seemed daunting. But so too was the prospect of being on the radar of some very unsavory dangerous people.

She sighed as she responded to Kate's urgings, "Kate my dear, I'd totally fight you on this, but I actually think it is a good idea. I need to regroup from this last ordeal and I am positive I don't want another. Also you should know that I called my friend in DC and he is sending out a big beefy guy to stick around and keep a watchful eye. He may be in this evening, or tomorrow at the latest. So I am thinking he can help get things pulled together to go out to the coast and he can drive us out there. I am just not prepared for any more of these attacks. My new protector's name is David; and my friend Jack said I'd like him, and that he was very good at what he does, and quite domestic for a bachelor type, oh yes and not bad on the eyes."

"So how about we plan for the day after tomorrow? Mac asked. "That will give me time to get things pulled together; get Mr. Beefy organized, and well, rest up a bit. I know you are eager for me to be baptized. I thought about it last night before I crashed and I agree. It is what I want and need to do. So would you set the plan in action? What do I have to do?"

"Good girl," Kate gleefully reacted. "Absolutely, I will get information for you and make some arrangements. You will have to attend a class before the baptism. I need to check on when they are scheduled. Just let me know when you feel you are ready. I really do think this is the best move right now. Things have just been too hectic and traumatic for the last many weeks. This way you can get some rest and feel much better going into the New Year. I am going to fix you a bit of breakfast and then head home to deal with some matters and clients. I'll be back in the late afternoon with some dinner and hang out for a while. And, Mac? Call Jamie now. Your son needs to know what is going on, whether he cares or not."

Kate dashed about the kitchen and in no time had some breakfast on the table. Mac decided to fold up her doubts and resistance and to give in to this idea—too tired to do battle over any of it now. She put through a call to her son but got voice mail. "Jamie, its Mom. Kate insisted I call and let you know I was in an accident. I am home and taking it easy and going to go out to the beach for a while to rest. Don't worry. But please call me on my cell at the beach. Jamie, I love you. Bye."

As advertised, Mr. Beefy, otherwise known as David, swept in with intentions to be as helpful as possible. He quickly grasped the details and had things organized by the following afternoon. It was just a matter of final details before they headed to the coast, with Mac's beloved dogs in tow.

David was an interesting man, and actually a shock. Jack had told Mac about him professionally, but neglected to add that he was a contemporary, that he was funny, articulate, surprisingly shy, and a wonderful cook. Oh, and that he was drop-dead gorgeous and built like a brick outhouse! Oh yes!

Winter at the coast can be stormy, cold, windy and overcast, but the scenery is so magnificent, it commands one's awe and enthusiasm, regardless of the weather. It was a great environment to work on the book, and the beach house was charming and very comfortable with overstuffed sofas and chairs, huge fireplace, roughly hewn wood beams, and rustic décor. Mac felt right at home and at peace, as if enveloped in a giant hug.

David was outstanding as a companion and guard—an excellent and creative cook, marvelous with the dogs, a pretty decent cribbage and backgammon player, pleasing personality, and without ego to prevent him from tackling whatever task faced us. He was tall at six foot three, thick gray wavy hair, dark blue eyes, a clean shaven face with few wrinkles. He dressed well, in a style that appealed to Mackenzie— casual in pressed jeans, loafers or cowboy boots, t-shirts, sweaters and blazers. Around the house he wore attractive flannel or velour sweat suits. She imagined he cleaned up well and looked stunning in a suit. Mackenzie was drawn to him in conversation, initially about their backgrounds. One evening after dinner they were seated in front of the fire playing cribbage and sipping brandy. Mackenzie felt so comfortable and drawn to this man, and she wanted to know all about him. "David, you haven't talked much about your family and growing up. Is that something you are comfortable talking about?"

David looked at her and smiled, "Mac, I don't seem to have much I'm not comfortable talking about with you. That surprises me, and unnerves me as well. But, since you asked. I was born Alexandria, Virginia. My Dad was a government employee, at DOD back then. We lived in a modest house off the parkway. I had two older siblings.

We had a pretty average life, nothing then was especially noteworthy. My Dad and I did typical guy stuff. He was not very demonstrative and believed in men being men. When I was 13, my Dad went on a business trip. I don't think we knew where he was going, but we later found out he had gone on assignment to Berlin. He was to be gone for two weeks, and about three days before he was due home we got a phone call that he had been in a plane crash and died."

"My Mom was destroyed and was never the same after that. We were never given details of the crash, where it happened, nothing. I tried to find out many years later, but all records were gone. My mother sank into despair and deep depression. My brother and sister were leaving for college, leaving me at home with her. I sort of became the parent, taking care of her because she just could manage nothing at that point. Her sister came to visit and decided my Mom needed to go into a home. She made the arrangements and then took me to live with them. They were good to me, but by then my family was pretty fractured. We all grew apart. I went to see my mother a few times, but she reached a point where she did not even know who I was, and died there a few years later. She was only in her late fifties, and looked like she was eighty."

"Fortunately my father had prepared for college educations and retirement, so we three had good educations and a small inheritance when all was said and done. I went to Virginia State, and then to Syracuse for graduate work. Once out of college I decided to explore government work. Initially I was with the State Department on the Middle East Desk. I spent about ten years there and then went to work on the Senate Foreign Relations Committee, and spent about five years there. Then I met our friend Jack and he recruited me."

"Oh David, I am so sorry about your parents. How tragic for them both and how difficult for you and your brother and sister. What about your personal life?"

"Personal life? In those early career days I was content being a carefree bachelor, where the women outnumber the men. Guy heaven! Once I joined Jack I was always traveling it seems. Oh I did have a desk assignment when I first joined, and at that time I had been seeing a marvelous woman for a couple of years. We were in love. She definitely made me a better man. We talked about the potential demands of the new job and what it would mean to our relationship, but she was sure she could handle it. So we got engaged and were to be married the following year. One evening she showed up at my house in tears. We sat and talked and she told me she had gotten a diagnosis of cervical cancer. It was terminal. We married quickly, I took a leave of absence from work, moved into her house and took care of her. She died about five months later." David's voice drifted off and a look of pain came across his face.

"Oh. Oh David. I don't know what to say. I'm speechless. I can feel your pain even now. How terribly sad for you both. I am so sorry for your losses. You have had more than your share."

David changed the subject and they resumed their cribbage game. Mackenzie knew they would one day talk of this again and felt all the closer to him because they shared the loss of the loves of their lives to cancer.

But with the passage of comfortable days and lots of free time, their conversations embraced a huge array of topics. During quiet times, Mac would wonder what was happening to her? It was a strange feeling, with which she was not altogether comfortable. She would have to talk with Kate about this, and knew Kate would be jumping with joy over Mac's awakening feelings, for David and God.

One day while David was at the store Mac called Kate to share her revelations, and as expected, Kate shouted, "Oh sweet Jesus. It's for real. We are now sisters in Christ. Oh my, I am overcome with emotion, yes and all blubbery too. And David? This is just too marvelous. So have you spoken about any of this with him?"

"No dear," Mac said. "I don't want to make him uncomfortable, and I don't know what to say anyway. It is rather awkward, even though we have had some personally intimate conversations. He has become a friend. I mean we are more or less trapped in each other's company day in and day out, so our time to converse has created a friendship. I just thought it might be a topic to explore one of these days. Maybe I could get a t-shirt with some clever conversation starter and go from there? Something like, 'Have You Seen Jesus Lately?' or 'Do you Feel Love in the Air?'" They could not help but laugh.

And so it was that the weeks of winter moved smoothly ahead. From the living room they could watch the waves and clouds, and the occasional brave beachcomber. On days with no rain David and Mac would take the dogs for a romp on the beach. He did the grocery shopping and most of the cooking, and Mac focused on the book. It was a great arrangement, and provided a level of safety she'd not felt in a long time.

Her time was free to research and write, and to analyze with clear head the events going on in DC, and elsewhere. They remained there till just before Christmas, when Mac planned to release David to return to other more pressing assignments. Jack however would not hear of it and insisted that David remain in Oregon with her, wherever she was, until they had re-evaluated matters. She was worried about keeping David from his own holiday celebrations with friends.

Over those winter weeks Kate and John came to visit, and there were numerous conversations and emails passing back and forth with Eli and Patrick. The planned trip was put off till sometime in early Spring. David remained on assignment with Mac and they managed transition from one year to the next in tranquility and with considerable joy.

CHAPTER EIGHT

Vision is the art of seeing what is invisible to others.
Jonathan Swift 1667—1745

John and Kate came out to the beach to celebrate their January anniversary, spending four delightful days of good food, too many ball games, a few walks, and lots of conversation.

It was during this visit that a most remarkable thing happened. Mackenzie was stunned and realized she couldn't explain it, she didn't understand it, and yet the simplest of explanations worked, in some cosmic way.

They knew that the Witnesses were all-knowing and seeing and were reminded of that with each email they sent. But on January 12 they all went to bed fairly early, tired from an active day. Now it is important to realize that Kate had dreams quite often, as most of us do. Where it got odd is that she dreamed in great detail and remembered every bit of minutia. Mac on the other hand may have had frequent dreams but remembered almost none of them.

The morning of January 13 Kate and Mac were up early so they built a fire, fixed some tea and plopped down in front of the fire. Mac started to relate to Kate a dream she'd had the night before that stood out clearly as if seen in a photo. She was particularly struck by the unusual detail, not normal for her dreams. Midway through her account of the dream Kate was desperately trying to muffle what would no doubt have been a real heaven-bound shout if she'd let loose.

"Sweet Jesus, I had the same exact dream! The same dream," Kate shouted as she leapt out of her chair. "The very same, identical dream."

Mac stared at Kate, "No way, that's not possible. Is it? No, can't be. You tell me the rest of your dream now and we'll see if it is still the same," Mac told her.

Indeed, they went through each dream to find they were identical, having to do with events in the future, later in 2008. As they divulged the details, they were both taking notes fast and furious, stopping for an occasional exclamation or sip of tea, both of them wide-eyed in utter amazement. Now the question was whether this was a fluke, a happening of utter uniqueness, or could it happen again.

Kate was so excited, she wanted to go back to bed and try to sleep again, to see if there would be more dreams, but they decided to let nature take its course that night.

Still, it had them wide-eyed and ever so slightly manic for the rest of the day as they went about their grocery shopping, card games, cooking of meals, walk on beach and finally sitting around after dinner watching a movie together. David and John, now accustomed to the two women's odd behavior, just shrugged and accepted things as they were. But Mac could tell that John was feeling ignored by Kate and there was a bit of tension in his voice.

In the middle of the movie he stood and said he was going for a walk, grabbed his gloves, hat and down jacket and left the house. Kate was concerned, so she donned her own gear and followed after him.

They headed up a road adjacent to the beach, and soon were out of sight.

Kate grabbed John's arm, "What's the matter? Why are you being so distant and aloof, not only to me but Mac and David too? What's going on? I want to help if I can."

John remained silent, ignoring Kate's pleas for some communication. Sure, now she wants to talk. He walked on in silence. Kate persisted, "John talk to me. If something is bothering you there is nothing solved in silence. So just tell me, is it something I have said or done?"

After a few more moments of brutal silence, John exploded with what had apparently been bottled up in him for a long time. His words stung, as he said "Kate, you have put God and Mackenzie before me and our family. You are obsessed with this stupid book project, and

141

with those two guys in New York. You spend more quality time with Mac then with me, your own husband. Frankly I am sick of it. Our marriage is a mess, and you are oblivious, as you pray to God, bow to God, embrace God and regard your existence as some divine mission. What's happened to you? I don't even know you anymore. And I am tired of being ignored, and playing second fiddle to everything else in your life. After God, your work, Mackenzie, this project, there is just no time left over. I have needs too ya know. And if you are no longer satisfied with your role as my wife, then perhaps you should pursue your own interests and we should end this so-called marriage. I've been silent for months now as you have traipsed around the country. Damn it, I can't take it any longer Kate. No, I won't take it."

John turned and looked out toward the ocean, stony-faced and obviously frustrated and hurt. Kate had not seen him this upset and angry in years. She knew he was hurt and she felt horrible for having left him on the outside during this extraordinary time.

Kate put her hands on John's cheeks, and speaking softly, said, "John, you mean the world to me. I don't want, or intend to hurt you, or make you feel left out. I know I have been preoccupied, and yes, obsessed. I have felt all along that I was doing this for us, you, me and the kids. I am sorry I have not been forthcoming with you about all that is going on."

"Honey I need you to understand. I need you to realize that there is great risk for us, our loved ones, our friends—everyone. I need you to realize that there is a force at work that would destroy us all, rip apart this country, our marriage, everything we hold dear. I can't explain everything, no one can. All I know is that Mac and I have been chosen by God to do his work by writing this book. We all have a purpose whether we know it or not, and Mac and I can't falter or turn away from this. The fate of our families, this nation, our friends, and neighbors are counting on each of us to do our part, sort of like they say in church, 'they are God's hands extended to a hurting world.' So of course, there are times when we have to sacrifice."

"That said, I can bring better balance back to our lives, and make sure there is time just for us. Believe it or not, I miss your arms around me; I miss the comfort and security of being close to you. I want that back too, and I want to give the same to you. Can you forgive me, and hang in, be patient and believe I'll try harder? One thing though—I can't share everything with you. You just have to accept that and not ask or expect me to discuss this stuff with you. And you need to understand that it is not personal, nor am I hiding anything. Mac and I were sworn to secrecy and one day you will understand why. Okay?"

John showed a visible sign of relief as he let a puff of air from deep within his lungs. He had hoped she'd say these things. He did not want to sound too pathetic or needy, but this business had become so all-consuming he was at his wit's end. He also knew he did not want to end their marriage but he could not continue as they were.

"Honey, I am relieved to hear you say these things. I guess I am feeling overly sensitive or needy, and probably because there is so much going on that I don't know about or understand, so perhaps I'm feeling threatened. Men really are babies. We need to feel we are all-important, come first; that you women can't survive without us. I have come to the realization that you can do very nicely without me, and it's tough on my ego. And if I am honest, I know I am difficult to live with too often. You are more than patient with me when I get into one of my snits."

Kate smiled, "John dear, we were babies when we got married. Neither of us knew how to be adults, much less parents and spouses. It took us quite a while to figure it all out. We each contributed to the problems, and we each have been part of the solutions. I will admit that it took you a long time to overcome the typical male attitude about responsibilities and sharing the load. It was hard on me and there were times I wanted to kick your ass. But hey, we stayed the course, God smiled on us, and we managed to get through those difficult times. We are being tested again. We once again need to stay the course, support each other, be patient, and work through our difficulties."

John and Kate returned to the house hand in hand, to find David in the kitchen tidying up, and Mac already retired for the night. David said goodnight and went to his room. They enjoyed the last embers of the fire and headed to bed, arm in arm. All was well.

The next morning Kate bounded out of bed totally beside herself, charging into Mac's room to waken her. She fairly dragged Mac to the kitchen and breathlessly told her of her dreams the previous night. Once she had a cup of coffee and could get her mind in working order, she realized that once again they were on almost identical paths in their dreams, which were divulging even more events to come during 2008 and beyond.

This pattern went on for the next two nights, dreams similar (some not), yet all revealing important information that they knew must be put in their book, *Chapter Eleven, The Final Call.* They kept scrupulous notes on each dream, each event, knowing that they'd have to do some background searches, and recall each detail. The dreams seemed to come in natural sequence, not randomly presented, so it was to that schedule that the book unfolded.

2008 literally flew by in blinks of an eye, and by the time the dreams had ended they both felt they had experienced the scope and breadth of time, but the stormy gray, bleak skies of January 2008 hovered outside the windows, reminding them that they were still planted in the present. The sea raged, sand blew and the wind, iced from its trek from Alaska, pummeled the windows. The year was but weeks old—could that be? Could they rely on their dreams and visions to be accurate indicators of what was ahead this year and beyond? They decided the dreams were insightful gifts and had to be used.

The four friends had been playing cards, watching movies, taking walks and generally enjoying the respite. On the last day of Kate and John's visit, the guys took the dogs to the beach while Kate and Mac built a roaring fire. The flames and red hot embers were in stark contrast to the stormy seas beyond their windows, the warmth of the fire welcome against the cold outside.

Mackenzie and Kate went to the kitchen to fix hot cups of cocoa. Waiting for the milk to warm, they reflected back on the stunning events of the last few days. Mac said, "I wonder if these dreams will keep coming, to cover more of next year and further into the future? It is unsettling to be presented with such detailed information. It is an enormous responsibility and frankly, it feels like we should be alerting people, warning them before some of this dreadful stuff happens."

Kate nodded in awareness, "No we must not make any of this known until the book is released. It is not up to us. The Witnesses will do what is expected and needed. We are vessels, nothing more; and it would be a disaster were any of us to interfere in God's will. We must not allow ourselves to get caught up in the future, not with anticipation or anxiety, not with worry or guilt, not with dread or fear. You must look at the information shared with us as merely that—information, to further season and flesh out the story."

Mac nodded with understanding, then with a mischievous giggle, reverting to her sharp wit, she said, "Gee, I wonder if Vegas has odds on predicting the future? We could clean up!"

"Mackenzie, how could you? That is a horrible thing to say. You wouldn't dare."

"Dear, I was just kidding. But on a more serious note, some of the information we now have has far-reaching implications that will affect so many people. I still think we should be warning people. We could save lives, fortunes, businesses, relationships. I am very conflicted. I know the book is intended to warn people, to raise issues, to get people talking and thinking. But there is economic, investment, social and other crises involved."

Kate continued to stare out the window at the wild sea, but did respond, "No. We need to do as has been made clear. We need to incorporate this information, as best we can, into the book. We can't stray from our appointed mission. In the bigger picture we have to stay focused and on point. We could share all the information with Eli and Patrick, but they know it anyway, so let's just keep to what needs to be done."

"John and I are leaving in a while you know. You have all the notes now, so I'm leaving it to you to determine what gets covered and how. When 2008 is nearly done, we'll have a good idea how accurate our dream process were, and even if they might continue."

Mac looked at her for a moment before speaking, "Kate, this is overwhelming. I mean, look at the stack of notes. How is it possible to dream in such exhaustive detail? We've got fluctuations in oil prices, fighting in the Congo, terrorist bombings all over the place, and who wins the U.S. election and that alone makes me want to take out ads warning voters. Right about now I am feeling like a fortune teller on crack! I am not sure how to unravel all of this, but I'll get busy on it tomorrow. I am going to miss you girlfriend. These last few days have been wonderful. I feel all warm and fuzzy. You are a wonderful friend and I love you."

"But I miss my home too. I really want to get back home. I have been thinking it's time to go back. I can't stay in hiding indefinitely, and I have the big guy who apparently can hang out for a while longer, so I'd be okay back at home. We'll remain here through this week, and then it's time to get back to reality. I love being out here at the coast, but I think I've had my fill of winter storms for a while."

Kate smiled and said, "Honey you don't need the big guy out there, because you are one of God's children and you have the big guy above to look after you. But just in case he is busy, or others haven't gotten the memo, it's good to have David with you. Besides, doesn't he make each day a bit sunnier? I see how you look at him. I even see how he looks at you when he thinks no one is watching. He adores you, ya know. And I think you adore him. You two are meant for each other, that is clear. So let yourself go, relax, be in the moment with David and let him know how you feel."

Mackenzie smiled broadly and nodded in affirmation.

Before long David and John, and two grubby dogs returned to the house. The men had promised the dogs would be clean upon their return so they all piled into the back bathroom for the scrub down.

Katherine and Mackenzie busied themselves getting Kate's things packed up, chatting, and laughing. By the time the dogs were clean and racing about the house, the gear was together and ready for loading into the car.

David and John loaded up the car then all sat in the kitchen for tea and cookies made earlier that morning. Before long it was time for them to be on their way back to Portland.

Mac wandered about the house and felt an emptiness, but also a sense of peace and quiet. Kate was after all at times intense and high energy. David sensed her feelings and set about cleaning up, busying himself with brushing the dogs, bringing in firewood, and cleaning up the kitchen, to give her time alone to adjust.

Mac sat and stared out the window at the crashing sea, and the white foamy waves beating the shoreline, before flying up into the air. Off in the distance she could see a line of dark clouds moving in formation for their next attack. A chill came over her, drawing her back into the warmth of the room.

"David, would you stop what you're doing and come here for a minute? I'd like to have a chat," Mac asked. "Absolutely! Would you like a refresher on that tea, or a glass of wine?" he asked.

"A glass of wine would be lovely," Mac responded. David brought in a bottle of wine, two glasses, and sat down in the overstuffed chair across from Mackenzie.

"This is a bit awkward for me David. I, well, I feel terribly guilty knowing that you are hanging around here doing stupid chores and looking out for me, when you have assignments waiting for you. I feel like I have taken you away from important work and you'll end up in some jeopardy and/or ridicule upon your return to DC. I also feel like I am fully recovered from the injuries, am rested, and am ready to go home. I have a lot of writing to do so will be holed up anyway. I was thinking it would be good to head home the end of this week. I also thought I'd call Jack and get you back into action. You poor guy, you've got to be bored to death here."

David smiled but paused, sipping his wine, and looking intently at Mac over the rim of his wine glass, before responding. "Mackenzie, you so misread me. You so misunderstand me. You of all people who know the depths of hell we operate in most of the time. I'd have thought you'd be far more intuitive. But you aren't so it's high time I set you straight. Now, listen to me carefully. Really listen."

David squirmed in his chair a bit then found the right position and leaned back into the cushion, stretched, then leaned forward and looked intently into Mac's eyes. He then decided he needed to be closer to

Mac, so he moved to the floor in front of her chair, on his knees, taking her hands into his, he began, "I admit freely that I was insulted and not a little pissed off that I was given this assignment without an option of refusal. It was an order from Jack. Oh he expressed it as a favor to him, but he would not take no as an option. I got out here and found it difficult to ratchet down from the intense schedule I'd been on. It was all so inane to me, initially. But there was plenty to do to get you safely moved out here, and in the process I got to be friendly with Kate and John, and yes with you. I learned how to relax. Do you know I've been at this bloody job for over thirty years, with only occasional breaks behind a desk, or on a vacation? No time for a personal life since Elizabeth died, nor did I want the baggage. I wouldn't even get a pet because I was always gone. Now I have these two buggers and they have grown on me, as has the peace and pleasantries."

"The most important thing is that I am comfortable. I feel like a whole new man with a whole new spirit. Our conversations about God have been enlightening and given me much to think about. But most of all, I have learned to appreciate this domestic scene, with a fire, the dogs, walks. I had no idea I was such a great cook! I had no idea I could ever learn to play bridge. I didn't know my heart could sing again. I didn't know I liked anchovies. Hell, I didn't know I could relax and be quiet.

"So what do you say to that?" David asked.

"Why David, I am so glad that it has been a good experience for you. I am glad that you have learned how to relax and enjoy some basic pleasures in life. That means you'll be headed back to work a new man, invigorated and raring to go," Mac said half seriously, half joking.

David look exasperated when he said, "Woman you are impossible. I am baring my soul here and you are not giving me a single break. So if subtlety doesn't work, let me be more direct. I like this gig. I don't want to leave. I want to stay around. I like you. I am going to tell Jack that I need to remain on here. And so it will be lady—for as long as you'll have me butting in and messing up. Oh yes, and I might as well let it all hang out by telling you that I am starting to fall in love with you, if memory serves me. So! That is it. You are not going to get rid of me, unless you really want me to go, which I sort of doubt. I am not brain dead; I know there are flames of attraction going on between us. Oh, we both have our barriers and shyness, but we know it is there. And Jack, being as fond of you as he is, and as protective, is not going to demand I leave. You know, I sort of think that he has secretly hoped you and I'd become an item anyway."

Mac sat there, afraid to move or say a word for fear of breaking the spell. She had been battling her feelings for David because she knew he'd be leaving shortly and they'd likely never see each other again. She too knew there was a strong attraction between them, that he liked her and was not unhappy hanging around. But she never imagined he'd say these things or speak of love.

"David. Oh my. I have not been paying attention have I? Well that is not exactly true as I have battled against my feelings for you. Oh I felt a connection with you, a chemistry yes, but I have believed your world would keep a hold on you. And as for me, I had given up on love or ever finding someone I could be happy with in the long haul. Wow. I am speechless. But I'd like to say one thing. I have feelings for you that I have been keeping in check. I have so often wanted you to embrace me, to hold me, but was afraid of my heart being broken again. To know I can relax about that is wonderful. This means that things will be even better; more relaxed, more fulfilling for us both."

"But David, there is one issue we need to discuss. You know some of what I am working on, and you know that I need to finish my work as soon as possible. There will be need to take a couple of trips back to New York before long. I will need to be focused and disciplined and not get easily distracted. There is a degree of urgency and importance in this project that I can't explain now, but it must be my priority till it is done. Can you accept that and not feel isolated, or left out?"

David was grinning, "Whew! When you said 'but' I thought you were going to give me a list of reasons why I needed to go. I know you have an important project. I won't bug you about it, and actually my being around to keep things moving smoothly will give you more free time to get your work done. All I'd like to ask is that we have one weekend day to do something fun, and whatever evenings you feel comfortable in freeing up. I have gotten too soft to get on any rigorous assignment and I think I'll keep it that way. I'd like to see how things go here; if that is okay with you? And that means devoting a bit of time to each other and building a relationship."

Mac suddenly felt quite joyous and fairly shouted, "YESSSSSS!"

They hugged, and finally, finally, he gave her a long passionate kiss, then he pushed her off to the computer and went to the kitchen humming. Mac could hear him calling Jack and smiled. "Jack old boy, this is David. No, no, nothing is wrong. I am just checking in. Mackenzie is mending well. But she is feeling pretty isolated out here, and she wants to get back to her house so she can be more disciplined in her work. I told her I thought it was not a great idea, but you know how she is. Anyway, I don't think we can leave her alone. Frankly, even though I am not privy to all she is working on, I have the distinct belief that her life is in danger while this project is being developed. Do you have any pressing need for me upcoming, or am I good to remain on here? Yes, absolutely. So. Yes. So, so we're okay? Yes I'll tell her. She is napping right now. Well, I'd like to make a fast trip back to my home to pick up more stuff, but I think I'll time that to take place as Mac is heading back home from her next trip. Okay Jack. Thanks. Yes you've got it. Night."

"David what did Jack have to say?"

David entered the room, "Well, he said I had a busy schedule, and would have to get back there soon. He wanted to know how you are doing, and said he'd find someone to replace me by next week. What? What?"

"Oh stop you devil. I did at least hear your side of the conversation. He is not pulling you out of here now is he? I am confident he is fine with the arrangement, right?"

"Okay you got me. He is more than fine. Elated even. Maybe he is so giddy because he can see retiring me soon, and cutting the budget. Whatever his reasoning, he is fine and was happy to hear you were on the mend."

"Now young lady, get to work. Enough of this frivolous foolishness. Chop chop!"

It was indeed time to make some sense of what she had learned about this brand new year. Her heart and soul were light and she felt far more able to handle the task than when Kate and John had left. She had not felt such joy in her heart since her time with Wayne, bless him.

The stack of notes was daunting but also exciting and intense, in a soup to nuts kind of way. She poured over the notes, and decided to get things into order with some cross-referencing. She knew she needed to do some additional research on a few of these items.

The afternoon and evening slipped by, as did a stream of clouds outside the window. David kept the fire hot and managed to create a marvelous soup, served with warm crunchy French bread. They sat in front of the fire enjoying their soup and some superb wine, chatting, enjoying the evening and the antics of the two dogs. Mac decided to put aside her work for the night. They played a couple rousing games of cribbage, listened to some great music, and then the little darlings had to take their last whiz for the night.

Mac had been up early each morning while Kate was visiting, so relished the chance to sleep in. She felt marvelous but was exhausted. It was probably due to being totally relaxed. She padded off to bed and was asleep immediately. David got the dogs taken care of and decided not to wake her. She looked peaceful and deep in sleep.

David rounded up the dogs and had them fed and out for a run before Mac was awakened by the smell of fresh coffee. She grabbed a cup, got dressed and was happily surveying the beach from the warmth of the window alcove when David came in from chopping wood, dogs trotting along behind.

"Good afternoon m'lady! Oh that's right, it is not quite noon, so good morning. Did you sleep well? Never mind, I know you did, if snoring is an indicator." He chuckled. "I have some muffins in the oven, and can fix you a poached egg, interested?"

"I slept so well I can't believe it, and what's this business about snoring? I don't snore! Do I? Tell me no. The last several nights have been tortuous at best. I had no idea how really tired I was, but when I crawled into bed I must have been asleep in two minutes and barely moved till thirty minutes ago. Yes I slept well, and now am eager for the day to kick into gear. Have had coffee but need something more, so that poached egg sounds perfect, and a muffin. You take such good care of me. Can I help, or should I get to work?" "WORK!" he shouted.

She pulled together several sheets of notes and started thumbing through them—a litany of bad news glared from the pages. There were to be numerous changes in heads of governments around the world. We will be facing new leaders in Kenya, Italy, Pakistan, Lebanon, Paraguay, and South Korea among others. The United Kingdom will fall under horrendous economic demise and issue a huge bailout to stabilize financial institutions and their economy.

The American dollar will go into decline while the Euro will increase somewhat in value, temporarily. There will be a buzz going on throughout Europe and Asia that America's economy is in trouble. Several countries will begin shoring up their own economies, in the event of American problems and a resulting ripple effect. Not helping matters, oil prices will explode to record highs per barrel, causing gas prices to soar. Another sign of problems in the U.S. economy will be the takeover of Bear Sterns by JP Morgan. Speculations about upcoming problems will cause most of the stock markets around the world to plunge, losing enormous percentages, from fear of a severe global recession.

Natural disasters will appear more severe in the months ahead than in past years, which would fit with biblical predictions. China will be hit with a powerful earthquake from which many thousands will be killed. A typhoon will hit the Philippines with major destruction and loss of lives; and in Myanmar a cyclone will kill over 100,000. Mac could not help but shake her head and sigh, in perfect timing to the call to breakfast.

"David, this looks great. I'm hungry. I see the kids have eaten and are content in front of the fire. You know, this project, or book is the better term, is daunting. Have you studied history much? Do you have a good view of this country's history? I am overwhelmed frankly. I so want to discuss it with you. Kate would kill me, and if she failed, God would likely finish the job. Still, it is so much for me to wade through and make sense of, and not just tear my hair out."

"Sweet girl, I don't want you to do anything you'll regret or feel bad about. You know you can count on me to support you in any way I can. I can be discrete if need be. I can be loud and bossy if need be. Or I can take up knitting and sit in my bedroom and knit one, purl two and leave the writing to you!" David said amid great chuckles.

They both laughed. Mac suddenly realized how critical David was to her overall mental health. This whole business could take most any person down into the depths of despair. It was just not enough, for her at least, to trust in God, to have faith. There was such seriousness in what had to be written about the near future, and the weight of responsibility was heavy in the extreme.

After breakfast Mac went back to the copious stacks of notes, putting the next batch in order, highlighting things that she needed to learn more about.

In the notes, terrorism will hunker in as a way of life in many parts of the world, with bombings in India, Istanbul, Israel, Algeria, Somaliland, and even at the Olympics held in Beijing. Later in 2008 Mumbai will be attacked, amid world-wide coverage. Terrorists out of Somalia will take to the seas as pirates, attacking cargo ships and oil vessels and holding them for ransom; shades of early American history when the Marine Corp was created to protect our ships from Islamic pirates.

Politics remains in a fevered pitch throughout the year, with endless advertising, speeches, debates and stops along the campaign trail with photo ops galore. The field of candidates will thin out as primaries reflect poor showings, and as donations dwindle. This year's campaign will have a very different flavor than in previous years, perhaps because of the especially long duration of it, everyone growing tired of each other, and voters tired of it all. But it will become quite ugly, with lots of finger pointing and accusations, mean-spirited advertising and rhetoric ad nauseam. The national party conventions will produce major surprises, if not upsets. The Democrat convention will move the first female candidate from the lead to also-ran, as the unknown candidate Nadir grabs the golden ring.

Meanwhile, the Republican convention, which is expected to be a snooze, will be energized by the nomination of the party's first female candidate, Sarah Palin, who will draw huge crowds and generate major excitement as well as hateful attacks that will continue well into the future.

The lagging war in Iraq will take center stage as the primary issue in the campaign, but the months of rumors about trouble in America will start to take the focus off the war and on to the economy.

The government's Fannie Mae and Freddie Mac will go into a downward spiral, and with that spiral the bottom appears to fall out of the U.S. economy. Lehman Brothers will go under, banks fail and the government under urgent pressure from the Treasury Department will opt to take over Fannie and Freddie, and to issue a $450 billion bailout to prop up Wall Street.

Mackenzie sat reading over the notes, feeling numb and on overload. She wondered how she was going to fit so much information into the book without the reader feeling overwhelmed or even terrified. And this was just one year. They had information in their notes that carried them to 2012 and beyond.

As she shuffled through the papers the phone rang causing her to jump out of her seat. It was Kate. "Kate dear, how are you? How was the drive back? I hope you feel rested and ready to resume the rigors of work? I also hope John had a good time out here. He and David seemed to get on very well and really bond. David said how much he liked you both."

"Mac, yes we are fine and the trip was uneventful. I wanted to check in on you. Are you doing okay? And what's the news of David remaining there with you? Have you started on the new material yet? John and I both feel rested. We actually needed that away time. David is a great guy. John thinks you two are a great match."

"That's great. It was super having you both out here for a visit. The events of that visit have me unraveled I have to admit. I have been pouring over sheets of notes just for this new year and it is staggering. Yes, David is a great guy. We had a wonderful talk yesterday, and he has been given approval to remain on here as long as he's needed, or wants to stay. I'm not sure I want him to leave, ever. Kate, we are going to come back home the end of this week. It is time. I am easily distracted here, from watching the waves, or the crackling fire, or taking a walk. Too easy to put off what needs to be done. I know I'll be more disciplined at home, and having David around will keep balance in the days. Besides, my pups are madly in love with him and would create a riot were he not around."

"Now Mac, you be sure to take it easy there and when you get home. I know David will keep an eye on you and make sure you are not overdoing. I need to run honey. Just wanted to say HI and see how you are. Clients just came in the door. Call me when you get home. Bye!" With that Kate rang off.

Mac went back to the kitchen to fix a cup of tea, looking once again out at the sea while waiting for the water to boil. She was struck by the miracle of God's creation in the scene before her eyes, as well as puzzled by the copious amount of evil and horrendous events to befall citizens of the World. To a novice like her, it seemed such a contradiction and was, to her at least, confusing. She likened it to a ying-yang, bitter-sweet, mean-kind sort of alignment. She reminded herself that she needed to study the Bible to get a better grasp on the meaning of all of this. But at some level she just accepted that for man to know good he must know evil; to appreciate peace he must know chaos; to embrace love he must know hate.

Mac knew that the Bible contained vivid descriptions and prophesies within the Book of Revelations, but it was the most complex scripture to understand. Still, from what the Witnesses had told her and what she and Kate had discovered through their dreams, it seemed humanity was now on a path to the End Times.

The teapot whistled, demanding attention. Mac sipped her tea, distracted. She realized David was not around and she did not see the dogs. It was quiet, but for the surge of wind whipping past the windows. The house was warm enough, she was warm enough, but couldn't help but shiver. She added more milk to her tea, and walked into the living room to sit by the window, stopping to turn on some music. Once at the window she could see two people bent into the wind, walking along the beach. She could not imagine a more unpleasant time to be there. The waves were huge and breaking close-in. The sky was dark gray, and trees around the house were bending and creaking with each gust of wind. There were so many trees around the house, each a liability in major storm.

In other times she'd have sat there, secure in the moment, enjoying the rather violent scene from the warmth of this home. But this afternoon, just then she felt anxious. Where was David? As she looked out of the window she thought she saw shadows moving near the hedges on the down-slope of the yard. She moved closer to the window to look again. Was that a man down there? Was that David? Mac grabbed the binoculars to get a better look. It was not David, but it was a man, a man not dressed for this coastal storm. She suddenly felt frightened. Where was David?

She quickly closed the drapes and started hollering for David. It seemed forever, but he came through the back door in a hurry, dogs racing behind him.

"Mac, what's the matter? Are you alright? What's happened?"

She could barely talk she was so scared. She pointed to the window, her voice barely audible, "I saw a shadow moving about down by the shrubs. I thought it was you, but when I looked through the binoculars I saw it was not you but a man, who was not dressed for this weather and definitely not a local."

David raced to the window, pulled open the drapes and looked down toward the line of shrubs with the binoculars. He told Mac to stay put, lock the door, close the drapes and he'd be right back. He grabbed his gun and raced out the back door and down the hill. Mac watched through an opening in the drapes as he ran toward the lower yard. She saw a man quickly exit that area and run south to the dead-end lane. He jumped into a waiting car. Someone peered out the window to see David racing toward the car; then putting their car into reverse they revved back up the alley toward David. Mac watched in horror as the window rolled down and a gun aimed at David started firing. She could see smoke from the gun. She looked back and could not see David. Now the car quickly sped up the side street near the cottage. More gunfire directed at the house, a window shattering. The dogs were barking and she was terrified, worrying about David. Her heart sank, her hands started shaking, and she was left with the realization that her whereabouts was once again known. How? Who?

She stumbled to the kitchen, grabbed a raincoat and ran out into the storm to find David. At the shrub line she saw David moving. She ran to him, "David are you hit? Have you been shot? Are you okay?" She rushed to his side to find him okay, but disoriented. Upon further inspection she found a gunshot grazing on his right cheek. "Let me get you back to the house and we'll go to the hospital. Oh they shot out one of the windows."

"Absolutely not. We are getting the hell out of here now. You can bandage the cheek, but we are not sticking around, period." Back in the house Mac tended to the surface wound, then went into the living room, sinking into the chair by the fireplace, shaking and crying. The dogs came to sit by her, sensing she was upset. Before long David came into the living room, still drenched. He went to the shattered window, closed the shutters and nailed a sheet of heavy plastic around the window frame.

He removed top layers of clothes and his boots, and standing in front of the fire he looked down at Mac. They did not talk. They both knew. David knelt down, took her hand and in a very soft voice said, "I'll not let anything happen to you. I promise. You are safe. I am going to see to it. Know it, trust it. And one more thing; if you give in to fear, you let those bastards have power over you. I know you don't want that."

She looked into his eyes and offered a pretty weak smile, before again bursting into tears. "I feel like a ninny. I was trained to be tough and fearless. But that seems another lifetime ago and now, I just feel exposed, vulnerable, weak, and like I have a target on my back." She knew her girlish bravado was long gone. She was too old for all this stress and worry. The tough broad she used to be had been replaced with a softer, more quiet, less daredevil, and more insecure woman of advancing age, yearning for a simpler and safer life.

"You know sweet girl, it is fully time for a cocktail, somewhere in the world. I'm going to get out of these wet clothes and build us something strong and delicious. You keep the fire burning. I'll be right back. And then I think we need to get out of here."

157

"I know we should, but my papers are all spread out and the bastards seem to have departed. I think we should stick to the plan and leave tomorrow, okay?"

Her peaceful little world had just been toppled, again. But one must keep on keeping on. She breathed deeply, and hugged the dogs; then feeling more relaxed, she returned to her desk still piled with stacks of notes not yet sorted through, and began reading, writing notes as she read, focused on the future events of that year.

Like a chain of dominoes in free-fall, other parts of the world will be struck with fear and their own economic woes. China will issue a huge $600 billion stimulus, while the European Union will prop up their multi-national community with $200 billion Euros.

"It's the economy stupid" becomes a renewed refrain, as Americans stand around in disbelief over the melt-down of the economy. Nadir goes on the attack against his opponent, and makes many promises to a population eager for something different. His call for change will prove a spell-binding, welcome chant to many. For some reason mainstream media will lay off this guy, never asking difficult questions; and supportive of any statement he makes.

Damin Nadir will be everywhere, consuming news segments morning noon and night. He'll create great support and equally great distrust. He is articulate and can spin a phrase that appeals to his audiences, but his talk of America as a bad member of the global community on the one hand, with talk of America's huge successes on the other, will divide people. His call for change will have people questioning him and his motives. He will talk at once of what a great, powerful and successful nation America is, but how we must come together to change it. Just thinking about all these contradictions had Mackenzie confused and doubting!

Over time, comparisons will be made between Nadir and Hitler; questions will persist throughout the year and beyond about this man's background; and people will question his associations, most of which are anti-American, at the least; and seriously radical.

Of course, these visions go to what she had been researching, so she would have a deeper understanding of just what would be going on with the campaign and election. She had lists of characters—dark and evil characters, which had surrounded Nadir throughout his life. What most people did not yet understand, and may never fully grasp or acknowledge, is that this group of characters had been woven together as if in a spider web, each connected to the other, where the typical six degrees of separation could be reduced to two or three at the most.

Those night-time visions reflected a time of chaos in the great city of New York and elsewhere. As if rooted out of the sewers that snake beneath the streets of Manhattan, men of evil intent and actions scurry to the streets like rats, hiding in the shadows, eager to pull a con. People hurt? Aw shucks, it doesn't matter. They are expendable; collateral damage; the cost of doing business. It's all part of the deal.

The 80s may have been about greed and personal satisfaction, but the groundwork was laid for an ongoing worship of money as the measure of one's worth and success. Now Mackenzie was not sure if those who acquired MBA's in the 1970s and 1980s were taught these criteria; or whether ethics was fully eliminated as a core value. It did seem clear that those most valued in the business world during these few decades had MBA's, and went on to lead many companies on a path to huge profits. Those leaders struck deals for ever-increasing bonuses and perks; and cooking the books was a term that one heard with increasing regularity.

Those left holding the fuzzy end of the lollipop were usually employees and minor investors, oh, and those with 401Ks. Their fates were an insignificant factor hardly worth consideration, while doing the deals.

Mackenzie recalled one day in the late 90s having a meeting with the CEO of a new tech company. He was in his thirty's, scruffy looking, in tennis shoes and jeans, feet propped up on his desk, arms folded behind his head, as he proceeded to tell her how they operated, and what their goals were in the short and long term. She asked him about the balance sheet and other financial policies, and what accounting system was being used. His reply was extraordinary to say the least, and later struck her as key to both the dot.com bust as well as the decline in various industry profits.

He spoke of high valuation for good will and future sales and for joint marketing alliances; and a strange way of dealing with sales forecasts as well as deferred losses. None of it made sense to her at the time or since, but this guy was full of confidence and ego. His was also among the first companies to disappear during those tech-wary times. The MBA-created marketing and accounting schemes designed to leverage non-existent assets for the emerging online companies did succeed in acquiring enormous investments by star-struck investors, but it was not long before all the red ink overshadowed any and all brilliant idea.

Mac refocused on her notes. Americans will grow campaign weary with advertising blasting party and candidate. It will be all-consuming and for most, over the top. With not a little irony, the strategy used by the Republicans will continue to be focused on the war, a strong suit for candidate McCain. But as the economy goes belly up, so too will the McCain campaign. The switch in emphasis from war to economy will give Nadir an entry and edge, one that he will maximize to the hilt.

During the campaign there will be behind-the-scenes events taking place that only a handful of people will know about. In secret meetings outside the U.S., and subsequent training of 'troops,' Ivan Schwartz begins crafting the 'buying of the big White House.' Ivan had long wanted significant influence over American government process, and a means of impacting the economy where he would have far more control than he did as an ordinary billionaire. His earlier attempt to buy the White House fell through as his chosen candidate, the controversial Senator, failed to win the election during the previous election cycle. Ivan had a lot riding on that election, not the least of which was many millions of dollars he'd poured into the campaign coffers. He was obsessed with defeating President Bush, no matter the cost. But he lost that election, and from his point of view, by damn, there'd be no more losses.

So he has his 'troops' at the ready. There are hordes of them working in the iffy states, to make sure that each state moves from iffy into the Nadir column. Of those troops, some are organized by his associates, aided by the dubious group called ACORN; and some come from the many organizations Ivan controls. They combine to create a massive wave of influence, supported by a barrage of advertising pro Nadir, and against the opposition. Nothing would be left to chance. That meant that Schwartz would make sure that within a number of states, there was 'intervention' at the precinct level—what would later be exposed as voter fraud, influence, intimidation and ballot fixing. His media machine proved highly effective in their use of propaganda; and making sure mainstream media reported (or not) on exactly what he wanted.

Now Ivan, being a smart man, did not want only his money supporting this massive national effort. So he will activate his Middle East network and through an innovative use of cutting edge technology, will be able to funnel millions of dollars into Nadir's coffers without the need of public disclosure, even though the money is illegally contributed from abroad. Of all the foreign influence Schwartz crafted, none was more important that the King of Saudi Arabia. He alone contributed vast millions of dollars, with many not so subtle strings attached. Schwartz was concerned in that he did not wish to share control, yet he was sure he could keep the King in his place. That proved a serious error in judgment for Ivan.

One of Nadir's school chums went on to be a computer genius who developed a unique means of processing credit card transactions for an early e-tailer; something he grew rich doing.

Nadir will invite him to join the campaign, for the purpose of tweaking this program, to enable foreign donors to contribute large sums into the campaign. No money trail, no investigation for breaking campaign laws, no charges of illegal activities, just an unprecedented sum of money with which to work, showing up as small domestic donations rather than the large foreign sums they actually were. And what about the influence garnered from such donations? There will be a price to pay for all that dough, and it'll be far more than a batch of cookies.

Schwartz lacked nothing in the ego and confidence departments. Aside from actually regarding himself as God (and comfortable with that role), he also regarded himself as his own State Department, better able to negotiate the rocky roads of international relations than anyone in government.

His disdain for America was overt and extreme. As an example, he viewed America as the "Fascist Fourth Reich" that duly earned the events of 9/11. He was against sovereignty for any country, but especially for America, which he believed owed a huge debt to the global society. His ideal conditions in America, which he was working toward, would be a secular open society with a full scope of drug legalization, a view he kept under wraps lest the public pick up on it. However, for the last twenty years Schwartz had funded most of the state-based initiatives to legalize drugs. He had been quoted as saying that he'd like to achieve a globalization of all drugs with no laws, no penalties and no government controls.

Schwartz had a business partner who was a major drug enthusiast, and joined Ivan in his support and work to legalize drugs. This partner, Jacob Evans, owned one of the major U.S. insurance companies, featured in an expensive national multi-media ad campaign. Mr. Evans was known to participate financially with many of Ivan's anti-American schemes and programs.

To achieve the level of economic control he had long desired, Schwartz had mounted a well planned movement to acquire significant chunks of a number of industries, such as the media. Of his media holdings, *The American Nation* was probably the most radical; articles written by numerous Communists, one of which was a former KGB agent. He supported media-related institutes and organizations that promoted liberal causes and over time had donated millions to these groups, courting their 'favor' and goodwill; and ultimately their compliance.

The man was a self-professed amoral financial speculator whose evil deeds have crushed millions of people around the world, leaving them in utter abject poverty. Whatever Ivan wants, Ivan gets and he'll spare nothing to that end, whether toppling governments and destroying currencies, or squeezing individuals till they bleed.

Ivan realized that political power and control is King in America, so he had invested time and vast sums of money in restructuring the Democrat Party by selecting specific candidates who reflected his most radical Liberal views. The transition from moderate and liberal

Democrats to radical leftists had taken many years, but it can be said that Schwartz owned the Democrat party. Politicians were obligated to him, shared his radical views, and did his bidding when it was time to draft or vote on legislation.

If 'Ivan's boy' was elected, they could expect amnesty for illegals, government paid abortion, drug legalization, big-bigger-biggest government, enormous spending increases, reparations in various forms to minorities and other countries for what Ivan perceived to be America's crimes; plus universal socialized healthcare, censorship, control over the media, overt training of activists, further corrosion of our school system, growing secularism with an increasing move to diminish any mention of God. Oh yes, and some form of nationalization of several industries.

People will watch the campaign evolve amid stumbles, gaffs, and a few high points played out before the country. Emotions will run high on all sides. There are those who vehemently disliked the current President; there are others who are drunk on the Nadir aura; and yet others who are just fed up and not liking any candidate. The contrasts are remarkable—youth versus seasoned maturity, inexperience versus multi-layered experience, brashness versus wisdom. But Schwartz played his cards close to his chest always, and there were secrets that no media had discovered, or at least would discuss. Only Schwartz and a handful of his inner circle knew that he had spawned a crop of 'progressive Republicans' and among them were existing Senators, including at least one major Presidential candidate.

In normal times experience would trump youthful promise, but these were not normal times. Leaving nothing to chance, Schwartz sets into action his plan and like a steel trap, it anchors into place a full spectrum of events, timed to near perfection. Oh there will be many events over the two-year campaign period, to gain exposure, influence voters, raise money—Iowa will be visited dozens of times, while the most U.S. donations will come out of California, mostly from the Hollywood crowd. Chicago will be the most visited city with 38 events scheduled during the campaign period.

Ivan was prepared to leave nothing to possibility—this was his time. Key to his plan was the financial involvement of many of his associates in the Middle East. Chief among them was Prince Al-Waleed Bin Talal from the Saudi Royal family. Then there was Nadhmi Auchi, an Iraqi relative of Sadam who bankrolled various real estate deals in Chicago, benefitting Nadir and his buddy Antonio Riesso who was an immigrant from the Middle East, and Chicago 'fixer' for the politically corrupt. Auchi, a colorful character, was in trouble for ripping off the UN's "oil for food program" and was under suspicion for numerous questionable deals, with dubious connections from U.S. governors to senators, and in the Middle East.

But Riesso's ten-year friendship with Nadir played a huge role in the initial launching of Nadir's political career. It was Riesso who hosted the first major fundraiser for Nadir at his lavish Chicago mansion.

Schwartz had a web of connections that was so complicated it would take a data analysis expert with a sophisticated software program literally months to make sense of it all. The convoluted web of associations was drawn into and removed from almost every deal Schwartz cooked up. Money poured into Nadir's campaign, aided by the clever software programming of his former roommate, leaving officials befuddled and unable to track fund sourcing. They may have suspicions, but they will opt to overlook them, giving Nadir just another 'pass.'

Mackenzie felt she knew Schwartz inside and out, and she reviled him more than any human she had ever learned about. She came to one particular conclusion about him after years of observation and study, gaining perspective on his motives and actions. That conclusion was that this man was the ultimate evil on Earth—he was surely one of two Anti-Christ's and he would do battle to make sure evil prevailed over good. She never verbalized that belief because she knew she'd be ridiculed. But nevertheless, she was as convinced of this nearly much as any other belief she held.

She put her pen down and patted the pups heads while vacuously staring out the window. How could one man be so evil, do so much damage and seemingly without one iota of conscience? Just as she was wondering where that drink was, David appeared with a pitcher of a peach-colored concoction.

"Here you are my dear girl. This will cheer us both. But be warned, this tastes so good, so smooth, so girlie, you may think it is very innocent. Au contraire dear one, this is very adult, and dangerous. Join me on the sofa—have a snack with me."

David had showered, was clean shaven, in clean clothes and chic even for at-home casual, plus he smelled of great cologne. Mackenzie curled up on the sofa, sipping this most marvelous drink, which may have looked girlie, but left fire in the belly. A tray of nibbles caught her attention and reminded her of a gnawing hunger.

After a few sips of cocktail, Mac felt her body relaxing, and leaned back with her head on David's shoulder. This delightful man made her feel secure and safe. She could no longer imagine him not being around. They had spent many weeks together now, and settled in to a routine and atmosphere that was cozy, comfortable, warm, and nurturing. She knew it was time for them to move into phase two, and feeling all warm and fuzzy, it seemed like an ideal time.

It may have been that peach dream of a drink, but they both felt romance in the air. David leaned over and kissed her—the first major, romantic kiss they'd shared. At Mac's age she didn't normally get all tingly and toes curled, but that moment of intimacy and that great kiss was a bigger turn-on than she had felt in eons.

She looked into David's eyes and said, "That was utterly fabulous and I've waited for some time for it. But I think we could do better, don't you?" He smiled and grabbed her close, giving a long, sensuous and sexy kiss such that she thought her toes would cramp up!

"So," he said, "does that qualify? Does that move us to premier status? It certainly did for me. I am thinking that we are on a new terrain here, stage two, and I like it. We both know that everything happens for a reason. God in his divine wisdom knew that we needed each other and that the timing was right. In another lifetime, or a different situation, we might not have paid each other any heed, much less liked each other. We are very fortunate that God smiled upon us."

They sat back, embracing, snuggling and talking for some time. Every so often David would get up to stoke the fire, and the conversation continued. Over the couple of hours they sat there, they talked of many things, each sharing dreams and hopes. It was during that conversation that Mac knew she would need to share the details of what had been and was going on. He should know. She could not share her life and make plans for a future with him, and keep secrets; especially not secrets as enormous as these, that put him at danger.

David interrupted her thoughts, saying "My girl, I am going to work some kitchen magic and get dinner ready. Or, would you like to go to a charming, romantic spot for dinner out? How is the book project coming? Are you going to get back to it now? Any chance I can read some of it one of these days?"

"Yes dear, I think I'll get back to the project and yes, I think you'll get to read some of the book. In fact, I think we are near the time for me to share the details of what has and is going on. So we'll plan a time for that discussion before we head back to Portland. Trust me, it is unnerving but I think you need to know since you are involved. What's for dinner? No, actually going out to dinner would be fantastic. We've been holed up here for a long time, and you've been so busy. Let's celebrate with a lovely dinner out."

David held Mac's hand as he spoke, "Celebration it is. Sounds good to me too. And Honey I am glad to hear you say that you will be sharing your story with me. I feel I can do my job better if I know exactly what I am dealing with. So I am all ears, name the time. As for dinner, I am going to make a reservation and surprise you." He chuckled as he grabbed up outdoor gear for him and the dogs and a quick walk.

Back at her desk she faced anew the copious notes she had on Schwartz, especially those related to visions into the future. It was evident that Schwartz would play a key role in the election, the U.S. economy, and the future of this country and it all looked bleak and foreboding.

Schwartz will unleash his cadre of 'influencers' across the nation. They've been trained, briefed, and prepared to handle any difficult situation, under the watchful, micro-management style of Johann Adler.

Their mission? To meet with select members of each state's Electoral Board, plus other state officials. They will also provide behind the scenes organization and impetus to the ACORN operation. On the front lines they will have a team of communication masters to manipulate public opinion, control media and their messages, and coordinate advertising messaging. They will promote Nadir but also hone in on the opposition, rendering them nearly impotent. And because Adler's army operates outside the campaign, they leave Nadir and his troops unscathed by the negative fallout. They are able to turn on a dime, in response to events of the day, including turning out advertising within 24-hours of any incident. As they get wind of rumors, they will stall media reactions, alter coverage in Nadir's favor, and have cameras aimed in whatever direction they want, whenever they want.

The Nadir team was tightly wound, determined, prepared, and willing to do whatever it might take to get the job done. Message control seemed key to their methodology, so interviews with the candidate were few and totally controlled. The fairly new concept of Town Hall meetings were also managed to a minute level, with the audience being handpicked, questions being approved, answers being rehearsed. Endless speeches were carefully crafted and nothing was left to chance or stumble, employing the latest technology including state of the art Teleprompters. Few press conferences were held or random questions taken from media on the campaign trail. Rather, the handlers opted to release speech text, or to control questions and responses, but most favored were prepared statements so media couldn't err in their interpretation of the message.

This campaign may be the most controlled of any in modern history. As slick and smooth as the Nadir campaign, the opponents make many a stumble. Of course, there is an advantage when one group operates outside accepted policies and procedures, if not even the law. Nadir's team is crafty and cunning in its movements, stepping outside the box, and pushing every envelope far beyond accepted limits. The opposition opts to play 'nice'—a huge mistake.

It should therefore be no surprise that Nadir prevails over the primaries, his ground forces handily doing as they were told. There are however, many issues and questions that will dog Nadir, not the least of which is his refusal to divulge any substantiated information about himself. Voters will be asked to accept him without question, and many simply won't. The Internet will be abuzz with rumors, speculations and doubts moving toward the Democrat convention and long into the future.

Certainly there was no track record to evaluate, no writings, no management experience, or leadership role to determine what sort of a President he could be. Of the issues garnering the most energy is the matter of Nadir's birthplace. He had written and spoken of his birth and childhood, but offered none of the normal documentation all national candidates must provide.

One tenacious and hard hitting reporter will dog these issues prior to the election, in an effort to quiet the madding crowd with answers, or lay to rest empty rumor. His efforts will be thwarted repeatedly, as he encounters one wall after another, erected by a team of high-priced attorneys.

So Schwartz's golden boy moves on, as if floating just above the fray, unaccountable to any, protected by many, especially mainstream media. Those people will dote on Nadir, hanging on each word, believing each promise, applauding each proposal. With the forces of vast sums of money, thuggary, and power are the sweet spots aimed at the engorged welfare state. By keeping recipients beholden and dependent, they will also be pliable, loyal, and serve to overburden all government systems. The perfect storm is a'brewin and its right out of the playbook by Cloward and Piven.

Schwartz has a detailed plan, and he will not be thwarted; not this time. He'll leave nothing to mishap, from registering voters to providing them transportation to the polls, and using his ground troops who have been highly trained. He will make sure any precinct in a blue state that is on shaky ground gets 'special attention' to ensure Nadir's success. There will be advertising, mud-slinging, innuendo, and the never-ending promises made by his boy.

In all of this there was no small irony. If you look back to the times of slavery when humans were shackled by bonds of ownership and servitude, it was the role of master to provide and care for their slaves, believing them to be simple-minded, unable to care for themselves. Was it any less a condition of slavery for people to sit in their government provided housing, waiting for government checks, free healthcare, furniture, etc.? Was it any less slavery for people to be promised so much over decades, promises never delivered? The promise of a better life was never intended, only the expectation and reliance. The desired outgrowth was the loss of initiative and pride that set Americans apart from the rest of the world. Gone too was the "can-do" spirit in far too many souls. They sat today no less indentured than their ancestors; merely less aware, and far less inclined to rise above.

If you looked at the American spirit from our beginnings, one saw all those qualities and great bravery within each person who embraced risk and challenge to make a new life in America. You saw such spirit take this country from raw survival to the most successful, accomplished, generous and vibrant nation in history—achievement based on hard work, determination, and drive.

Naturally among voters in the upcoming election there will be concerns and grave doubts, while another segment of our society will be elated—elated that they can support a man of mixed-race; a man whose finesse at a lectern and the glossy promises seemed to lift people up above the realities of the day, with new hope. Euphoric elation will follow the election, as Nadir supporters eagerly await the joyous Swearing In Day. They believe—with all their might, that this man will 'fix' whatever ill, whatever gripe, whatever void; still others believe he will fix government and its excesses, lessen the greed, improve efficiency, better serve the people, stop the war.

Based on what? How will so many people hold such depth of belief in a man who flew in on a cloud, leaving no trail behind him? How can words of promise rally so many? What will it all bode for the people and the country? The visions foretell answers to come quickly and in ways many do not expect, or want.

There will be a collective sigh of relief across the nation as the holidays near, relief that all the campaigning is finally behind us. Many will talk of campaign reform, a need to limit the duration and spending.

If only. Amid holiday decorations, Christmas shopping and unusually cold and gruesome winter weather, Nadir will organize and prepare to hit the ground running. Our current President, under urging from The Fed and his own economic advisors, will agree to an unprecedented economic bailout for Wall Street that will start a rumble of discontent across the nation.

Quite typically, President-elects and their staff operated behind the scenes, pulled together their game plan, hired key people, vetted Cabinet nominees, and got briefed in areas of vital importance. Typically that was the case, but not this time. Damin Nadir seemed to thrive in a campaigning mode, so he will not appear ready to give that up. He will continue with speeches, appearances, travels around the country and abroad, appearing at once as if a candidate and an already sworn in President.

Rumors will reach a fevered pitch about his Cabinet choices, priorities, meetings and staff selections. It is not often that those early choices draw much attention, and rarely do they elicit negative reaction. This time will be very different as the country learns of those individuals who will be advising the President and who will have ready access to him. With barely an exception, those surrounding Nadir will be people who hold radical viewpoints, share radical ideology, propose radical concepts, and vow radical actions. All of which suggests that there was more of a 'cloud's trail' than had been previously thought.

Here, for Mackenzie, was a stumbling block. The visions were clear about Schwartz's influence on the election, and on recruiting key people he wants in various Administration positions. It is clear that the win, while questionable in some respects, is a done deal. What will become a huge mystery will be the nature of a secret meeting that will go on between Schwartz, Cora Lamia and Nadir—a meeting that the visions had defined as a huge scandal, taking place in Colorado just prior to the convention.

Try as she might Mac could not imagine what such a meeting or scandal might be. Unfortunately, as fabulous a resource as the Internet, it did not yet allow users to delve into the future. She made inquiries, but was unable to get a handle on any possibility. Mac decided to put it on the back burner, and to keep digging till she learned what it was all about.

Unity in hope and charity; racism to melt away; bi-partisanship the order of the day within the hallowed halls of Congress; and an open, honest and transparent form of government—this will be the foundation of promise in the new Administration. We will not all be convinced, not all assured that what we hear will match up with what we will see and read. Yet most will agree that this will be a whole new direction and we will need to be patient and give the new President time to prove himself and to carry out his plans.

New Year's Eve will appear to be more a time of reflection and contemplation, than celebration. Perhaps it will be the economy, perhaps the nasty weather, or perhaps anxiety over so many unknowns. 2009 will arrive with more than a few concerns on the minds of the American public.

###

CHAPTER NINE

The grand essentials of happiness are: something to do, something to love, and something to hope for.

Alan K. Chalmers

The weather remained stormy and cold. It was not much fun going for walks at this point and snow was in the forecast all the way down to the beach. Global warming? Seems more like global freezing, Mac thought.

She decided it was time to get serious about loading up and heading home. David had been cleaning out the garage, tidying up the wood stack, and came in to the kitchen, stomping his feet, rubbing his hands, and hollering, "Its bloody cold out there. My hands are numb, my toes surely have broken off, and I lost all feeling in my body more than an hour ago. Who's for a cup of hot tea? Me Me Me!"

Mackenzie could hear him rustling about in the kitchen and the eager whistling of the teapot beckoning. She went into the kitchen, was handed her cup of tea, and they pulled up chairs in the breakfast nook. The tea was warming against the brewing storm outside.

"David dear, I think we need to get serious about packing up and leaving. The weather is more like a hurricane than an Oregon storm. It's time to get things organized. In fact, I'd like to be on our way tomorrow morning, or even today if that is possible, but definitely tomorrow. This storm is making me edgy and there are just too many noises in this old house. I am worried about those two huge trees by the garage that are not looking like they'll last many more days. This is not my house, so I can't just start doing things, but those trees need to come down. I'll let Kate know, but let's get out today okay?"

David smiled, "I knew you were going to say that. Well, you'll be happy to know that the trunk is already loaded. I have some things in the kitchen yet to pack, and your papers need to be boxed up. You take care of your clothes, and I'll bet we are ready to leave in no more than two hours. Does that work for you?"

She could not help but laugh. He so 'got' her it was at once funny and scary. "You do give me a giggle. This is what I call a heightened sense of anticipation. Okay then, we'll press on. After you get things loaded up, you'll need some dry clothes. It won't take me long to pack, and I'll gather up the doggie items. I'm actually excited about getting home."

They went their separate ways, wasting no time. Mac thought they were both motivated to flee before a tree fell on the house or a window blew out.

Before she began packing she called Kate, "Kate hi; we are leaving shortly for home. The storm is right up there with a pretty decent hurricane. I don't have time to chat now, but wanted you to know that the two trees by the garage are looking precarious and I don't think either of them will last another day or two of this. Do you want me to call someone?"

Kate sounded concerned, and anxious, "Mac, please call our tree guy. His card is on the fridge door. Tell him I asked for him to come out today and get both trees down, or at least to inspect both and determine their status. Also ask him to call me from there once he's checked things out."

"So, you'll be back into town this evening. You sure it is time to return? Seems you'd be a lot safer there, except for this storm," queried Kate.

Mac felt a sense of urgency as she spoke, "Kate we are coming back tonight. No longer safe here, no time to talk. I'll call the tree guy now. But really, can't talk now. We've got to get out of here. Some warnings have just been posted on television, and there are some areas that are being evacuated. We are coming home. Now, I've got to run. I'll call you tomorrow."

With that, she picked up speed and within an hour had things ready to load into the van. David changed clothes, loaded the last 2 boxes and they did a tour of the house to make sure everything was packed, locked up and secure. Mac put in a hurried call to the tree guy, left him a message and instructions and they locked the door and left.

As they drove north on highway 101, trees were toppling, followed by mudslides. They dodged a few flying items and proceeded with caution. David's face was grimly attuned to conditions around them as he made the turnoff to Portland. The road twisted through the mountains, with snow coming down. They drove slowly, and eventually dropped down from the coastal range and heaved a sigh of relief.

David was visibly stressed, saying "I'm not sure I've ever had such a tough battle to keep a car on the road. That was intense. Ordinarily I'd not have ventured out, but it was obvious we were in more peril by staying put than getting out. I'm just glad we made it over the mountains in time. But the winds are still fierce, so it'll take us a bit longer than planned to get to your house. Hang in there sweetie and try to relax."

Mac decided it was not the time to have an important conversation, or do anything to distract David from the road so she sat in silence. The dogs napped on the back seat, oblivious to the dangers outside the vehicle. Mac's cell phone rang. "Hello? Oh hi Honey. Is it stormy there? Yes, we are headed home right now. The storm was like a hurricane at the beach. Trees are coming down right and left. Listen, I'll call you tomorrow. Things are pretty gnarly on the road now. Love you too."

It was late enough by the time they made it into Portland that the rush hour traffic had dwindled and they had a fairly easy trip across the river and home. But once home it was also obvious the storm had been an issue there too. She had a good size tree uprooted and hanging on the back fence; some roof tiles were flapping about, and some gutters had blown loose, but nothing that couldn't wait till tomorrow.

The house was freezing, but David had a fire going in no time, and turned up the heat. They unloaded the car of essentials, deciding to leave other things for the morning.

Having warmed up and gotten things put away, they both realized they were starving. Fortunately David had brought grocery items back with them, so he set about making a delicious omelet, hashed brown potatoes and tea. It really hit the spot.

After dinner, they curled up in front of the fire with a snifter of brandy and Mac decided it was time to bring David up to date and to share some information with him.

"David, I think it is time to share some information with you that will explain what I am doing, and why some things have been happening. I was told to tell no one, so I have to be careful in what I share and what I can't mention. You understand that the areas that must remain secret have nothing to do with you, or me for that matter, and I am obliged to protect them and honor their wishes."

"This is a complex story, long in development, so I am going to skirt some details and get to the key issues."

She began to relate the story from the time when she and Kate had met, and how the trip to New York came about, plus what happened there. She mentioned their meeting with Patrick and Eli but without giving their names, and avoiding their roles as Witnesses. She then moved on to details about Schwartz, and Nadir. It took her well over an hour to give depth and breadth to the many issues, characters and events that had taken place. She skirted over how the book idea came about, and the dreams that she and Kate had simultaneously.

It was easy to tell that David was shocked, occasionally agitated, frequently angry, and essentially blown away. He'd occasionally interrupt with an expletive or few, but he kept mostly quiet and heard Mac out.

When Mac acknowledged that she was done, he said, "No wonder you are writing a book. This stuff can't be made up! This is such a strange story it would have to be true, or else from the mind of a very perverse person. I have heard about Schwartz before, but had no idea he was so evil, or far-reaching. You must finish this book. It is a story that must be read, regardless of political persuasion, age or location."

"David there is more to this, most of which I can't get into. But I will tell you that last week when Kate and John were at the beach, she and I, well, now promise you won't think I am insane and don't laugh, but Kate and I had the exact dreams each night for three nights. The dreams were in amazing detail, having to do with the next two years, what happens in this country and around the world; and what happens with our political scene. Yeah, I can see you are amused."

"For the record, it was not amusing, just frightening, to see so much information off into the future. We compared notes in detail and everything matched to a 't.' I've been plagued with the responsibility hanging over my head, knowing I have to treat this information with kid gloves. I've poured over the notes, trying to see patterns, and to glean some insight beyond the two year timeframe. Most of all I am struck with how unnerving it is to have seen the future. So many times I have wanted to tell you all about what is going on, but Kate and I were warned to not share any information."

"Now you know that the threats and attacks are related to what I know, and by that I mean both what I have learned recently, as well as earlier research."

David sat quietly absorbing all this information with the keen and well trained mind of a professional. He instinctively knew that this plot was global; he knew there were near and present dangers, as well as into the future. Because he was a man, one trained in solving problems, it was his tendency to leap into the game; to solve problems. But he was no fool, and knew this was a pretty tricky situation that could have him bound and gagged by his magnificent Mackenzie in mere moments. He opted for the calmer, low-key approach.

He began slowly, "So, if I understand correctly, you and Kate have had the exact visions at exactly the same time? Visions of the future? Knowledge of who is going to be elected, what's going to happen?" He was about to burst out laughing, believing it was a joke, that Mac was pulling his leg. But as he looked at her he could see she was dead serious. David managed to smash the burst of laughter he was about to emit, just in time. "For a moment I thought you were doing a number on me. I can see that is not the case. So that leaves me without words. I simply can't grasp this whole thing."

Mac nodded in understanding, "I know, I know. Imagine how I feel? I have been stressed just holding so much knowledge and unable to share it. I mean, I could change the direction of things by warning people in advance. But it was made very clear to me that the repercussions of my doing so would be dire and far reaching, and going against God's will. It was told to me that God finds the state of the world unacceptable; that the U.S. and other parts of the world have slipped too far into behaviors that are aligned with evil, and that support the growth of evil. It is what the End Times are about—to purge all the evil, to let non-believers suffer and find their way to Jesus; and then to rebuild anew. Now that is of course very simplistic, and I have to learn more, but that is the Reader's Digest version. It is hoped that the book will warn enough people soon enough to seek redemption, to repent, and to accept Jesus into their hearts and souls. So that is what we have to focus on, difficult as it might be. I have all these visions, but I also have to do research, to identify what exactly is being referenced, the allied associations, the possible impact. The visions are a guide. There will be a lot of work to do as well."

David sat there, silent and still, while the magnitude of what Mac had just told him sank in fully. He stood and went to the fireplace to stoke the fire and add a log, then sat down again. Mac waited, watching him.

"This is very heavy Mac. I honestly don't have anything in my background, ever, to prepare me for this. I feel totally awkward and out of sync with this story and the implications. Forget the details that you have not shared—I don't even want to know. The only thing I can offer you in all of this is to stand by you, support you in whatever it is that is to come; and to work my best to keep us safe. I can and will do that. I suspect we are going to need some help from above on this one." David sat very still, hands dangling at his sides, as if Mac had just punched the air out of him.

Finally, "God Mac, what have you gotten yourself into? Does Jack know any of this?"

"No, Jack only knows about my interactions with Schwartz and the various assaults. And it must remain that way. You know Jack. If he got wind of all of this he'd have some sort of team organized and into action before we knew what was happening. This is God's will, and so it must be."

"David I feel like a nice warm chai latte, would you like one too? No you stay put. I am going to fix it. You haven't learned your way around my kitchen yet."

Mackenzie went to the kitchen, dogs padding along behind her. They were happy to be home in their own environment, more relaxed. Well heck, she was more relaxed and happy to be in her own home too. She returned to the living room with two large mugs of chai latte.

The two sat in silence watching the fire, both lost in thought. Mackenzie was afraid that David was so stunned about her information that he'd bolt out of there never to return. She could well imagine him thinking her a nutcase. His silence did not calm her worries. Of course, deep in her thoughts was the apprehension that she was nuts to have gotten involved and nuts to believe all that had presented itself.

David was looking at her, "What's going on deep in that terrific mind of yours? Speak to me." Mac managed a smile when responding, "Honestly, I am doubting myself, all of this, and knowing that you have every right to think me a loon and bolt out of here. But also I realize that if I had none of the details, say from the dreams, I'd still wish to carry on, feeling I could make a small contribution to this country. Now, knowing what I know, I'd not be able to live with myself if I did not continue. I now know this country is in peril from evil forces, from within and outside the nation, and I could not now turn my back on doing my small part. I can only hope that you can understand in some small way, and hang in with me."

"Now let's be clear. I do not think you are a loon. I am not about to bolt from the best thing to happen to me in a long time (those two dogs have captured my heart)." He laughed loudly. "And I do understand, especially about helping in whatever way you can to protect this country. I am right there with you."

Mac emitted a huge sigh of relief. "You know, I am exhausted. It's been a long day, battling weather, loading up, driving, unloading, getting things operational here. I suddenly feel so weary I could fall asleep here and now."

"You go on to bed. I'll lock up, get the dogs out, and make sure we are battened down. I also want to get the fire quieted. Sweet dreams.

Sleep well and don't fret about anything. We are going to be just fine."
He gave her a big hug and kiss and moved her toward her bedroom.

Morning came with sunshine streaming in through the shades.
Finally some sunshine, Mac thought as she prepared for the day. She
entered the kitchen to find David busy with breakfast, coffee made,
dogs fed, and a cheerful smile on his face. Life is good she thought.

"Good morning sunshine," he said. "Your favorite to be plated in two
minutes. Help yourself to coffee. Say, I was up early, got everything
in, figured out where most things go, but there is a stack over there for
which you'll need to give some directions. And I have an idea to throw
out, understanding you want a routine. But, we've had such wretched
weather for so long, and you've been working hard. So I thought we
could play tourist today, you can show me around your city, and we'll
get an early dinner at your favorite place. How does that sound?"

"You know I was so excited when I saw the sun this morning. We've
not seen sun in weeks it seems. I'd love to play hooky today, show
you around, share a meal at one of my favorite spots. What a lovely
way to get back into the swing of things here. I made up my mind this
morning while showering that I am not going to allow Schwartz and
his goons to scare me or keep me isolated and holed up. I have you
with me, and we'll be observant, not take risks, but we are going to
live a normal life. Besides, the book will be done within a month I am
guessing, so then it is on someone else. So yes, let's go out and have
fun. It's cold but we can dress warmly and be just fine."

They shared the delicious breakfast, got the rest of things put away,
and bundled up for a day in the sun. Mac decided the first stop would
be Multnomah Falls in the Columbia Gorge. It was one of the region's
most spectacular sights. The falls were about half frozen, providing
a glistening white frame to the threads of water making their way to
the pool below.

From there they went across the Bridge of the Gods to the Skamania
Lodge for cocoa, cookies and a great view of the Gorge; then into town
to tour around. They walked and drove around the river and a shopping
and dining area where they stopped for dinner.

The restaurant was aglow in candles and soft tones of green and peach, with pale peach table cloths and lovely artwork on the walls. Mackenzie had been here before and always found the food perfection.

They talked over cocktails and a delicious meal, touching on many topics, including their budding relationship, and the mounting responsibilities and potential threats from Mac's involvement in the Schwartz issue.

Feeling fully sated and content, they headed home. Once there, David asked, "Do you want to get back to your writing, or can you play hooky till tomorrow?"

Mac smiled as she spoke, "I should get back to writing, but this has been such a grand day of freedom, I don't want it to end. What did you have in mind?"

"Now that is the question isn't it," David laughed. "I thought a fire, sipping an after dinner drink, some soft music and dancing, some kissing, and whatever else might come up."

"Great minds think alike and I like the way yours thinks," Mac said. "How lovely and what a fitting way to bring a perfect day to a close. I am all in. You fix the fire. I'm going to get comfy, and then I'll pour us a nightcap."

David lit candles around the living room, built the fire, and selected some DVDs. By the time Mac entered the living room, drink tray in hand, the room was softly lit, a fire was going strong and dance music filled the room. They spent the evening in each other's arms, dancing, cuddling, and engrossed in each other without any outside interferences. Even the dogs sensed that it was time for them to chill out and not be pushy. It was a night of perfect romance that enveloped them in intimacy and eventually peaceful sleep in each other's arms.

David rose quietly so as not to disturb Mackenzie. He went about the usual morning tasks waiting for her to rise. As a manly man used to being tough, he was not used to how he was feeling, but so elated over his new found joy, he was sure he never wanted it to end. It had been so many long years since he felt true happiness and peace.

Mackenzie fairly floated into the kitchen, smiling widely, and clearly happy. "Good morning sweetie. Wow do I feel great. Yesterday was the best day, and night, I have had in so many years. I feel at peace, comfortable, loved, fulfilled; well I just feel joyous. Thank you for making me so happy."

David was equally effusive and openly happy about their time together, commenting "I rarely display this side of myself and for the life of me I don't understand why I am now, but it just feels right, and as such I am going with the flow. Now young lady, I don't want you getting mad at me for keeping you from your work, and boy could I ever. You can at least go to work with a smile on your face."

"You are right dear. Besides, the sooner I get done with this project, the sooner we will have lots of free time. So I am going to get back to work. I need to be disciplined so please help me. What will you be doing today? Grocery shopping would be good. Kate's number is on the note board in the hall if you want to get your hair cut."

"I planned on grocery shopping, and am going to take the dogs to the park. I'll get the haircut later in the week. Now you get to work. We'll catch up over dinner."

Mackenzie settled in at her desk, selected one stack of papers to review and double check some data, and then began writing. She was well into 2009 and grappling with the litany of bad news to come.

The inauguration will take center stage across America. The promise of hope held tightly by many, and the promise of change will cause rejoicing far and wide. Many, however, question just what 'change' will really mean. But most people will want to give the new president a chance, lest he be judged too quickly.

As inaugurations go, the Nadir soirees will be grand and elaborate, and the costs astronomical. Some will liken the combined events as befitting royalty; some will feel them ostentatious at a time of economic crisis. Whatever the opinions, things will be carried out without a glitch and end with the new First Family entrenched in their new home, and President Nadir eager to get to work making changes.

The primary story for all of 2009 will be the failing economy. It will impact everything, and America will be jarred into a new reality that is at once uncomfortable and unsettling. Americans, being used to a perceived status quo that has implied stability and comfort for generations yet to come, will begin to question just what is real and what wishful thinking is.

Most people understood that the prior Administration left an economic mess for the new Administration, and that it would take a lot of work to turn things around. Most Americans were hopeful, but cautious. Typically a new president spends his pre-inaugural period pulling together a staff, identifying possible advisors and cabinet, vetting primary candidates and organizing a plan of action for those first few weeks.

For those who follow closely the workings of an Administration, flags of concern will appear. Appointments will be an immediate concern, due in part to a lack of experience and in part to the beliefs of many nominees. As for staff, they will be found to all come out of an existing operation in the Presidents home town. But unbeknownst to most citizens, many of the appointments will be people associated with Ivan Schwartz's think tank, otherwise referred to as his "shadow government."

What bothered Mackenzie about the newly formed Administration was the lack of vetting, and the common ideology among staff, advisors and Cabinet members—a belief system that could only be described as radical, leftist, even Communist. Mackenzie had researched most that were named, and found their ideology alarming. She was also concerned that no one in the Administration had any experience in real world endeavors. They were either career politicians or from academia. The combination of radical views and lack of experience will become a huge issue for most Americans.

The first six months of the Administration's operation will display a near-manic, reckless pace, with money flying out the doors. In short order the deficit and debt will grow, the budget will be expanded, and various bailout packages will seek to minimize economic demise. An aura of arrogance will waft from the entire Administration, initially taken as abundant self-confidence, eventually regarded as windbag bravado.

With all the startling signals and red flags waving in the rarified air of Washington, the country was divided. It will seem that the unified hope for unity and correcting the ills of government and our society will be dashed on the rocks of partisanship and disagreement. A buzz will eventually be heard—at first low and barely audible. As the year moves along the buzz will grow louder and elevate in intensity above the madding crowds and urban denizens. Tea Party gatherings spread across the country, reflective of a population very unhappy with Washington. The buzz will become loud, embracing all nature of Americans with all nature of political persuasions. Herein rests the loss of unity that most had expected when they voted for Nadir.

2009 will see vast sums of money in the Trillions doled out for one vague purpose after another. Promises will continue without production, unraveling with the passage of time. And it is still, "The economy stupid." Nadir's Achilles heel will prove to be his sweeping healthcare program that will ignite enormous controversy and ire, made worse by the underhanded shenanigans of Congress and their collective resolute refusal to heed public ire. The year will also see growing controversy over the global warming issue, and by year's end it will be referred to as a colossal global scam to make a few very rich, based on fifteen years of rigged data.

Record breaking foreclosures, bank failures, bankruptcies, 401K investment losses, retirement portfolio losses, stock market fall, job losses, unemployment claims—this is what 2009 will be all about.

Mackenzie pushed away from her desk, sad and discouraged and headed to the kitchen to see what David was up to and when dinner would be ready. He handed her a glass of wine as she entered the room and firmly moved her to a barstool.

"So miss wordsmith, you've been at it for hours without a break. I looked in on you and you were so engrossed in your papers, research and writing, I decided to let you select your time for a break. I hope you at least took one? The pups and I had a great walk. I drove up to that mountain aka hill just to our east, and we went for a hike. It was cold and windy but sunny for the most part. A few snowflakes flew about, but it was just a tease, sufficient to get the boys worked up chasing them. Bought some groceries, and have had a lovely time here getting familiar with your kitchen. I hope you are hungry. I sort of went overboard for our first meal at home."

"Honey, I am starved. I haven't eaten since breakfast. I did have a cup of tea and that was my break for the day. I could eat a half a cow about now, but hopefully you have something a tad tastier," she giggled. They spent the evening enjoying their meal and conversation, retiring early, the dogs snuggled on their bed to keep warm.

The next morning Mackenzie was awakened by a phone call much too early in the morning. "Hello?"

"Mac, its Jack. Have you opened your email yet?" "Jack, its just 5 AM. I was planning on sleeping another 3 hours. No I have not seen my email. Why? What's going on?"

"I sent you a report on a top secret meeting that is coming up. The word that I have gotten is that this meeting is will bring together Schwartz, Al Talil, Nadir, the mystery head of World Bank, someone from the EU and a couple of others. The White House was asked for comment about the rumor and denied it categorically. But my source in France confirms the meeting will take place at some mountain chateau in the Alps. I am told Nadir will secretly fly out of Andrews while weekending at Camp David."

"So what's the purpose of such a meeting, and what can I do about it? Really Jack, its pitch black outside. Why the urgency?"

"You have a woman in France and we need her. I want you to set it up that she'll be working at that chateau soon and will remain there for the conference plus several days after. Her record is clean right? I want you to get over to France and get her up to speed, and in place at the chateau."

"Oh Jack, after the last many weeks, and now you want me to go to France? I am not going without David. No way am I moving in on any Schwartz territory without him along. Isn't there someone else, really? I have other urgent matters I need to keep on top of, and I'm just worn out."

"Sorry old girl. I would not ask were it not urgent. You know that. Listen, I'm sorry for waking you. I just got word on this. I'd like you to get over to Paris in three or four days tops. You are already up to speed on the players so you can hit the ground running. Mac I am sorry. You don't deserve this and I feel like a dog. But if what goes down that I believe will, we need details as soon as possible."

"Jack I understand. But what can we do with Nadir involved? He's the President now, not a candidate. How can we prevail over the power of the White House?" Mac questioned.

"Mac, I just don't know. But we've got to play it out. If nothing else, it's the stuff of a good mystery novel eh?"

Jack rang off and Mackenzie looked at David who was now scowling and shaking his head. "Mac this is not right. Jack needs to rely on someone else. You have got to start saying no and mean it. So, I heard the essentials of the conversation and know we are going to Paris. Hey, that sounds romantic. It won't be all work and no play, I guarantee you. Of course, the weather will be horrid, but for romance, we'll make do. Now let's not worry and go back to sleep."

They awoke at eight thirty, the dogs eager for their breakfast. Mac took a quick shower to wake up, dressed and joined David in the kitchen. "David, I'm going to get on the phone and make some plans. No time to waste. Can you just bring me some tea and toast for now?"

Mackenzie opened her email and there was Jack's message with some details. She read it over and decided to call Juliette first thing. "Bonsoir Juliette, its Mackenzie. Am I interrupting anything? Can you talk? Okay, great. Listen, we have an assignment you and I. I need you to take a job at a private facility up in the Alps. You'll be there for probably two weeks, maybe longer. Can you do that? Excellent. Now, I am going to fly into Paris in three to four days so we can go over everything. I'll also make sure you get hired on at the facility, and get you in place. I'll send you my itinerary as soon as I know it. We'll need to keep a low profile. I'll be in touch once I get into the hotel. Do you still have a car? It would be best if you drove your car to the resort. Please don't mention any of this to anyone. I'll explain everything once we meet up. Thanks Juliette. See you soon."

She proceeded to make airline reservations, and then track down information on the chateau where Juliette was to work. Before long she had a lead on the owner of the chateau, and was making inquiries as to whom she could use as an introduction.

It was then time to let Kate know she was going to be gone, and to make arrangements for Saundra to come in and stay in her absence. "Kate. You are not going to believe this but David and I are going to Paris for a few days. A friend of mine is getting married over there, a rather rushed arrangement, so we decided to go help them celebrate. Pretty exciting and I'm thrilled to be spending a few days with David in that romantic city. Anyway, I wanted to let you know."

"Mac you can't go now. What about the book? You have a lot of writing to do and it's needed soon. What do we tell Eli and Patrick?"

"I'll give them a call shortly and tell them what is going on. I have been working on the book. I have covered the research I did, and gotten into our dreams through 2009. When I get back I'll start on 2010. Don't fret. It is coming along. I'll have my laptop with me and may find time to do some writing over there, though I am not counting on it. We're leaving day after tomorrow. We go from here to New York, then nonstop to Paris. Now then, I've got a lot to do. I won't have time to stop by before we leave, but will try to call. Take care. Oh yes, how is your research going?"

"Okay Mac, give a call and be sure to be careful. At least David is going with you so I can relax. Research is going alright. I am not as adept at ferreting out information as you are but I am making headway and apparently we are not under much of a time crunch otherwise you'd not be going off to play. Now take care of yourself and call or write when you get in to Paris."

"Kate, do I detect a tone of disapproval? Could that be?"

Kate was abrupt as she responded, "Oh never mind. It just seems odd, after being out at the beach for several weeks. But what do I know?" Mac was quite peeved with her friend's reaction.

Within three hours Mac had managed to make all the arrangements, but for a few errands that needed to be done. She decided to spend that day packing and doing errands and the following day writing.

The night before their departure, Saundra came over for last minute instructions and the house key. David had all the bags by the front door for the early morning departure; they had a light meal and went to bed early.

The trip went smoothly once through the rigors of security clearance. Comfortable business class seating, a good movie and decent meal, and they were in New York. On layover Mackenzie decided to put in a call to Eli. "Good Afternoon Eli, Mackenzie here. I wanted to let you know that I am taking a sudden trip to France and will be back in a few days, probably a week. It is a necessary trip but I'll be back on the project as soon as we get back."

Eli was not surprised with her call or information. Darn, she just could not keep in mind that those two were all-knowing. "Mac, yes I understand. I figured a trip was soon on the agenda. I could save you the hassle, but it's better to proceed through normal channels and process. Besides neither Pat nor I wish to utilize our knowledge to alter the natural course of events, except to educate and warn people while there is still time. Mac, I don't believe you will have any problems over there and you'll be gone before trouble presents itself. So relax and enjoy the wonders of the City of Lights. Call when you get back. Now have a great trip. Bye."

David and Mackenzie settled into the VIP lounge awaiting their departure, playing a game where they try to guess information about each passenger—what line of work, why the trip to Paris, married or single, etc. They never knew if they were right or wrong, but they most often agreed on their guesses. This one time however, there was a man seated near the window, deeply engrossed in a book. He'd occasionally look up, glancing around the room and out across the tarmac and return to his book. Mac guessed him to be British, a long time resident of the U.S., on way to Paris for a funeral. David disagreed on all points. He thought the man was American, in his sixties, retired, and going to Paris to visit family.

They spent twenty minutes arguing back and forth on the signs and clues, remaining at odds. Mac could not stand it so she went over to the man, apologized for interrupting, and asked "Sir, my friend and I often try to guess information about people we do not know and often agree. You however have proven a rare stumbling block so to settle our argument, I wondered if you could answer a couple of questions?" The man was taken aback, but in a British accent replied he'd try to help. "So, you are British?" "Yes, but I've lived in America for over twenty years." "You are single?" "Why, actually I am. I was married but divorced about ten years ago." "And the last but most important question, what takes you to France?" "Well, my sister, who lives in France now for thirty years, is ill. She is not expected to live much longer and I am going over to help her out and see her through this nasty end business." Mac extended her sympathies and thanked him for his kindness and time in allowing her to pry. She returned to David beaming ear to ear. "So, we win—we're both a little right." They laughed and continued chatting till it was time to board their flight.

The flight over was delightful. They had seats that reclined into beds; the food was remarkably good and plentiful with food service throughout the flight. They enjoyed their dinner and a good movie, played a couple games of cribbage and fell asleep.

Charles de Gaulle airport was always chaotic, somewhat like the French in general. It took an hour to clear customs and get their bags. Fortunately Mackenzie had a car waiting so they did not have to battle taxi lines. The driver took them into the center of Paris to a hotel Mac had stayed in one night and found utterly divine. They arrived at the Champs Elysees Plaza where she had booked a small suite. She figured that to be dragged out in winter to Paris on short notice, they should spoil themselves.

The boutique hotel was elegant, with superb and regal décor. Mac thought David would enjoy the gym and sauna, while she knew she'd love the massage and sauna. Their small suite was tres chic, in shades of grays and plums, high ceilings with windows from floor to ceiling, opulently draped, some opening to a small balcony from which one could view the local denizens out and about on rue du Berri below. The king size bed was plump with down bedding, 1000-thread count sheets and soft faux fur throws. Grand, simply grand. Mac could hardly wait to leap into that fluffy bedding.

It was a busy location, though off the beaten path, so that Mac felt it would make it easier to disappear into the crowd. Plus they were within walking distance of the shopping and fine dining around the Place de la Concorde, and major roadways to get around to other parts of the city. For the week they'd be in Paris, Mac knew they'd be comfortable, pampered, and every romantic whim catered to—heaven.

After unpacking, Mackenzie rang Juliette, "Bonjour Juliette, I am here and nearly settled in. Can we meet tomorrow morning? How about that café on Rue Dauphine in the Saint Germain, do you know the one? It has a red canopy over the front door and ivy up the side of the building. Fine. Let's say about eleven? Bon. See you then. Au revoir."

David was quite pleased with the suite and hotel, perhaps not so with the location. "Mac this is lovely and luxurious; I am very happy even without fresh air at night."

Mac smiled, "I thought a busy area would allow us to come and go without much notice, as opposed to a quiet hotel on the Left Bank. And if you'll notice, at the bottom of every other French door window is a sliding vent that lets in fresh air and with these massive drapes closed, we'll not hear a thing. Happy now, you baby!" she laughed.

"So here are my thoughts. It is morning here, but night for our clocks. What if we go out for a walk, have some lunch and come back and go to sleep till, say eight o'clock? Then we'll clean up and go to some fabulous spot for dinner, get to bed at a reasonable hour, and be on local time in the morning. Sound good?"

"Perfection." David was eager to get going. They headed out on the rue du Berri, passing a modern Starbucks, so they grabbed Chai Lattes so as not to interrupt their upcoming sleep. They moved along various side streets till they came across a charming café where they had a delicious lunch and bottle of wine. They wandered a few more avenues before they headed back to the hotel for a lovely long nap.

Dinner was a gastronomic tour de force within an elegant old townhouse that was transformed at the end of the War into one of the world's great restaurants, Taillevent. It proffered classic French Haute cuisine in an intimate and opulent setting where service was in a class all its own. It was a romantic evening, a dining adventure, where superlatives could barely do justice to the experience.

Mackenzie and David took a taxi to the hotel, exhausted, sated, content and falling in love. They snuggled in the fluffy luxuriant bedding and soon fell off to sleep, unable to fight their exhaustion.

Room service awakened them in the morning with a pot of steaming French coffee, warm buttery croissant and jam. David decided to explore the Champs Elysees and hit the gym while Mac was at her meeting. Mac grabbed a waiting taxi and headed to the Saint Germain area. She was early so opted to walk around the area before meeting Juliette. Just before eleven Mac entered the café, busy with locals taking their morning coffee break. She took a table toward the back facing the door and waited for Juliette, who came along shortly.

The two women embraced and spent a bit of time catching up, chatting about old times when they shared some work and leisure time in Paris. Realizing that they had much to cover, Mac maneuvered the conversation into the task at hand. Mac explained the necessary background and issues that had raised concerns among a few. They talked about some of the problems in Europe and how we were all being drawn together where one's failure was everyone's problem.

Finally Mac mentioned the reason for needing Juliette's native French, her powers of observation and her pristine discretion. She was adept at thinking on her feet, her mind was sharp and she could talk her way out of most uncomfortable or compromising situations.

"Juliette, there is a regal chataeu, Avenieres, up in the Western Alps, a place that is privately owned, but is leased for celebrities who seek total privacy, as well as small private functions such as weddings, business retreats, family gatherings. The chateau is near Cruseilles and an easy drive from Geneva. I am going to arrange for you to go to work there. I spoke with the manager who was thinking about using you as a chamber maid, but that does not serve our purpose. You will need to be in dining service where you will be able to remain in the dining room and listen to what is going on. You will speak only French and let everyone know you do not understand English. How is your

Italian? You could offer to speak Italian should that help with some of the guests."

"The meeting will take place in 10 days. I am assuming that a security group will come in a few days before to sweep the entire property and check out workers. I've arranged for you to have a verifiable employment record of 4 years with a resort in Switzerland, and 3 years with a hotel in France. You can indicate that you are up there to enable you to ski on your off time, and to heal from a personal tragedy, the tragic death of your husband, my brother. Here is a folder with photos of a few people. I know for sure that this guy will be there, as will this one, and probably this one. The rest we are not sure about. But it is these two that I wish you to focus on. What they say is of utmost importance."

"Now Juliette, please listen carefully. This guy, Schwartz, is dangerous. He is smart, and observant. You should be as bland as possible to blend into the woodwork so they don't realize you are around. At the same time, on your toes so if water is needed, or a clean ashtray, or more bread, whatever, you have it there before they have to call you. Do nothing to attract attention to yourself. If possible, use your cell phone, from the kitchen or through a window or something to hide behind, so you can get photos of all there; that would be great. Don't risk anything to get them. Here is a recording device. You should be sure that it is well hidden before the security sweep (like tucked under linens, or in the silverware drawer), and once the sweep is over, keep it hidden till the day of the arrival. That morning you all will be checked again—so don't have this device on you till after you are checked, then without being seen, get it and tuck it in your pocket like you would a regular pen. It works as a pen, so use it to take orders, and then return it to your pocket. Click here to activate its recording ability. It will go on one cartridge for about 2 hours. You will need to hide 3 other cartridges. Following the meeting take all cartridges to your room and keep them well hidden till the first opportunity for you to ski; then go to the village and mail them to me, along with the pen. Memorize my address; don't have it written down anywhere. Same for my phone number, remove it from your cell till you leave there. Now I've done a lot of talking. Do you have questions?"

"Mon dieu! This is greatly more than expected. I hope accomplish well this job. What do I do if the man wishes my pen to use? What if I get, how you say, fired? Or what if the man wishes me out of the room?"

"Yes it is a lot Juliette and I am sorry. You will do fine. Your job there will be secure. The owner will be told that you are the widow of my brother who died recently; that you need work desperately but something that is not too demanding and is isolated. I will indicate that I have a mutual friend of hers and that I've been meaning to stay at the chateau. In the meantime could she provide you with work, even if temporarily, because you have been kicked out of your apartment in Paris. And as for a man borrowing your pen, just let one without hesitation, but get it back right away. If you are asked to leave the room, do so, but try to stay by a door so you can overhear. It might be possible to leave your pen nearby and out of view so it can continue to record. You'll have to check on that once there and decide."

"Now Juliette I believe we have covered everything. I'll call you when I have the job securely lined up. Be sure to take your skis and ski clothes with you. Guard the pen and cartridges with your life. Only call me when you are away from the chateau and only in an emergency. So this is it. I wish I could go with you, but it would never work, since Schwartz knows me."

"I am expecting at least Schwartz and Nadir to come in by private plane, unmarked with security on board. But as I said, an advance team will arrive a day or two before. They will probably land at Geneva and take a helicopter to the chateau."

"Actually, I think that a friend and I will go up to the Chateau and check it out and talk personally with the owner. We can take a train up for the day, perhaps spend the night. That will make things go easier and give me a chance to get a sense of any possible problem areas. So I'll call you when we get back. Now I need to get going. Take care of yourself Juliette."

They hugged and walked out together, each going their separate way in silence. Mac's heart felt heavy. This whole business was unnerving and the stakes were so high. Down deep she prayed Juliette could handle the assignment and not get caught.

Mackenzie walked for quite a distance along the Seine. The aromas of freshly baked bread and dark French coffee wafted in the air; the Bateaus Mouches glided by filled with tourists; and street artists captured crowds of onlookers on every block. She stopped for a moment to watch an overly enthusiastic mime perform (wasn't that an oxymoron?). He bounded about a parking lot adjacent to a restaurant with amused diners watching from the windows. A crowd gathered to watch his antics as he interacted with several of them. To the side of the crowd was a middle-aged woman and her son, probably about 10 years of age. They were very well dressed, the mother in dress, heels and fur coat, the son in slacks, jacket and trench coat. Mac thought they might be English or German, and was surprised when she heard them talking to learn they were American.

The mother was looking about the area as the boy delighted in the antics of the mime. Suddenly the mime grabbed the boy and took off with him. Mac could see the mother panic and start to chase after the mime, until she realized the mime was coaching the boy to mimic the mime's actions. Within moments the duo was sneaking beneath the restaurant's windows, popping up and waving, continuing the full length of the windows. The mime then grabbed the boy's hand and they paraded through the restaurant, acting like buffoons. The boy enjoyed himself, the mother, not so much, but she did not want to make a scene.

Eventually the boy was returned to her amid a flurry of French. She nodded, smiled, said merci, and moved on as the crowd clapped in approval.

Mac wandered on and decided to stop for a coffee au lait. She found a café with a sunlit patio, took a seat in the sunshine and sipped her coffee while observing the passersby. She loved people watching normally but in France it was especially fascinating. Parisians, while they could be rude and obnoxious, were stylish. They had a joie de vivre that was reflected in how they ate, dressed, drank, made love, and even in how they walked. All was done with a special zest, yet in moderation that offered a reasonable balance in most things. That they were liberal loons was another matter entirely.

Mac paid her bill and returned to her walk. She decided David would be finished with his gym, so she hailed a cab and returned to the hotel. He was in the shower, humming an unrecognizable song. She smiled, feeling that warm and cozy thing she felt whenever around David.

He came into the room, "Well there you are. How did your meeting go? I had a great workout, a good sweat session, and am now sparkling clean, raring to go. So where are we going?"

She gave him a kiss on the cheek and said, "it is lovely outside. How would you like to do something very touristy but fun?" He was enthused. "I thought we could take a boat trip up the Seine on the Bateaux Mouches. Then find a lovely restaurant for some classic French food and wine, and perhaps a nightcap at a little boite. But wait, there is more! We are going up to the French Alps tomorrow for an overnight. Too much excitement all at once?"

"It all sounds perfect to me my sweet. I am along for the ride, so I'm happy no matter what we do. But why the Alps, and just for one night? David questioned.

"Well, I need to check out this little hotel, and make arrangements for a friend to get a job there. I thought it would be better and of course more fun, to do it in person, than by phone. While you get dressed, I'll check on the train schedule. We can take one small bag of essentials and a change of clothes, and leave everything else here," Mac suggested.

Soon the couple, hand in hand, was walking along the Seine; a place of romance featured in so many films over time. The moment was not lost on David, "You know, I have seen this scene or similar scenes so many times in the movies with so many couples walking along this path. It is far more romantic here and now. I have to admit, I was not keen to pack up and head out from your home so soon after just returning. But now that we are here, I am glad we made the trip. Or, I am glad that you included me; all the better because it is all on Jack," David chuckled.

They continued to the Bateaux, got their tickets, and went on board. Yes it was touristy, perhaps a bit cheesy, but the glass covered boat provided an inspired view of both sides of the river, and a perspective on Paris you could only get from the river.

The boat was far from full, and the commentary was fortunately done in English as well as French. They enjoyed the historical presentation covering buildings, moments in history such as the French Revolution, and French culture. The sun cast sparkling highlights on the Notre Dame Cathedral, as it did on other impressive structures. It was late afternoon when they returned to the dock. Since they did not know where they would be dining, they decided to walk the East Bank and find an interesting dining spot frequented by locals.

They dined with the locals in a romantic cafe that proved to be a delightful experience with friendly people and delicious food. It was a leisurely pace that prompted them to linger over dessert wine and coffee. By the time they departed, Mac had a change of mind, "Sweetie, would you mind if we did not go to a club tonight? I thought it would be nice to just go back to that fabulous suite, maybe get some champagne, and have a bubble bath. How does that sound?"

"Club? Who wants to go clubbing. I've had a hankering for bubbles all day. Now help me find a cab so we can brew a bath," David said as he grabbed her hand and headed to the main boulevard.

The evening was utter romantic bliss—a warm bubble bath and perfectly chilled champagne; massage with citrus oil; they were in love, and so well suited to each other. Being in Paris took them to a whole new level in their relationship, bonding them to each other in a more solid and enduring way.

Morning came early with a wakeup call. They gathered their things into one bag, grabbed the heavy winter paraphernalia and hurried out to catch their train. The time went by quickly as they passed through valleys and into the Alps. The scenery was breathtaking, dramatic, and grand. Snow glistened in a pristine way so that around every curve a vista appeared as if on an expensive greeting card. They arrived in Geneva, rented a car and headed to the château.

They pulled up in front to be met by a charming man who introduced himself as the butler, Pierre. They went through a brief sign-in while Mackenzie made some inquiries of the desk manager. "Can you tell me when Madame Trussant will be available? We spoke on the phone and she agreed to meet with me while we are here."

"Madame is busy with kitchen staff at present. I'll let her know you have arrived. Someone will fetch you when she is free. You can come to that room across the hall. It is our small salon. She will meet you there for tea."

David and Mackenzie were taken to their rooms—a lovely suite with mountain view, fireplace ablaze and smelling of fragrant wood, magnificent bath with luxurious robes and towels. It was elegant, relaxing, and sumptuous and the bed, oh that bed. Mac dove onto the bed, falling into the fluffiest down duvet she'd ever seen. She could imagine people coming here just for the beds, remaining in them all day.

"David dive into this bed. It's incredible. We could get lost in here. This suite is so gorgeous. I could stay here for days and days. But at these prices, Jack will have a fit over one night. So we are going to enjoy every moment here. I'll have tea with Madame Trussant and get my friend's employment arranged then we'll go exploring."

David was smiling widely as he took in the surroundings, saying, "I am going to check out what our options are and will have a plan in place when you get back to the room. This is a touch of heaven isn't it?"

There was a knock at the door. "Mademoiselle, Madame Trussant is in the salon waiting for you." Mackenzie responded, "Tell her I'll be right down. Merci boucoup." The maid responded, "je vous en prie."

As Mackenzie entered the Salon, Madame Trussant was seated at a tea table. She smiled, extended her hand and in perfect English said, "Welcome Mademoiselle. The accommodations are to your liking, oui? Have a seat here. We'll have some tea and you can tell me what it is I can do for you."

The room was filled with sunshine from the many windows facing the valley and a line of snow-covered trees nearby. It was a room decorated in a soft Wedgewood blue, off-white, and touches of amethyst. The furniture was Louis XIV; luxurious softly colored Aubusson and Persian rugs, taffeta and velvet drapes hanging from the 20-foot ceilings. There were two enormous antique urns on either side of a very large fireplace; gilded mirrors, antique paintings, and personal items on occasional tables completed the décor to perfection.

Madame Trussant was seated at a round tea table draped to the floor in a deep blue velvet. An elegant silver tray, and pots sat on the table, along with a dainty set of tea cups and saucers. Madame was a beautiful elderly woman who had obviously been a world-class beauty in her youth. Her thick gray hair was knotted on the back of her head with an ornate hairpin. Her skin was like porcelain—fine in texture, pale and delicate with minimal wrinkles, carefully made up with understated precision. She was wearing a royal blue dress with matching jacket, adorned with a lovely butterfly pin made of exquisite gemstones, matched by princess-set sapphire stud earrings. This woman was a study in perfection, elegance and confidence. Madame had spent a lifetime in charge; a woman accustomed to having her way, being surrounded by wealth and comfort, and admired by men and women. She was stunning still.

"Madame Trussant, a pleasure to meet you. I have long heard about you and this fine chateau from our mutual friend Jacques. It is even grander than I had been told; it's very impressive and truly lovely. Our suite is perfection in every regard. I am only sorry we can be here for just one night."

"Ah oui, it is an experience here. The weather is glorious is it not? You and your husband should take a sleigh ride. I'll have the kitchen prepare a thermos for you, if you'd like."

"Why thank you. That sounds marvelous and so beautiful an environment. Madame, I am hoping you can be of help. I have a sister-in-law living now in Paris. Her husband was my brother and he died the latter part of last year. She is having a difficult time of it emotionally, and financially. Before they married she had worked in Suisse and Paris in luxury hotels. She has been given notice to leave her apartment within days, and while she could find some sort of job in Paris, she needs to get away from the city for a while. The memories are too painful for her. We were talking about this chateau and she felt it would be an ideal location for her skills, and the sort of isolation she needs."

"Mademoiselle, may I call you Mackenzie? Your young woman, is she crying and emotional? You understand I can't have someone in tears around our guests. Has she a security check recently?"

"Madame, no she is not in tears. She knows how to put business ahead of her problems. She just needs a break from Paris for a time. And as for a security check, I believe she had one done about three months ago, if that is recent enough? She has excellent references too."

"Excellent. It happens that we have exclusive guests here for a few days and need extra help in preparing. And after that group, we are booked up for the next two months, so her assistance would be most welcome. Do you have copies of her references? I am willing to accept her on your word, and that you come to us from Jacques Landreaux. Have you seen him recently? How is the dear man?"

"Here are the references for Juliette Honor. I have spoken with Jacques on the phone twice in the last couple of months, but it's been nearly a year since I saw him. I think he is doing well. The heart attack really affected him, and his outlook. He seemed to age rather a lot in a short time. But he has rebounded, seems fit and back in good humor. We are having lunch in a few days and I am anxious to see him. So Juliette can come up here? How soon should she arrive?"

"Please have her arrive this coming Saturday, if she can get here that soon? Will she come by train? I can send a car for her if I know her schedule. Tell her she will have a private room with bath in the adjacent building where staff resides. She will get one day off per week, and occasional half days depending on our occupancy. A bus comes by here to pick up skiers, if she skis. Now, please give Jacques my love and best wishes, and tell him I'll be very offended if he does not come to visit soon. Oh yes, she needs to bring her security check, passport and a health record with her."

"Madame, the arrangements for Juliette work perfectly. She is a quick study and very discrete and diligent in her work. I'll give her your instructions. She will be driving up, so she should be here early Saturday afternoon if that is acceptable. I shall indeed give Jacques your message."

Madame Trussant smiled, saying "Now my dear, I must excuse myself. I have things to take care of. I'll get a thermos made up for you and the sleigh will be around to the parking lot side awaiting your arrival. I bid you adieu and wish for you to enjoy your stay. Perhaps I will see you at dinner?"

Mackenzie smiled, nodded, and waved to Madame Trussant, then headed back to their room. "You are all smiles. So you had a good meeting?"

"Madame Trussant is charming, very elegant and regal. She is a sharp old lady. She has arranged for us to take a sleigh ride. It is ready for us now if you'd like? We are to stop at the desk to get a thermos she had made up for us. I'm excited, it should be wonderfully romantic. Yes? Okay, let's get going then."

They stopped at the front desk to get the promised thermos then headed out the side door to the waiting sleigh. Mackenzie caught her breath, "Oh David, this is right out of Dr. Zhivago. Have you ever seen such a magnificent sleigh? The driver helped them into the sleigh. There were toasty warm pillows to rest their feet on and an oversized mink throw lined in velvet and filled with down. They settled into the soft padded seat, pulled the throw up to their shoulders and off they sped, led by two beautiful white horses. Mackenzie was a sucker for such romantic adventures, and this one was right up there with the best.

David opened the thermos and poured a creamy mixture into mugs. "Oh mama! This stuff is just too good," he raved. "What do you suppose this consists of? It's like hot chocolate only thicker, like a brandy Alexander only hot, like Bailey's only denser. Wow, we've got to get this recipe. It's addictive."

The sleigh, all sparkling white, silver and red, slid along a well groomed trail into the woods and open fields. Bells tinkled from the horses as they pranced along the trail, happy to be on the run, proud of their rig.

Off in the distance the Alps rose to meet the bright blue sky, like points of a glorious crown festooned with tiny diamonds sparkling in the sunlight. Mackenzie was in awe as she quietly spoke, "This vista is a marvel of God's creation, perfection in its simplicity, so regal and profound in its scope. We are but two tiny specs flitting along, ignored by these majestic mountains. Sights like this make me feel humble and insignificant. Even the worldly troubles we face pale in comparison to God's design. Surely in the Book of Revelations it is not meant that such majesty should be sacrificed? How could that be and for what purpose? It is man who has made the mess." She sighed and rested her head on David's shoulder, sipping the lavish liquid from their thermos.

David said, "Mac darling, you are at times such a poet. That was beautiful, what you said. Life is made up of brief moments, and of them a few form those lovely memories we cherish into old age. This shall be one of my most memorable till I die. I'm so grateful to be sharing it with you. We must work on creating more of such memories, even amid the chaos and problems, of which we've spoken."

Onward the sleigh carried them, in blissful silence but for the tiny tinkling bells and occasional snorts from the cold noses of the horses. Ahead of them was a field surrounded by dense forest. The angle of the sun cast a rainbow affect across the snow, and a halo over the trees. Mackenzie asked the driver to stop near the line of trees and position the sleigh and horses at an angle to the stream of sunlight for a picture. He obligingly arranged the team and rig, then stepped back and shot a number of photos for Mackenzie.

The sun was edging its way behind a towering mountain and before long it would be dark. They decided it was time to head back to the chateau. By the time they reached the chateau they had consumed the entire contents of the thermos, vowing to get that recipe no matter what.

A fresh fire had been lit in their sitting room, a welcome treat after the chill of the outside. They decided hot baths would be most welcome before dressing for dinner. Mac told David to go ahead, as she had to make a couple of phone calls.

"Juliette, its Mackenzie. Everything is arranged. You should be here in the early afternoon on Saturday. You will have a private room and bath, one day off a week plus occasional half days. Madame Trussant will not be easy, but most definitely fair. She is a charming, lovely lady. Remember all we spoke about and don't forget your favorite pen but there is no place here to get refills, so have extras with you. Ski clothes are a must. You'll be fine here. Madame said there are special guests coming in shortly, and then the chateau is booked solid for 2 months. Now call me on your off hours, or if you need anything. Take care Juliette—be very very careful and don't break anything on your body. Adieu."

Next Mac rang Jack to update him on arrangements. As seemed to be the norm, she woke him in the wee hours. "Jack Hi. You awake? Okay, listen up then. All the arrangements have been made. Juliette will be in place on Saturday. I met with Madame today, she is delightful, and a shrewd, regal grande dame. I liked her."

Yawning, Jack asked, "Have you been around the place? Do you see any potential for problems? How is the place in general?" "Oh Jack, this place is ultra-luxurious, grand, and magnificent. We went for a sleigh ride this afternoon and it was pure heaven. Not eaten yet, but am sure it will be great too. And the room, well it is fit for a queen."

"What do you mean 'we went for a sleigh ride'?" Jack prodded. "Oh, I told you I was bringing David along, remember? I have no intention of going anywhere alone at this time. So David came along; we took the train up, and car over to the Chateau. We will be going to dinner shortly, and yes dear, spending the night. You'll hate the bill, but just think how welcome this respite. But I knew you'd blow a gasket if we stayed on another day, so we are going back tomorrow. Anyway, Juliette will be driving up with her ski gear. She'll do fine as long as she does not take risks. You know how aggressive she is on skis. I told her to cool it since she's not been on skis for some time. But she is eager to start work, she has polished up her favorite pen you gave her and is ready to take orders and keep everyone comfortable. I'm sure she and I will speak from time to time. I've a couple of people, old friends, I want to meet with in Paris before David and I head home."

"So Mac, how are things with David? I mean, is there something special, something going on? You know, special? Oh hell, is there romance? Falling in love stuff?"

Mackenzie broke into laughter at Jack's charming clumsiness and concern. "Why Jack, isn't that an invasion of privacy? Or sexual harassment? Or some such thing?" She could not keep from laughing, and could hear him squirm over the phone. "Damnit Mackenzie, you know exactly what I mean. You're just trying to agitate me. You also know that you and David are friends of mine and that he was not a casual arbitrary selection. I've long thought you two should meet and you offered the most ideal circumstance. So I want to know if my hunches were right."

"Yes Jack, your hunches were spot on, as usual. You have not lost your touch dear man. We grew close as friends, and when it seemed he'd need to return to duty, we both realized there was more. And since I can't be alone, I'd far rather have David with me now, than some stranger. Anyway, he figured you'd be happy to let him cruise out of work and retire. Not yet, but one of these days. So I thank you for your brilliant planning. Now are we all set on this venture of yours? Nothing else to be done, right? And for me, I've got Juliette settled, and will touch base with some old friends and all will be good. We'll head home on Friday. I'll drop you an email. Now you go back to sleep and rest well knowing all is in order here, David and I are better than good, and we'll be home in a couple of days. Night Jack."

"Goodnight Mac. I am happy for you. Give David my best, and tell him he better take damn good care of you or he'll have me on his case." Jack chuckled as he hung up.

Mackenzie poured two glasses of wine and went into the bathroom, handing one to David. She sat on the stool and sipped the wine. "I just spoke with Jack. He was embarrassed, uncomfortable and terribly nosey, wanting to know just how things were going with us. I did not make it easy for him, but he knows now. Oh and he said to tell you you'd better take damn good care of me or you'll have him to deal with. He is a dear, but a tad grumpy in the wee hours. Hey you look pretty cute covered up in bubbles."

David blew bubbles at her, "Hey come on in. The bubbles are fine, water warm. My toes were numb after all that cold air so it feels great in here. Mac was torn between bubbles and the jets; she wanted both but then she'd have churned up enough suds to fill the entire bathroom, so opted for bubbles only. "Come on girlie, join me."

Mac took off her clothes and climbed in, sighing from the nice hot water. They snuggled in the hot water and bubbles, sipping their wine and talking about the chateau, the ambiance, the sleigh and life in general. David said he'd done a bit of research on the chateau. "I went into the library and there were some books on the history of the family and this beautiful structure. It seems that Madame was orphaned at an early age. Her parents were Swiss and died in an accident when Madame was a child. She was sent to live with an Aunt in Paris, who was regarded as very avant-garde for her time. She attended college for three years, and while visiting her Aunt for Christmas she met her husband Charles Trussant. He was an officer in the French Army, from a prominent Parisian family, a dashing man some years her senior. They met at a society ball and according to the book, fell in love immediately. He was sent on assignment to Germany, it was in the twenty's, and when he came back two years later, she was waiting for him. He got out of the military and joined his father's company, and they married. She was apparently worrisome to Mr. Trussant's family, who regarded her as a bit of a renegade, wanting to do things her own way. Seems Madame liked to shock, by smoking and drinking, going to parties. As a young wife, she was not especially domestic, but she had a great head for business. Charles opened new business channels for the family company but it was Claudia who really expanded the operation, and invested their money. She ended up dabbling in real estate. The family had a number of homes around Europe. By the time their two daughters were raised, Claudia and Charles divided their time between the social life of Paris and their country home, this château."

"There was something that happened within the family, and their wealth was threatened. I could find no details, but Charles died amid rumors of suicide. Claudia sold their home in Paris and bought an apartment for when she visits her daughters. She moved full time to the Chateau and turned it into this grand hotel, tending to every aspect of the operation. She never remarried, and has lived quietly since her husband's death. Sort of sad don't you think?"

Mac was fascinated about Madame Trussard's life, "Yes sad to have lost her husband, and to feel she must abandon her former life.

But this is a determined woman of strength and character. She has lived a privileged life, yet she is resilient. I wish I had the time to get to know her. You just know there are some amazing stories she has to tell. Perhaps one day before long we can come back here and I'll interview her." Mac's stomach grumbled and they both realized it was time to dress for dinner.

They had been told that during the week appropriate attire is casual dressy, but on Friday and Saturday Madame requests guests to dine in black tie. So Mac slipped into a knit dress with glittery embellishment, David in a silk turtleneck sweater and blazer. They entered the dining room arm in arm to find the restaurant nearly full and surprised to see so many people, many of them there just for dinner.

Dinner was no less elegant and memorable than the sleigh ride, or the Chateau for that matter. Madame Trussard had created a special place—her home that she shared with a select few who knew they had been favored by a woman of intrigue, accomplishment and stellar taste. While waiting for coffee and dessert, Mackenzie went over to Madame Trussard's table, "Madame Trussard, this has been one of the most memorable experiences. Thank you for sharing your home with us. I was wondering if you might be willing to let me interview you about your life, at a time when you can take a break from daily oversight of the property? I would love to learn your story and perhaps write a piece for a magazine; but only if you'd agree. And the interview would be only when you have cleared your schedule and have time, whether here or in Paris, or wherever you like. Think about it. I'll contact you later in the year. We will be leaving in the morning. Juliette will be here by auto on Saturday. Thank you again for allowing her to work here. Goodnight Madame."

The next morning Mac and David had their coffee and rolls in their suite as they packed and leisurely prepared to leave for their return trip to Paris. Mac, sipping her coffee, decided to check her email. There were dozens of unread messages that she skimmed through. But two caught her immediate attention.

One was from a reporter friend who had become an intrepid sleuth, digging in every aspect of the last campaign, candidates, and now the new Administration. He was obsessed, and believed things were not as they seemed; a belief with which Mackenzie agreed. The message from Brian read as follows:

"Mackenzie: I have been following some leads to information about the two Conventions last year. I am in Denver and have had two meetings on the QT that are explosive, as in the atom bomb of news flashes. There was a secret meeting during the convention between Schwartz (your buddy), Nadir, Lamia, and the party chair. They decided to take some precautionary measures to arm against a bunch of rumors going around (since when does one have to arm against rumor if they are just rumor?) Anyway, they decided to prepare two separate "Official Certification of Nomination" documents, which were faxed to each state's Electoral College following every convention.

"So Mac, it seems that Schwartz wanted the standard legal wording changed. This is the actual legal wording standard to each such document following a nomination. *"THIS IS TO CERTIFY that at the National Convention of the Democrat Party of the United States of America, held in Denver, Colorado on August 25 through 28, 2008, the following were duly nominated as candidates of said Party for President and Vice President of the United States respectively and that the following candidates for President and Vice President of the United States are legally qualified to serve under the provisions of the United States Constitution."*

"This document was signed by Lamia, the DNC secretary, and officially notarized. But guess what? The document was not, repeat, not, faxed to any Electoral College office. Instead, a second document was created MINUS some of the above text ("*—and that the following candidates for President and Vice President of the United States are legally qualified to serve under the provisions of the United States Constitution."*) The notarized document sent out was without this "legally qualified" statement, while the other one was filed as part of official permanent record with the DNC.

"I can't prove it, but my guess is that Schwartz paid off the notary, who seems to have retired. Mac do you know what this means? It means that the whole country has been scammed and duped, that the team elected is not eligible, and that a conspiracy does exist. And Schwartz and Lamia are in the eye of the storm. Could the Devil have done any better job?"

"Now get this. I've tried to get some major media outlets to run with this story and none will touch it. NONE! So I put in a call to CFP and am meeting with them on Monday. We need to talk. Where are you? Can we get together? Write me back. This is explosive and yet my gut is telling me it is going to be buried."

Mackenzie sat there staring at her laptop, stunned at what she had read. She could feel her heart pounding and she knew this was the secret meeting in her vision. She could never have imagined it would be so insidious and far-reaching. She gasped, unable to catch her breath, causing David to spin toward her.

"Mac are you okay? You look like you've seen a ghost. What's going on? Can you take a deep breath?"

"Oh David. Oh, this is not good news. Read this email. I just can't speak about it yet."

David read quickly, his eyes growing larger in disbelief. "Wow, explosive is an understatement. My mind is racing, wondering what would happen if this were widely known, exposed in the media. But he says they won't touch it. Good God Mac, what's going on? I don't like the smell of any of this because it seems all Americans are being played with, fooled, cheated, and scammed. This seems an act of treason to me. I'm speechless."

They hugged each other tightly, realizing they knew very dangerous information. Mac said, "I hate to even check my email. All my networking is bringing forth news that is just plain frightening. There is another message, but I don't think I can bring myself to look just yet. In fact I am not going to read it now. Let's get on our way and I'll review things in more detail on the train. Are we about ready?"

The car was waiting for them, and the sunny beautiful drive to Geneva. Once settled on the train, cup of tea in hand, Mackenzie decided to once again view her email. This time she opened a message from a friend in D.C. Andy, otherwise known as Andrea, had been a long time friend and colleague. She was always off on some new assignment, sometimes working in a U.S. company, sometimes abroad. She wrote now to indicate that she had been set up to go to work in the Administration and was in place now. Her area of specialty was global economics as an advisor to the President.

Mac smiled, knowing her friend as a quick study, whose mind could absorb complex data at rapid-fire pace with remarkable retention. But, global economics? Now that was going to be a challenge, especially since she'd have to acquire knowledge on a daily basis. But if anyone deserved a plum assignment it was Andy. Oh how she wished she were in D.C. to pick her brain on a daily basis.

She wrote, "Mac, this is unreal. I've wanted to call you, but have been so busy. The hours are long, longer than long. When I get home I crash immediately. But I had to write, and I have to talk to you. I don't know where you are these days. Jack said you'd had some problems. If you get this message, call me tonight, but not till after eleven PM my time. For sure. I'll be having scrambled eggs. I miss you Mac and hope you are doing okay."

David was watching her, "So, more bad news?" Mac felt edgy, "I don't know. Something is up, but what I don't know. Do you ever get a feeling, a mild sensation, that something is wrong? That there is an undercurrent, one you can't see, feel, or describe, but you sense an ominous force? How do we battle against just a feeling?"

David was curious, "Yes Mac, I have had those feelings, often vague. And as often as not, I just brush them aside. So what is going on? Is this a new feeling or a vision?"

"This is a new feeling. I guess it's been brewing for several days. It's a feeling that something is seriously wrong, beyond that which I know about or see into the future. It's as if, oh I don't know. I can't describe it. This is a new feeling. In my gut I feel apprehensive, anxious; perhaps someone died. I don't know, but I don't like it."

She settled back and closed her eyes as if to shut out any more foreboding thoughts. David took his camera and went to the lounge car to take a few pictures. He picked up two cold lagers and took them back to their seats. Mac was awake and smiled as he handed her a beer.

They chatted lightly for the duration of the ride, and were back in Paris and in their suite in no time. Mac calculated the time difference and determined she had to make a call to her friend in D.C.

"Hello? Andy is that you? How are the scrambled eggs sweetie? Great. Now girlfriend, what is so urgent? I read your note this morning and got a knot in my stomach, in part from the urgency, in part from your new position, and in part from all the other stuff going on. Okay, I'll shut up. Talk to me."

"Mac, I am not sure I know where to begin. In this job I am in private meetings, meetings with people and conversations that are supposed to be secret. There are people being driven to the far side entrance in SUV's with dark windows, past the media; then in through a private entrance. My knees shake at times. I have been asked to gather economic outlooks on many countries, prepare graphs, and then I sit in a chair in the background as these men talk about what they think is going to happen, what they want to happen, what they can make happen."

"I tell you Mac, I feel like I am committing treason. There are discussions going on about American financial matters, and how things must get worse. There have been a dozen meetings so far and the same two men are in many of them, with a few others. Now get this, they have a way to ramp up a housing crisis, and it was an idea presented by one of the men who arrived in secret and is there often. His name is Ivan Schwartz. Do you know of him? He scares me Mac. I know this will sound crazy but it seems as if he is determined to destroy the economy of this country. How can that be? Anyway, there is some grotesque Russian man, and a German who heads up a hedge fund in Europe; and I don't have the names here with me but I can send them to you. There is someone else that gives me chills and that is the Chief, to whom I report. I am not sure if all the names of staff are even out yet, but his name is Ari Auerbach. He is a nightmare let me tell you. He's a runt of a guy and very effeminate, but he swears more than anyone I've ever been around. He gives a whole new meaning to the term potty mouth."

"You'd swear he has brass knuckles in his coat pocket, switchblade in his back pocket, and a gun in his belt. He is little more than a gangster personality, a thug who loves to intimidate and treat people badly. You know the type, the Napoleonic complex on steroids. Gee, I am just rambling on and on. It's been so long since we talked, and I've wanted to tell you about this cast of characters. You'd normally never see them in polite, civilized company, because they all come across as thugs. So aside from all the gossipy stuff, I need to tell you that there is a plan underway, certainly embryonic at this point, but a definite plan and objectives. I don't hear everything, and occasionally am asked to leave the room so I know there is a lot more going on that I don't know about. But from all I have been able to surmise, these men wish to foster chaos, elevate our financial problems, weaken the dollar, and make us indebted to foreign interests, namely China and Japan. Ari and Ivan Schwartz have been to China once already, and I heard a secretary talking with someone about a travel schedule for Ari that shows him headed to China at least 5 times this year. Now why would someone in the Administration be getting chummy with China, and in the company of a billionaire?"

Mac's face formed a frown and her stomach churned, "Andy, I feel sick. Is there anyone working with you who knows all of this? Have you been sworn to secrecy and silence, I suppose? Now I know this is upsetting, it really angers me, and I know it would be our natural instinct to call Jack or one of our media contacts. I can't explain my reasoning, but I need to ask you to not tell anyone else. I wish it could be otherwise, but trust me on this. I have a good reason, but it too must be kept secret. I can tell you that there is a master plan that goes beyond you, me, and even those in the White House. We are to let things evolve. A time will come when all of this becomes known and while it may be too late to redirect the forces and intentions of the White House it must be left alone."

"Now Andy what you can do is to keep me informed. First of all, I am writing a book and your information can be added, plus it fits with a project I am working on. But you must be careful. I'd like you to get a pay as you go cell and use it only to talk with me. Keep it in your car hidden, or at home hidden. You need to know that the people you have mentioned are dangerous, as you have surmised, only much more so. Also, nothing you will hear or discover will ever be too outrageous to mention, because at this point I'd believe anything. You should give no one reason to give you a second look or regard you as anything but a number cruncher. If things get too rough, you can resign."

"Oh Andy it is so good to talk with you. I miss you. I hope we can figure out a way of getting together one of these days. To do so means we'd have to meet on neutral ground, like a sunny beach in Mexico. Now you take care of yourself. Don't email me at all from your office computer, and if you use your home laptop, use a separate account just for our exchanges. Call me when you have more information— scrambled of course. Oh and one more thing. If you hear rumors, there is likely substance to them, so dig around, just don't draw attention to yourself. Night."

Mackenzie closed her cell phone slowly, closed her eyes and let out a soft moan. David had left the room to give her privacy, but he could hear the moan and came back into the sitting room. "So your face tells me that your feeling was justified, that things are already happening?"

"Yes, oh yes. I am shocked actually. I would not have expected things to start so quickly. And I wonder why the rush. What are those people trying to do that requires this full court press? There is time to destroy America. But I am getting the sense that we are not operating on normal time, we are not operating on Nadir's time; it looks like we are operating on Schwartz's time, and he must be in a big hurry. David, I need to just process for a while. I need to just be quiet with this information. Can we not talk about it till tomorrow and just go out and have a nice dinner and a walk?"

"Of course sweetheart, whatever works for you. I am hungry, and a walk would be great after sitting on the train all that time. Do you think you'd be more at ease if we cut our trip short and headed back home tomorrow? If this environment is not relaxing to you, then it is not serving its purpose. Think about it; it's strictly up to you."

"Honey we are due to go home day after tomorrow anyway. There are some fun things we could do, like a day trip to a nearby wine area to sample wines, though I admit the weather is not great for that. Or, we could tour Versailles, and then have a grand dinner tomorrow night. Work for you?"

"Sounds perfect. Now let's get our duds on dudette, I could devour a horse." Mac laughed, saying, "Excellent, that is one of the specialties in most bistros."

That night in bed, Mac said, "David, this stuff going on, well I need to sort of compare notes and go back over what has come up in the visions and see how it all fits together. So I'm going to dismiss it from my mind for now so we can just enjoy our last day here."

Their last day in Paris was delightful; the weather cooperated, the tour of Versailles was marvelous and not too crowded; some last minute shopping produced some great buys; and the dinner was tres magnifique in food and atmosphere. They walked down the Boulevard Champs-Elysees soaking up local culture, stopping for a brandy, and then back to their suite to prepare for their return flight early the next morning.

####

CHAPTER TEN

For I have sworn thee fair, and thought thee bright, who art as black as hell, as dark as night.

William Shakespeare
1564-1616, British Poet, Playwright, Actor

The flight home dragged, like it would never end. Mackenzie was eager to get back to her home, and to dig into the seeming disparate events, present and future, and try to make sense of things. She felt restless, and then realized she was annoyed and taking for granted this wonderful first class flight, comfortable and luxurious. Spoiled brat, she thought.

They got home quite late. David took the dogs out for a quick walk and Mac gave a glance at the mail on the desk, and then checked her email. A message to call Jack, a note from Kate, and a note from Eli, but it was too late to call so she dropped each a quick email and indicated she'd call in the morning when she got up.

They wearily trundled off to bed, happy to be back home. The dogs were elated to have Mom home, and David was happy to curl up in his own bed. He thought to himself, "wow, I've come to already regard this as our home and our bed. I'm a cooked goose, happily."

The smell of fresh coffee brought Mac to her feet. It was good to be back to their normal routine, or at least what had become normal. Sure enough the dogs were fed, coffee ready, much of the unpacking done and poached eggs almost at the ready. David spoiled her; he was a marvel and she loved him. Yes, she said to herself, she did love him. Wow

"Good morning sunshine. You slept well. You didn't even hear the phone ring this morning. The pups and I have had a bit of a walk, and all is well on the home front. And now, a poached egg for m'lady."

"Oh David you do spoil me! And I love it. One of these days when I am cleared of this project, I am going to spoil you rotten, I promise. But for now, I need to get back into the groove. There is so much to do. I have got to try to make sense out of all the bits of information. I am so confused now, and overwhelmed. But right now I am starving. Let's eat!"

Later Mackenzie settled at her desk—notes spread out, laptop open, and began returning phone calls.

"Kate, Hi honey, it's Mac. We just got back late last night. Oh yes, we had a marvelous time. Paris is such a romantic city, plus we spent a night at the most divine chateau in the Alps. The whole visit was perfection."

"Mac I've missed you. I thought you were going to email or phone. Surely you weren't that busy? So what all did you do? How was the wedding?"

"The wedding? Oh, it was lovely. Small, just family and a few friends, but charming. They scurried off to a honeymoon in Greece, and David and I did our own thing. We had some great meals, walks, and tours. The weather was for the most part not great, cold and rainy. The overnight stay at a mountain chateau was magical. But it's good to be home, back with the pups and into our routine. Listen, I've got a bunch of calls to make, so how about we chat later, and get together soon? How about you and John coming over for dinner toward the end of the week? Great, I'll call later."

"Jack Hi. Yes we got back last night quite late so I did not call. I've not heard from Juliette, but she just arrived there today and the guests are not due there for a couple of days or so. She'll be in touch so relax. So what's up?"

Jack sounded out of sorts, "Oh Mac, I'm not sure. I'm tearing my hair out here, and we both know I don't have much to work with. Between your information, and what else I have come across, plus some recent reports, and this upcoming meeting; it's all got me rattled. I know what

I know, yet I feel like I don't know the most important stuff. I feel like I am in the eye of a storm; all is quiet and still around me, yet I know out there just beyond my reach is a killer wind. I know, it's all nuts."

"Actually Jack, I've been feeling somewhat the same way. I also feel on overload. But like you, I know there is something missing, some magical key that will put things into perspective and make sense out of the disparate insanity. But I have an embryonic idea that I am going to spend today exploring. Don't even ask, as I have no clue yet. It is just a germ of thought and I am going to have to step out of my comfort zone and let my mind travel where it normally does not. If I strike pay dirt or gather some sort of insight, I'll get back to you. But Jack, if you don't hear from me do not assume there is a problem. I'm going to call if there is one, so no news is good news for you. Okay?"

Jack sighed, "Okay. Sorry, but I feel spooked of late. I am thinking about resorting to tea leaves, or palmists, or Tarot cards, anything to give me a leg up. I wish we had finished all of this before the election, because it would have been much easier to get information, ask questions and get help. But it is what it is. Okay Mac girl, keep me posted, stay out of trouble, and may the Good Lord give you a sign of some sort. Say Hi to David and how is the bugger doing anyway?"

"He's just great. Bye Jack and take care of yourself."

Mackenzie took out two folders of notes, spreading the contents of one folder out on the floor and then sat in the middle, looking from one to the next—2009, on the move, with much happening. Her visions were reduced to condensed notes yet reflected a degree of intensity and speed with which the new Administration was jumping in to impose change.

It is said that the best way to figure out what makes a person tick, and the nature of their character is to see who they associate with. Our mothers always told us, 'pick your friends carefully because you are judged by the company you keep.'

The biggest buzz seems to be over Nadir's appointments, and discussion of his associations. Mac had a list of both, had dug into each one, and her findings were worrisome at the least. To date she had not found anyone who was not a Communist, Socialist, Marxist, or who had a history of radicalism in their work, education or activism. She had found their speeches given at various universities and organizations, video clips of presentations, and books they'd written; and so far she had not found one who had a straight or honorable background. Plus, Nadir was bringing in mostly academics, hardly anyone who had real life experience, had a business background or had any management experience. America no longer had a Democracy, but instead, a Neocracy, a government of the inexperienced.

People have been appointed to oversee just about every aspect of American society and business, each with their litany of radical views. It was a reflection on the new President, and emblematic of a prevailing attitude in this government. Those around him seemed wedded to radical ideas and objectives geared to move this country to a weakened state, wherein we will be more in tune with much of the rest of the Marxist, Socialist and Communist world.

And what does this say about Nadir? How can he not be in the same camp, if he has surrounded himself with people who hold extreme, radical views and a desire to tear America down? If one runs with gang bangers, is not one likely a gang banger? Is it not reasonable to assume that one's scope of associations would be vastly different than their own composition? Part of Psychology 101 is that people seek out those who are most like themselves, from the standpoint of comfort, ease of relating, and sharing more in common.

Just more puzzle pieces to be worked into the whole. As Mac sat there, a nagging thought kept bugging her. She had a feeling that there was more to the process of the mind in terms of psychology and philosophy going on here, more than mere politics and party partisanship. What was needed was an expert mind to pick. There was a professor at Stanford who had written several books on the human condition, history, and philosophy among other topics. He had a good grasp of early political thinking and the conditions of the time.

Mac put in a call to Stanford and tracked down Doctor Galt. A student answered his office phone and put her through to the good Professor.

"Dr. Galt, this is Mackenzie Honor. I am working on a very complex project that has me confused and even stymied, and I need a

Renaissance Man from whom to draw some clarity and understanding. I was wondering if you would be able to spare me a couple of hours next week. I am at your disposal and will fly in at whatever time works for you."

"Ms. Honor, a pleasure. I'd be happy to meet and allow you to pick my mind, though a Renaissance Man I am not. What exactly are you seeking from me? In other words, how can I be of help so that I might be prepared before you arrive?"

"Dr. Galt, I wish I could say exactly. But I can't. So let me explain the bits of a puzzle I am trying to pull together. I am trying to figure out what the common denominator is within the current political thinking in Washington; how it measures up to events and actions in this country and abroad; and what it all suggests for the future. I know I am being vague, but I have a wealth of bits and pieces of information and I know it all fits to a bigger picture, which alludes me."

"Ah, well in that case, yes I think I might have some information that would be helpful. I have been following things somewhat myself, and a few things seem rather clear to me, and I expect you will find them interesting and thought-provoking. So it will be fun for me to open that door for you. Let's see, my schedule is open on Monday. I have no lectures or obligations. Do you suppose you could be here by noon? I'll have lunch brought in."

"Monday it is. Yes I'll be there at noon. Thank you so much Dr. Galt. I look forward to meeting. Goodbye."

Mackenzie was pleased with herself. She had a good feeling about Dr. Galt and was excited to learn from him. She returned to her notes about 2009. While most of her visions of 2009 have been put to rest, the Administration's actions continued to create a separate area of concern and public outrage. An on-going point of conflict will be the Attorney General's secret appointment of about a dozen attorneys who have defended various terrorists who have attempted attacks on America, and his continued refusal to reveal their names.

There will be a lot of discussion about the people who visit the White House, from outside the Administration and Congress. Ivan Schwartz was there far too many times; but the primary visitor who appeared multiple times a week was Drew West, the head of one of the most powerful labor union in the U.S. But as time went by information emerged that Drew had been bleeding the union funds, using that money to promote and build an international labor union and to feather his own nest. Of course, labor unions by now had toppled American industry and manufacturing through outrageous demands, salaries and benefits that removed American companies from any competitive posture. Job losses meant less income to unions.

Corporations, especially many multi-national entities, invested in the Nadir campaign, and it became clear that their interests were not political, but pragmatic business dealings. As such they made deals with the Administration to gain advantage. The expected return on their investment gave them clout and they put on the pressure, with deals getting cooked behind closed doors.

By the end of 2009 the majority of Americans will be concerned about what they have heard and viewed; they will be wildly outraged about various pieces of legislation, disgusted with the lies and deceit, and generally fed up with Washington. The clarion call around which a grassroots movement will spring forth is "Throw all the Bums Out."

No matter the visions, the research and early warning signs did not bode well for the nation in 2009, or beyond. Our economy will plummet, and with it will come job losses, a national real estate crisis, bankruptcies and escalating foreclosures. The rest of the world will teeter on the brink, as will the global economy—all watching the U.S. with concern.

Mac pushed herself away from her desk and sighed. The near future was looking grim, and very unpleasant. But it was Friday and she needed to prepare for the trip to meet Dr. Galt. She made a list of questions and points she wanted to cover in their meeting. Once finished, she decided to put her work aside and to have some fun. She put in a call to Kate, "Kate dear, can you and John come for dinner tomorrow night? I thought we'd have game night and a good dinner. Just relax with no work talk. You and I can meet on the following weekend to go over our work. So what say you?"

"Mac that is perfect. John and I need a break too so the timing is ideal. What can we bring and what time do you want us there?"

"Bring yourselves; oh throw in a bottle of red if you like. And plan on 6:30. We'll have a snack and drinks first, maybe play a game, then dinner. I am up to my eyeballs in all this stuff, and need a couple of days away from it. By the way I am going to California to meet with a professor who may hold the key to this massive puzzle. Okay sweetie, see you tomorrow evening. Gotta run now."

David soon came into the kitchen, pups scurrying along behind him (oh were they in love with him!). "Hi doll, how goes the work?" he asked.

"It is going very well indeed. In fact, I had something of a breakthrough earlier, and realized I need some high level professional input. I tracked down a noted expert who is a lecturer and professor at Stanford. I am flying down Monday morning to meet with him, and will fly home that afternoon. We spoke on the phone and I am very excited to gain his insight, though I have a feeling it is going to be highly intellectual and difficult to grasp, but if I am right, it will be the key to solving this puzzle."

"Also, I decided to take the weekend off. I invited Kate and John for dinner tomorrow evening for a game night, and I thought we could prepare the meal together after hitting a good farmer's market in the morning. But I was thinking of maybe going to the movie this evening? And on Sunday, how about we go out for brunch and a walk?"

"You clearly read my mind. I was feeling a need for some special activity and some time with you. Your whole agenda works for me. We can keep dinner simple and easy and make a movie. You decide what movie and I'll start something."

By the time Kate and John arrived on Saturday evening, Mac and David had created a special dinner and were ready for a fun evening. John was in good spirits, but Kate seemed out of sorts. David fixed cocktails and chatted with John while Mac took Kate to the office to chat. "So girlfriend what's up with you? You don't seem a very happy camper this evening. Talk to me."

218

"Mac, you seem to have taken off on your own. I know you are exploring lots of things we have not discussed and I thought we were to work on this stuff together. Now you are going to San Francisco on your own. I feel like you are leaving me behind. And I am not happy about it."

"Kate, David and I went to a wedding and a mini vacation. That was our time and there was nothing to do with the book. I have been pouring over all the notes you gave me, plus my own, and am trying to find a way to have it all make sense, which it doesn't quite yet. Plus, you work full time; you have a busy family schedule and many demands on your time. I don't want to put more demands on you, and you to feel overwhelmed, and then sit and wait for some point in the future when you find a bit of free time to work on the project. We need to get this done. Plus you don't write, so since I have all the writing to do, I need to bring the information together in a way that makes sense to me. The professor I am meeting with may well provide the missing link to all of this. I am hopeful."

Mac continued, "Now I don't want you to feel badly, and you are not being left out, but I am trying to move things along. I want to get this done and back to Eli fairly soon, as I have some other work that I'll need to get to before long. So honey, just perk up and let's have a nice evening. We've got a delicious dinner, and I am ready to kick some butt at our favorite game."

The four friends had a good time, drinking wine, playing board games, and sipping brandy in front of the fire. By the time Kate and John left, she was in better humor, but still seemed a bit resentful. Mac determined she'd address the issue in more depth next week after her return from San Francisco.

David and Mac spent a wonderful weekend together, just relaxing, enjoying each other's company and exploring Portland. By Sunday evening she was getting her notes together, and preparing for her brief trip. David dropped her at the airport on Monday morning with the understanding he'd be back for her when she returned.

On the plane Mac reviewed her notes, added some more questions, and soon was in a rental car headed down to Stanford in Palo Alto. It had been some time since she'd been on the campus and as always it looked lovely. She quickly found her way to the professor's offices.

Professor Galt greeted her at the door, hand outstretched. "Miss Honor, it's a pleasure to meet you. We have spoken on the phone of course, but meeting in person is far preferable. I'll never get comfortable with all this fandangled tech stuff. Now, it is my understanding that you seek information on the possible beginnings of our economic and political condition, or at least what promises to be that condition based on what we know of the new President. Am I correct? What else?"

"Yes, Dr. Galt. I am trying to put together a strange conglomeration of information and things are not making complete sense so I know there is a missing piece and I believe you might have it."

He smiled, adding, "I hope I can be of value to you. Let's get some lunch in here while we visit." He asked his assistant to bring in the tray. "Now here my dear, help yourself. We have sandwiches, salad, and assorted drinks and cookies. My assistant spoils me rotten."

Dr. Galt said, "I talk a lot at times so if I am getting too windy, just stop me. Now to start off, there is a quote from *The Rise and Fall of the Third Reich* which references Georg Hegel. I can quote it because it stuck in my mind since my days as a political science student. It goes, "the State has the supreme right against the individual, whose supreme duty is to be a member of the State…for the right of the world spirit is above all things." Which is to say, individuals are answerable to the state, must abide by all rules of the state, and must do as they are told, as a part of the state. No free will. No freedom; all in support of the so-called greater good."

"Hegel, do you know of him?" Mac shook her head no. "He was a German philosopher in the 1700-1800's, whose ideas and philosophies were used by Karl Marx and Frederick Engels, and served to support their Communist economic theory. But now, this theory impacts most all social and political thinking globally. I once took a class on early formers of political thought, but we've not the time to school you in the nuances of each. So I will give you a simplistic definition and then a basic explanation. Essentially, Hegelian Dialectic is a framework or guideline to move our thoughts and actions into conflict and from there to a predetermined outcome or solution."

Mac's eyes rolled, "Doctor Galt, could you put that into even more simple terms? My brain is shutting down here."

He smiled knowingly, "Well, Hegel studied human behavior and certain patterns emerged. He determined that if you manipulate people into a frenzied, yet circular mode of action and thinking, where they defend against or fight for any specific ideology, we can then move people into a dictatorship over the proletariat. The Marxist agenda is still alive and thriving, and moving throughout the globe at break-neck speed. If we wish to stop it, we must step outside dialectic patterns, or predetermined, controlled and guided thought, and not do what is implicit in our battle against that ideology."

"Now, be clear here, Hegelian Conflicts permeate every aspect of life around the globe, from global organizations, companies, and governments, all the way down to local committees and school boards. It is about building consensus and dialogues; and fear and intimidation; all are acceptable means to an end. And the end? Well, at the top of the Hegelian pyramid there is and has always been one world government. It was Marx's goal, it is what Marxism, Socialism, Fascism, Communism—it is what they have all been about, each with a piece of the pie, each directing some form of the conflict. And each has believed they were working toward a perfect utopian state."

"I see you are frowning. Let me give you a hypothetical example. Let's say there are two communities separated by a river. One of them is a thriving city doing very well economically, with strong infrastructure, school system and so on. The other community is a small sleepy town with no real prospects for growth but still stable. The Mayors of both communities meet from time to time to discuss their challenges. At one meeting the Mayor of the bigger city suggests that both communities could benefit from a bridge across the river, providing access to cheaper housing for city dwellers, more shopping and cultural opportunities for the burg dwellers, and an all around boost to both economies. The small burg Mayor raises the issue of how it can be paid for. The big city Mayor says, 'by increasing taxes of course.' The small town mayor says that neither of their communities would allow such a thing, and since both communities were doing fine, there was no justification."

"The city Mayor says, 'well all we have to do is make cuts to school and fire department budgets, then get busy with our development plan. As time goes by parents and home-owners will be fearful of the impact of reducing both budgets and will ultimately agree to a tax increase. During that time both groups will be in conflict about where the cuts should come from, and eventually they will just accept cuts from both"

"So here we have conflict, fear, manipulation, acceptance and reaching the objective. Imagine Group A holds a belief that the Constitution is a vital document that is the foundation of American law and order. Then imagine Group B believes that the Constitution is a living document and should be changed to suit modern times. The two groups are at odds, doing battle over divergent, opposite beliefs. Hegel believed that given time and enough discord, two differing groups could come to 'C'—a blending of the two to form the third. And Hegel further believed that you could produce a conflict with 'C,' making C another A at odds with a new B to form a new C and so on. Essentially there has never been much reasoning within his philosophy. One more thing, Hegel's ideas placed all the emphasis on collective reasoning as to what's best for the individual, not on the individual determining what is best for himself. I hope this simplifies it for you. You will see in time, if not already, that our government has placed itself over the individual, as elitists who believe they are superior, and therefore better able to determine what is best for each of us."

"Frankly my dear, I am glad I am an old man and won't live to see most of this come to reality. I've seen too much already and I don't like what I see, not one little bit."

"If you study those who stand in the forefront of economic manipulation, government, and social change, you will find people who are skilled at orchestrating conflict, one against another, be it idea or action. Hundreds of organizations have been formed for the sole purpose of manipulating—attitudes, beliefs, media and their content, needs, expectations, business methods, ideology—Ivan Schwartz is one you should look into, as he has hundreds of such organizations that he funds and which are very successful at what they do."

"Today we are in conflict over capitalism versus big government; freedom versus government controls; God versus NCLU; race versus race; free-markets versus government jobs; rich versus poor; good versus evil; environmentalists versus land owners; pro choice versus pro life; Christians and Muslims, Muslims and Jews—well you see, it's everywhere."

Mackenzie's eyes widened as the pieces started to fall together, and she was horrified. "Doctor, to me this is terrifying. Based on this information, we are perilously close to global Communism in some form. That means that a single group of people would control the world, and the people, the citizens of the world, would be nothing more than chattel, to work and slave on behalf of the state, which would then decide what meager subsistence we will have."

"Doctor, isn't this also in line with Cloward-Piven?"

"Yes indeed, wonderful you know Cloward-Piven. It is a central force in the overall plan. They proposed overloading the system, which goes to creating conflict from the top down. It's all a huge web my dear. It's been in the works for a long time. Today there are so many followers all over the world, in the highest of places. Some of them were radical, pot-smoking activists in the sixties. They now call themselves Progressives, at least in this country, because Socialism is not popular."

Mac felt a knot in her stomach.

"I need to add one more issue for you to consider. Today there is not one single politically-based issue that is not driven by this dialectic; not one. Working as an intangible influence, it is used to control every conflict and its outcome, and then redirect the divergent sides into yet another conflict. There is no intention of ever achieving harmonious resolution because that would disrupt the flow and progress to the ultimate goal."

"In addition, there has been a unique progression in American politics over the many decades. Things have changed remarkably, and not for the better. The changes have been both in politics and in business. The term Machiavellian takes root from a Fifteenth-Century

Italian philosopher, Niccolo Machiavelli, who promoted an especially controversial philosophy about war. The term now refers to those who practice devious and deceitful despotism to gain advantage in politics. Don't they all? (He chuckled). Nowadays, it is a term that suggests the end justifies the means, and that no matter what is jeopardized, the end is the objective. He believed that suffering and misery was a tool to keep people in check. Machiavelli believed that while it was good to be loved and feared, it was more important to be feared."

"Now does all that have a ring of familiarity? Think about Schwartz, Nadir, Madinski; the cast of characters is long who seem comfortable with this philosophy."

"In modern times psychologists have studied the human mind and personality sub-sets. They have defined a 'dark triad' of personality types—Machiavellianism, narcissism and psychopathy, and all share one common trait—to lie, deceive and manipulate others for personal gain. Here in the U.S. there are far too many players in what is going on that can be identified with that characteristic."

Mac thought for a moment before responding, "You know, it strikes me that there are forces at work in America that would drag us down, would make us into an impoverished Third World country and I've long wondered why. The answer seems to be clear now. In order to create One World government with passive followers who willingly work for the 'state', there can't be one or two powerful countries that have highly educated, aware citizens who would do battle against any efforts to weaken this country, or create the One World order. I see now that this effort has been ongoing for some time, from decades of dumbing down our educational system to weakening our dollar, taking us into economic decline, shipping our manufacturing abroad—it all goes to creating our decline to prepare us for what is to come. Now I wonder how many Presidents and Congressional leaders have contributed to this. Oh my! May God help us!"

"My dear, you seem shocked. This has been on the horizon for some time. But I must tell you, Hegel was one of the great con artists. His premise has not been proven, but it does have a record of success; none more so than in Europe and America. Here in America, in 2003 and thereafter, all our foreign and domestic policy is based on Hegel's 'communitarian' thinking, yet those Americans directly affected have likely never heard any of the terms. By the time the transition takes place, almost no one in this country will know what went wrong; they will not understand that we are the ultimate accomplishment of Hegel/ Marxist theory, brought about by agents of change to implement world justice, social equity and world peace, terms we'll be hearing more about in the coming months and years, as the scene is set for government intervention, confiscation, and redistribution."

"One colleague says that we have been duped by elitists and their propaganda into believing conspiracy theories which then causes us to not believe anything else. It is like the child who cried 'wolf' too many times, so when the wolf really showed up, no one paid attention or believed the child. When we hear about something seemingly outrageous, we just don't believe it. We are primed for a totalitarian global takeover of all people, property and produce. And this can well take place before Americans know what hit them. It has already begun."

"Doctor Galt, I appreciate all your time you have given me. It has made my trip to meet you very worthwhile. It seems that each expert I speak with, whether economics, politics, or religion, I find I am faced with a whole new quandary."

"With all the conflicts going on, with the implied actions of the new Administration, it seems that it all boils down to a battle of good and evil, or God and the anti-Christ. Thank you again for your generous time and lunch. May I call you if I have questions in the future?" Dr. Galt shook Mac's hand and enthusiastically said yes.

As Mac sat on the plane for the relatively short return flight to Portland, she reviewed her notes from her meeting with Dr. Galt. She realized that in the linear continuum of liberal and conservative ideology that began with the founding of our country, we have moved back and forth. The big difference is that the back and forth movement was to the right of center until the last few decades, where we have moved back and forth within the center of the continuum and right. But since about 2005 our margin of movement was to the left of center and going farther left each year. It was truly upsetting and Mac sat there feeling inadequate to the challenges facing her.

Moreover, the leftward movement promised ever-increasing secularism, with God and Christianity being withdrawn from our culture. God was in control now as ever, and Mac pondered the scope of meaning to all of this amid an emerging monster headache. It was obvious that if God and Christianity were eliminated from U.S. culture, faith and hope would vanish as well; and with their passing, people would be so disconnected, they'd go along with anything.

David was curbside at the airport when Mac emerged from the terminal, happy to see his smile, which made her relax. "Hi honey, how was your visit? You look a bit haggard. Here's a big hug, with kiss yet to come."

"Oh David, it's so good to see you. I am feeling like Alice in Wonderland when she fell down the rabbit hole, into a whole new dimension of existence, with nothing looking normal and sane; at least until I see you. I'm glad to be home, but the meeting was extraordinary, mind bending really. I'll tell you about it once I have a martini in hand. Let's get home!"

David knew she'd be tired and likely upset, so he made plans to give her a hassle free lovely evening at home. He ordered dinner delivered from one of her favorite restaurants; had a pitcher of chilled martinis ready to go, and had drawn a hot bubble bath just before he left the house. When they got home he took her by the hand to the bathroom, to the still steamy and bubbly bath in candlelight. It was just what she needed. "Oh my, how did you know? This is perfect. All I need now is a chilled martini with olives."

"Your wish is my command." David flew out of the room and by the time Mac was submerged in the water, he was back with a small tray with a shaker of perfect martinis, a bowl of extra olives, plus a two iced glasses. He poured her martini as she leaned back in the hot water up to her neck with a huge sigh of relief. "Heaven, pure heaven," Mac purred.

David smiled, pleased that he had, so far, hit the right tone. "I had a feeling a bubble bath would hit the spot; and I knew a martini would be the drink of choice. So far so good. But there is more. You have a twenty-minute soak, and then put on some glamorous robe and join me in the living room. I'm taking my martini with me as I have something to do."

Mac felt all the stress evaporate out of her body and smiled, feeling content and blissful. After about ten minutes she showered off, combed her hair, and put on an elegant robe. When she got into the living room a fire was going, cushions were on the floor, the room was lit by more than a dozen candles, and an amazing meal was on the coffee table in front of the fire.

"Oh wow, this is amazing. You cooked all of this? No, this looks like it was made at Paley's Place, right? My favorite! David, you spoil me so, I am blown away. This is perfection. I am starving too. Now we'll have no serious talk about the meeting or any of this other stuff. Tonight is just for us."

The next day over breakfast Mackenzie told David about the meeting, working from her notes. When done they both sat in silence until David let out a low whistle. "You know, I have been after bad guys for a long time and I came to believe they were spread around the globe, each with an ax to grind, each with anti-American motivations. I never imagined I'd be sitting here in America and realize our biggest enemies are within. This is so depressing. I feel like I need to run off and enlist in something, somewhere. Sweetheart, you indeed have fallen into a rabbit hole. Looks like we all might be joining you."

"I know. And this is the tip of the iceberg. I need some spiritual guidance, both to ease my worries, and to explain some of the events that are playing out over the next couple of years. This is a lot of pressure. I am going to call Kate and have her go with me today."

"Kate, Hi. Listen, can you call your minister and see if we can get in to see him today?"

"Hi Mac. Why? What's up anyway? How was that meeting in San Francisco?"

"Kate, this is all just too much. I feel overwhelmed and tense all the time. I can't back out of this, but I need to find some peace in all of it.

I thought some spiritual guidance might help, both in giving me some peace, but also some insight into all the events upcoming."

"Okay, hold on and I'll call him from the other phone. Mac, he said he could free up some time this afternoon about four o'clock. Do you want me to come along or is this another of your private meetings?"

"Come on Kate, you're not being fair. You've been quite a bit removed from all of this since we got back from New York and certainly since that last visit at the beach. I'll trade places with you today if you like. I'll do the hair, and you go out and gather information and write the book. Fact is, this is other-worldly, in a dark and evil environment where two plus two no longer equals four. Even if Schwartz's goons aren't after me, I feel an evil presence all around. The more I find out the more difficult it is. So let's go see your minister this afternoon. In the meantime I am going to work on the book, but also need to check in with Eli. I'll come by your house at 3:30."

Kate looked at Mackenzie for a moment, then said, "Perhaps your actions and attitude are attracting the evil and feelings of fear. Maybe you need to get closer to God, and gain some faith."

Mac was stunned as she replied, "Are you serious? Kate, I don't know what has gotten into you lately, but I am not liking it. Yes you know me, but how presumptuous of you, really! I think I'd best hang up before I say something I may regret. I need to rethink this afternoon. I'll be in touch later."

Mac sat sipping her coffee, pulling her thoughts together and trying to make sense of Kate and her strange behavior before she placed a call to Eli. She took a deep breath as she heard the phone ring. "Hello. This is Mackenzie Honor. Is Eli available?" "Hello Miss Honor. Hold on, he wants to talk to you. He is on the other line."

"Mackenzie? Are you alright? Pat and I have been hoping to hear from you. I'm guessing that you are feeling under a great deal of pressure, and you probably are pretty horrified about all that you have been learning. I understand. I really do, but you need to keep yourself focused, not allow your emotions to get in the way, and certainly don't allow fear to worm its way into your thinking. You need to know that things are as they should be. God is in control. He must again play out the battle once and for all with Satan, who right now has gained far too much power. Remember what we talked about—that repenting is necessary, for each of us, and prayers for our nation as well. God wants the Godless to feel his displeasure, to feel the pain of not having him in their hearts. We know what you know, and as such, we know that you are under stress. It is good for you to seek counsel from a minister."

"Eli, you know only too well. Yes, things are as you imagine. I am overwhelmed and doubting that I and even Kate, are the right people for this book job. She is already too busy in her personal life, and frankly she has been acting very strange and quite snarky of late; and I am feeling much too inadequate to this task."

"Self doubt, not a luxury you can afford Mac. You are in this position for a reason. It is not for us to question what the reason, just to know it is as it should be, and you need to finish. How far along are you?"

"I am not sure. I think a bit more than half way. I am dealing with future issues and events now. It is difficult to know how to present events that have not yet happened without sounding like a loon. But I have more than enough material. It is just keeping focused and disciplined. One problem though. Bits and pieces of information come my way, and I then dig further into each and uncover yet more information. I am afraid I have too much, yet I can't seem to stop with gathering mind-blowing information. As example, I met in San Francisco with a Dr. Galt. He provided information that seems to bring all the pieces together, by way of Hegelian Dialectics. Do you know about this?"

"Yes, we are up on it. I know it is hard to grasp at times, but these are not normal times, and as such they call for extraordinary measures. Mac it is vitally important that you stay focused on the project. It must be your priority till it is handed off to us, and perhaps even thereafter for a time. Meanwhile, Patrick and I will be using our bully pulpit to bring truth to as many people as possible. At some point we hope to influence many to repent, but that is not the main focus right now. Now we must inform, bring light into the darkness, expose the evil that is growing in our midst."

"Now then, about Kate? I have not heard from her in over two weeks. She is succumbing to a debilitating degree of jealousy. She was the sole voice of translation of the Bible, you relied on her, and she felt she had the upper hand. Now she feels she is not needed, and is not in control. Kate needs to be in control and now she feels resentment. Mac it is her issue, not yours. If Kate is going to bog you down, emotionally or even in process, then she must be left to deal with her issues."

"Eli, I saw Kate last week socially. She seemed out of sorts. She is also not very communicative which is not like her. I have been wondering what is really going on. She has expressed being upset that I had a trip to Europe for a friend's wedding, and that I took a day trip to meet Dr. Galt. She did some research and delivered her notes to me, and now I have to figure them out and meld them into the rest. Your explanation makes more sense than anything I have come up with, sad to say."

"I may give her a call this week," Eli said. "You are better prepared for this sort of situation, than is Kate. It is not for me to give her a pass, or even guide her decision about what she wants or needs to do. She needs to see this through as we all do, but if she feels she must stop, that must be her decision alone."

"Eli I'd appreciate it if you did call her. You might glean more insight into what is troubling her. I'd like to be of help or support for her; and at the same time I need to stay on this project. My goal is to have it to you next month. Now that I have met with Dr. Galt, I feel better prepared to deal with all these visions, and I have a much better grasp on the end-times issue. The pieces of the massive puzzle are finally fitting together and the picture has become far clearer."

"Mac, on the matter of end times, you have probably learned that there are many interpretations on just what it will look like, be like. But beyond that, there is no set time for it to happen, and there are many dates and events that are believed to foretell its coming. None of us can say with any level of certainty when this time will be. Now Pat and I believe that a series of events will take place in 2012, some natural, many contrived, but it will not be Armageddon. That might not happen for ten or twenty years. There is no question that it will happen, but it will be on God's terms and timeframe, and it will be to ultimately cleanse evil, and punish those who hold evil in their heart, who don't believe or have faith, those who have turned from God, and those who have aided Satan."

"Listen Mac, once I have talked with Kate, Pat and I will decide when to have you two back here. I am thinking in two to three weeks, before you near the end of the book. Now, one thing, we had a message from Al, with news you'll no doubt find of interest. He said that Madinski's financial empire is crashing and he has been caught cheating investors out of billions in some sort of ponzi scheme. He was just over in Europe, apparently hiding a large sum of money before they arrest him. Al also said that a secret meeting was about to take place. The topic will be how to topple the US economy for the long term, and repay financial favors owed by Nadir to some backers in the Middle East. More details are coming, and we'll go over everything when you are back here."

"Eli thanks for calling. I was going to call you today actually. And thanks for the information. I gather your phone is safe?"

"God I hope so. Yes it is. I am not in the studio. I am at an office of a friend. Why?"

"Well, I may know something about that secret meeting. I was asked to get someone into the facility where a secret meeting is to be held, so I got a colleague from Paris hired at the hotel. I am expecting to hear from her shortly, as the meeting was the end of last week. The people arrived on Friday night were to leave Sunday. I don't know exactly who attended, but was told that it was Schwartz, Nadir and a few others. Is that what you heard?"

"Yes, exactly. Would you drop me an email when you've heard more?"

"Absolutely, Eli. I am sure I'll hear by tomorrow, given the time change. We agreed that she'd not call until she got a break to go skiing. Eli do you know if your email and phone are secure? Have you had them checked or put secure devices on them?"

"Actually I am not sure. I figure that Pat and I are open books given how our programs go. But you may be right. I'll look into that right away. Okay Mac, take care of yourself. No further problems, since you got that bodyguard with you, right? I'll drop you a note or call once I've chatted with Kate and my secretary will send you the travel information, probably by the end of this week. Bye Mac."

"Bye Eli. Give my regards to Pat."

Mackenzie decided to wait to hear from Juliette, so turned her attention back to the papers on her desk. Looking forward to the rest of 2009, the country would remain in economic trouble, Nadir would kill several efforts to develop oil, offshore, at the Bakken field, and up in Alaska. On a purely logical evaluation, knowing that the U.S. had to decrease its dependence on foreign oil, it made no sense to block domestic development, when we were reportedly sitting on untapped fields holding far more oil than in the Middle East; sufficient supplies to last us nearly 300 years, or longer by some estimates. Nor did it make sense that Nadir had sent $20 billion to Venezuela for their oil exploration; no sense until one realized that Schwartz had invested a few billion into the Venezuelan oil industry, so the U.S. money would ensure that Schwartz made yet another monster profit.

The year will see a growing resentment among voters toward all of Washington; scandals, charges of corruption and growing divisions. Nadir will continue to spend a good percentage of his time on the road giving speeches, to the point of over-exposure. Spending will quickly reach the outrageous as zeros are added to every category of the so-called budget. The economy started and will end the year as the number one crisis from which various summit meetings will be held during the year.

Of the numerous scandals to explode, none will be more loathsome than the disclosures pertaining to global warming, wherein we will learn that the numbers and reports were fixed, the research was sketchy, the results tampered with, and the conclusions, based on false numbers and assumptions, were wrong. Still, the year will close out with a handful of would-be billionaires sticking to their premise of global warming. There will be a slight economic up-tick in late 2009 and well into 2010, but it proves to be temporary, much like the calm before the storm. People will appear hopeful but very cautious, as if unwilling to trust any news, not wanting to expose themselves to greater risk.

David came into the office to announce that he was headed out on errands and were there any requests. Mac replied, "Popcorn please. We don't have any and I am craving some. And pears. Oh and those great cheesy breadsticks. Then I'm good. You know, this year looks like it is going to be a tough one for most of us, certainly for the country. I'd say we should escape to some other place, but darn, it does not look like there are any good places left unscathed. Should I tell you what's coming?"

"First of all, I don't want to know. I don't like surprises, but I don't want to dwell on what's around the next corner. I know you'll grab my arm if a truck is about to hit me. So no my love, keep the scary stories to yourself. And as for the grocery requests, you shall have them post haste! I am out the door now."

Mac returned to her work. She seemed to have 2009 pretty well covered. There were a few visions that were just not clear, and she did not want to commit them to paper unless and until she could make more sense from them. There were just too many Schwartz-originated actions that were complex and yet on their own made no sense, and/ or would appear innocently obscure. But for Mackenzie one thing was certain—there was nothing innocent or obscure about anything Schwartz was engaged in, regardless of its nature.

The lingering impression that gnawed at Mackenzie's thoughts was that of American history, going back to the times of FD Roosevelt. When FDR took office this country had a history of citizens being self-reliant, moral, believing in God, and supporting limited government. FDR decided that 'programs' were needed to limit the Depression; so he instigated many social programs, and so began our decline with the worsening of the Depression and the generational acceptance of government assistance.

People were caught up in fear, and weakened by hunger—the ideal conditions to get people to go along with anything. History easily repeats itself if lessens are not learned. Mackenzie could see the U.S. going down that dark road once again. We were being fed huge doses of fear, so of course she wondered what would happen to our food. This concern arose due to a vision where one or more government agencies would be taking over food production, eliminating the ability to grow one's own food. One official report would expose government experiments with our food and water supply, including putting a birth control substance into corn crops and certain of our water supply.

There is evidence of genetic altering of food within numerous secret projects, some of them in existence since 2001. To what end? One can only imagine; and Mac had not been able to find out. But if fear is a leveling agent and hunger topples, then comments made by a Nadir czar/minion held ominous meaning. He comments late in 2009 that Americans are weak; that the government must take control of manufacturing, production, and food supply, as example. Ominous, extreme, but possibly linked to the fear and hunger control patterns.

Mac further learned that government officials have determined that Americans are getting more agitated, angrier, more emotional and disturbed, so they proposed a mild tranquilizer be added to the public water supply. The study is to be completed within the next year and trials will take place during that time.

Communism has taken a seat in this new Administration, once again repeating history from the FDR era. Back then Communists were instrumental in creating labor unions, with a strong-hold on the CIO. Russia was then our ally and Communists were encouraged to participate in our government. Communists were also active in the leadership of unions. Today as we move further into 2009, things have a remarkable similarity to those pre-war days of FDR.

Mackenzie knew that there could be no positive influence or outcome from Communist, Marxist or Socialist influence over our government. Labor unions had a strong foothold even before the election, and quickly forged a sphere of influence over the Administration, which grows well into the future, to the detriment of workers and citizens alike.

Mac recalled a time long ago when she was barely twenty and worked on "The Hill" when LBJ was president. He had been elected in part by the unions to whom he promised a repeal of Section 14B of the Taft Hartley Act. In the first year he tried to push through the vote and failed. In the second year he was 'urged' by unions to get that vote passed. In essence, repeal of 14B meant that anyone could get a job in a union shop, but in order to keep the job, you had to join the union within 30 days or else be fired. Mac was working on a project when two union bosses came into her office to see the Congressman for whom she worked.

They sauntered in, saying, "So hey there little lady. Now aren't you a cutie. How about shaking that fanny of yours and let your boss know we need to talk to him." Mac entered the Congressman's office to announce the arrival of the union boys, but she felt compelled to say to her boss, "Sir, how can you in all conscience vote for this bill? Those guys are standing out there in their $1000 custom made suits and fancy imported shoes with a limo and driver waiting at the curb; they have their $50 haircuts, manicured hands, gold jewelry and fancy silk ties. What do they know about what is good for the common man? You must not vote for that bill."

She recalled his comment as if made yesterday, "Mackenzie, you do not understand. I promised Johnson I'd vote with him. If I don't keep my promise he will ruin me and my family. He has a dossier on all of us in Congress and he'll use it to destroy anyone who goes against him. Those guys out there are from my state, and they can make additional trouble for me. I must vote with the President. It's called survival Mackenzie."

Mac showed the slick and slimy union bosses into the office and closed the door. Later when they emerged all smiles, the Congressman's Administrative Assistant chatted with them, indicating they should avoid the young lady in the other office because she was pretty upset about their proposed legislation.

"So little lady, Alan says you don't like us much; or our legislation. But we know what is best for the worker and this bill is it."

"No I don't like you at all. I don't know where you get off believing you know what is best for workers, since you are so far removed from them, in your custom made suits, imported shoes and ties, and limousine outside. You are only interested in expanding your coffers, not helping the working stiff. No indeed, I don't like you one bit."

Mackenzie knew today's union bosses were a totally different breed, and far more dangerous than back in the LBJ era. Their radical communist-like beliefs and strong influence over the Administration gave them a level of power they had not known since their earliest days. They were usually doing battle against big business and government, but no longer. Now they were in the driver's seat.

Mackenzie decided to put 2009 to rest. It was time to organize 2010 and 2011.

###

CHAPTER ELEVEN

Whoever wishes to keep a secret must hide the fact that he possesses one.

Johann Wolfgang Von Goethe
1749-1832, German Poet, Dramatist, Novelist

Notebooks filled with notes and comments still cluttered Mac's desk. She had made considerable progress on the book since returning from her Paris trip, by staying focused. She had been aided by her meetings with professionals who shed light on some of the more complicated issues. But she wanted to get it finished so she could take it with her when she and Kate head back to New York. The project was far more time-consuming than Mac had ever imagined.

Then too, she now had a life and she was determined to give time to it so it could grow and strengthen. David was the most important part of her life now and she was not going to allow anything to detract from the marvel of their relationship.

She smiled as she thought of David, who was not yet back from the store. The ringing of the phone interrupted her, "Hello, Mac here."

"Bonjour Mac." "Juliette, I've been hoping to hear from you and eager to learn about your job."

"Oh Mac, this has been a strange experience. You were right; Madame Trussard is a lovely woman, a strong task master but fair. I got to the hotel before noon, was shown to my quarters, and asked to report to the dining room as soon as I changed into my uniform. She had someone give me some training, showing me where everything was and how the kitchen service worked. Fortunately I had a few days to get comfortable.

Initially I was assigned table service for the meeting, but the woman who was the room host was not feeling well, and Madame asked me to take over that duty. So I quickly changed again, and returned to the dining room. I was asked to greet the guests and show them to their table, take drink orders, and remain in the background. I do so. A waiter was to take food orders, but Madame had decided to serve a lavish meal without ordering. So I stood tableside while courses were delivered. I used drink orders as an excuse to stand nearby. There was a man from the Chinese government, a prince from the Saudi royal family, an American who was a friend of your Schwartz and though I am not sure of, from a comment, he has something to do with your Fed banking, a short man? There was also a man whom I took to be an Arab but from what country I do not know. But my impression was that these men operated outside boundaries, and laws, and are how you say, renegades? Your President was not there for all of Sunday. He had Saturday dinner with the group, and he talked with them in the morning and then a helicopter came and took him away."

"He is an odd man. He flashes smiles easily, but he is ah, froid," "ah chilly?" Mac said, "You mean cold and aloof?" "Oui, Juliette agreed."

"Yes, cold. He was also stern with everyone, and he swore a lot. But strange, he also had courtois? You know?" "Ah, courtesy?" Mac smiled, "courteous, you mean courteous." "Oui, exactement! laughed Juliette."

"He listened on every word said by Schwartz. He silenced when Schwartz spoke. But he was arrogant. And when Schwartz finished, your president would seem very angry, bang his fist on the table and holler at others. One moment I was standing opposite him pouring water to the Arab man and I looked across to see his face. His eyes were black and empty, a truly horrible look on his face that showed utter contempt and ire. Mac, I found them all to be very upsetting and scary men, but especially Schwartz and your President Nadir. More than once my arm hairs stood up."

"President, he made like a little speech telling each man what he wanted them to do. One objected on some point and the president he shouted. He told them no excuses, no questions, no changes. And then whoosh, he flew off. But the other men remained and their chat was hushed but Schwartz, he was in charge and was stern. I heard him shout and swear too. We were all ordered out of the room. I stood in the hallway with my pen on, and picked up little this's and that's, and I heard a bit more when overseeing service or getting beverage orders."

"So Juliette, what is the bottom line on your observations and what you heard. By the way where are you now?"

"I am at a nearby ski resort, and going up the lift soon. Safe for you. Okay, bottom line. These men were talking about storing money in a safe place, about a crisis to come, about Nadir and can he be trusted, and how they will bring America into line and the dollar down. They talked about what each should do and I could not hear that. But I think, from words, they will create a diversion and use it to their advantage, and get money out of it and that money will go to the safe place. Oh I know this is a bit vague. I had such a hard time hearing. English is not my first language so I struggle sometimes. But Mac, I did not get the impression that this is happening soon. It seems they wish to make certain things happen first, so they have a time in mind. Did I make a mess of it?"

"Oh no, Juliette. You did just fine. It is valuable to know about the different people, how Schwartz and Nadir behaved, and the nature of what they were talking about. It's now up to me to gather more information and piece things together. Good job Juliette. I knew you'd do just great. Now then, how much longer are you staying there?"

Juliette laughed, "You know it is so marvelous here; I don't work too hard, I have a very nice private room and bath, and I get to go skiing two times a week. I decided to stay on here for another month or two. In another two weeks I'll get three days off in a row, so I'll drive back to Paris and take care of some things, and then return here for perhaps a month. It is okay?"

"Absolutely, Juliette. I am thrilled that you enjoy your time there so much. Anyway you are free to work wherever you wish. I only ask that you do not discuss our arrangement or anything you heard there. Madame would find out and she'd probably contact the authorities."

"Yes Mac I understand, as always. The lift is coming. We'll chat soon no? Au revoir Mac."

Mac hung up the phone, thinking about the bits of information she had. The secret meeting mentioned by Eli is likely the same meeting.

Now she wondered if Madinski was the other person with Schwartz, and just where he had gone to hide his money. In the end, she knew that all of these characters were up to no good, and would stop at nothing to get their way.

But Ivan Schwartz stood alone in many respects. He lived, but only among elite and wealthy; he appeared human and of skin and bones, and his face at rare times exhibited a softness nearing likeability. But he used such characteristics to disarm people, to keep them from seeing beyond the mask. Beneath the mask was darkness and evil. There was no humanity there, no warmth, no compassion, no regret or remorse, no love, no caring. Stripped of his human exterior there was a machine. "The wicked are estranged from the womb: they go astray as soon as they are born, speaking lies." And like every other time she thought of him, Mac shivered.

Mac decided to call Eli and Jack before she got down to the work at hand. "Hello, this is Mackenzie Honor. Is Eli available? It is urgent."

"Mac? Hi, Eli here. I've only got a couple of minutes before I have to go into the studio. What's up?"

"Eli, I spoke with my associate regarding that secret meeting. Did you hear more from Al? Anyway, I learned that Schwartz and a 'friend' of his were there, as well as an Arab from some country, a member of the Chinese government, a man from the Saudi royal family, and Nadir. She said Nadir was there for the Saturday evening dinner, and for a short time on Sunday morning, and while there was swearing, banging his fists on the table and being obnoxious. Can you imagine? She also said that the discussions were most often held in private, and she heard only that they are intent on creating a diversion of some sort, and bringing down the dollar and collapsing the government. She said Nadir and Schwartz were intimidating and scary, but we knew that."

"Okay Mac. Now study your visions and you will see where this scenario fits. We can't be certain of timing since that is up to God, but I am sensing it will be late in 2010 or sometime in the first half of 2011. Keep that in mind as you go forward. We are not in control of timing, nor are any of the evil ones, even though they believe they are. God controls everything. God is in charge. That applies to visions of things that will happen in the coming months, as well as to 2012 when many believe we will enter the end times."

"Now I know those times are coming, but I do not believe they will happen that soon. So don't get caught up in timing Mac."

"Alright Eli I understand, but what about the Book of Revelations; the Mayan calendar, and St. Malachy's prophecy? They all seem to point to a specific time, 2012," Mac questioned.

"Actually the only actual date mentioned is associated with the Mayan calendar. Revelations does not mention a specific time, even though many people have interpreted a time. And St. Malachy's prophecy is many years later. The fact is that those who write about end times, Armageddon, Tribulation—they are based on a series of events and timeframes, and each has been interpreted very differently. To one interpretation a year is one span of time, but to another a very different timeframe. We can warn of what is coming, we can urge people to repent, we can even give examples of events that will mark those times."

"Eli, I know we have discussed this, and I guess I struggle with the whole concept. So I need to revisit the issue now and then, to make things more clear, as I go through all the notes. It is very frustrating to me Eli. But I shall heed your advice. I am just now moving into the future visions. I'll be in touch if I have further questions. Do you know when you will want Kate and me back there?"

"Not yet. I spoke briefly with Kate yesterday. She had someone with her, so I did not want to press her with questions. But I did sense a strain in her voice, some sort of tension. I am to call her this evening. Now Mac, take care of yourself. The remainder of your writing is going to be hard on you. I don't wish to alarm you, but as you articulate future events, you will find it stressful, even scary. Just remember that we are going to be okay. We'll get together soon, I promise."

No sooner did she hang up than the phone rang and it was Kate.

"Mackenzie, its Kate. Are you going to be home in a couple of hours? I'd like to stop by and have a talk, after I run an errand. I won't be able to stay long because I have appointments this evening."

"Hi sweetie. Yes of course, I'll be here the rest of the day. Drop by any time. Anything I should be prepared for in advance?"

"No. I'll see you in a couple of hours. Bye." And with that Kate hung up, coolly and crisply.

Mac rested her head on her hands thinking. What was going on with Kate and why? How would she present an accounting of the future without sounding insane, or scaring people to death, and how could she tell the story and keep things in perspective without succumbing to her own concerns and trepidations?

First, a chat with Jack, as she punched in his number. "Jack, it's me. I promised a call upon talking with Juliette. She called a bit ago. Nadir was there for Saturday evening and Sunday morning and behaved badly, like a petulant brat. Not a lot could be overheard, but there is a plan simmering for the right time. I made a couple of inquiries and it is likely late 2010 or by mid-2011." Mac related the players at the meeting and the focus on manufacturing a crisis to serve their purpose. The two chatted briefly and then bid each other goodbye.

Mackenzie was spent, emotionally and mentally. She realized her shoulders were up to her ears, so she forced herself to relax, deciding a cup of tea would help.

Sitting before her notes sipping her tea, she wished for a moment that she could wave a wand and make it all go away, like a bad dream. But that was not possible, so it was time to get into it. She must have dozed off because she was startled when the doorbell rang. It was Kate.

"Kate dear, it's so good to see you. How about a cup of tea? Something to eat? How is John, everything alright? You caught me dozing off; am so tired."

"Yes, tea would be great. John is okay. Mac I am not here for idle chitchat."

"Whoa! Since when is asking about your husband, my friend, idle chat? You have been out of sorts now for a while. Really, ever since you left the beach house and David and I left. You have been rather pissy girlfriend, so what the heck is going on?"

"Well now that you ask. I am very upset that you and David went off and left the beach house during the storm, without seeing that those trees were taken down. You seemed to take for granted being out there, and I expected some sort of consideration for your time there. Then you come back and were all lovey-dovey with David, and just moved on without me, doing your own thing on this book, without my input, my advice and contribution. I was to be involved. I expect to be listed as co-author, just so you know."

Mackenzie sat there in disbelief. She felt her temperature rising, yet was speechless. She sipped her tea, about to speak when Kate said, "And now you sit there and say nothing? I don't know why I bother, I really don't."

"Okay Kate. I am pretty stunned about all of this. I am trying to get my head around all of it so I know what to say. I am feeling a bit angry myself right now, so I wish to weigh my words carefully. First of all, we have been close friends for quite a long time. That friendship means a great deal to me and I don't want to say something that will jeopardize that. So let me deal with each point. First, leaving the beach house. You may recall the winds were ferocious at hurricane levels, and we felt in jeopardy. David wanted us to get over the mountain while the getting was good."

"In addition, we had a man lurking about outside that David went after, but the guy got away by car after shooting at David. We both felt it was time to get home. The storm was vicious and we barely made it over the mountain as it was. I did call the tree guy and gave him your instructions. He did not seem very amenable to coming over and cutting down trees in those high winds, and frankly I don't blame him. He could have been killed."

"The house was shut up tightly when we left. Now about me and David. I'd have thought you'd be happy for me, for us. I have been alone for eons, and only occasionally do I see my son. I never begrudged your happiness with John all these years. Yes I have devoted a lot of time to David, when not writing. And that brings me to the book. You did the minimal amount of your assigned research and provided me the notes and I appreciate that. But we both know you are generally over-committed, stretched too far, with so many family responsibilities, and the never-ending string of crises. I did not wish to burden you further.

But it is important to point out that you are not a writer. You have good ideas and you have helped in offering input now and then. But the book must be finished soon; you do not have time to participate according to your own comments; and you are not, as I said before, a writer. Your input about the Bible has been helpful in giving me a generic overview but I have asked repeatedly for details that you apparently were not willing to dig up and share. So I felt I needed a more scholarly input."

"There has been no intent of taking you for granted, or not appreciating your assistance, especially in providing me a safe place to recover from the accident. I did not know you expected me to pay you for my stay. You needed only to tell me. Now that I know, I'll get you money right away. But let me interject something here—we are reducing a close friendship to dollars and cents. We are bickering about matters that should be of no consequence. I don't know what has prompted all of this, but I am shocked. And Kate, I am very disappointed."

"Mac I am sorry you feel that way. I think my points are valid, and deserving of your attention. John feels the same way."

"Ah, John, he feels the same way. Now I get it—and how transparent. It is John who is upset about the cabin's use. He feels I should pay for that. Okay, I will, but you should have told me you expected to be paid. It was an offer that did not appear to have strings attached. Anyway, what is this business about you being ignored, about the book?"

"Mac you seem to have things all worked out. My contributions are not needed, even though it was I who figured out the secrets of Eli and Patrick; and they made it clear that we were chosen by God to do this work, not you, but both of us."

"Yes, that is how it was put to us by Patrick and Eli, I grant you that. What was not addressed is just who would do what, based on what skill-set each of us has. Now I may be totally off the mark here, but once you had done your research, I figured you were already stressed out, and it made sense to just get going on the writing. I write quickly because that is what I do. You have always struggled with writing. In fact I don't remember a single paragraph that has been clearly written. It is not your strong suit, so I thought I was being of help to you. Right now I just don't understand where all of this is coming from, out of the clear blue?"

Kate responded quickly, "I think we can trace this back to our time in New York. You were quick to take charge, you were having secret meetings, you were keeping secrets; you know, sort of like now. I complained then, and I am complaining now."

"Well, here is what I suggest. I think we should take some time apart, think about all of this, and in a few weeks get back together and talk about things in a rational dispassionate way, and try to resolve things. One issue about that though is that Eli and Patrick want us to go back to New York in a couple of weeks. Eli said he spoke to you about that. So how does that sound to you?"

"I suppose you are right. No harm can come from thinking about things a bit longer. But as for New York, I don't think I'd be comfortable in going back there with you at this time. I don't think the guys want nor need my input. So no, I won't go back to New York. I have my family to think of," Kate said rather petulantly.

"Kate, I appreciate your perspective and I'll not pressure you. Let me ask you one question. Is our friendship of any import and value to you? And if so, why; and if not, why?"

Kate sat in silence for a time before responding, when she said "I have always thought it was very important, but now I am not really sure. I've been thinking about things, and talking with family and friends and they think you are using me. They have pointed out things I did not notice before, and yes, it does seem you are using me. I don't like that Mackenzie."

"Wow. Kate, have you stopped to think that some of your family or friends might be jealous of our friendship, and travels? Or have some other ax to grind? I don't understand any of this. But I am opting to give this a rest and revisit it in a few weeks. Meanwhile, if you have any questions you know you can call any time. And before you leave, I'd like to say one thing. Kate I love you like a sister; you are one of my best friends; we have been close and shared a great deal over the years. I do not want to lose your friendship; and I want you in my life. We both need to be true to ourselves. I believe strongly that our friendship will survive these issues. I'd like you to pray about this Kate. You always find truth in your prayers. I am not the enemy and I know at some level you know that. We also need to be united in a battle against the real enemy."

Kate was stoic, but as Mac talked about prayer and their friendship, Mac could see Kate's eyes tearing. She walked with Kate to the door and gave her a hug.

This is a very strange occurrence Mac thought. And then a light bulb went on and she knew what this was all about. It was Satan's purpose, to divide, create conflict, disrupt and drive a wedge between individuals, groups and countries. We were small fish in a big sea, but doing God's work, so we had been targeted. She would let Kate reflect on things for a while before discussing her belief. For now it was time to carry on with her work.

Back at her desk she began writing from her research notes, the visions, and information provided by others.

While President Nadir had moved quickly in 2009, 2010 is to be even more frenetic. His three dozen czars, each with extremely radical views, are busy pursuing changes that affect most of America. Before the end of 2010, there is serious talk of a nationwide plan to bring censorship to broadcast media. The 'diversity' czar establishes new guidelines for the Federal Communications Commission, whereby there are stringent rules and regulations on private ownership of media, making it no longer possible for a group of investors to own multiple media outlets.

"And this is the condemnation, that light is come into the world, and man loved darkness rather than light, because their deeds were evil." So it is that this government will persist in operating in secret, behind closed doors, in the dark of night. Evil is as evil does.

Among the rules and regulations Nadir establishes are the requirement for broadcast media to have a totally balanced commentary and content (racially, ethnically and politically) as well as advertising. To police such content there are to be those pods scattered around the country to monitors all content. If a station is found to be less than balanced, it be fined and taxed. Each station is to be scored quarterly and if scores don't meet determined standards, they are shut down; all this is in an effort to silence conservative broadcasting. Silence dissent!

2010 will see an unsuccessful assassination attempt on President Nadir, causing extreme safety precautions to be taken and a number of public appearances to be cancelled.

Swine flu re-emerges and this time around it is determined to be one of the worst pandemics in history. Along with it, old diseases long dormant reappear. They are blamed on parents for not getting their children inoculated, but an investigation turns up an intentional act, eventually attributed to terrorists. It is later found that employees within Departments of Agriculture and Health had been responsible. The employees are labeled rogue, fired, and sent to prison. However the data does not point to an act of revenge; rather to an attack on the weaker of our citizens, who overwhelm the system and are left to die.

Ivan Schwartz turns out to be involved with two large pharmaceutical companies that manufacture vaccines. These companies are reputed to have added viruses to certain vaccines, initially having trial tested them in Russia, and then in the U.S. One thing is certain, whatever Schwartz is involved in proves to be dangerous, dire and negative for the U.S., and along the way he is sure to make a great deal of money.

The White House outlaws all large public demonstrations, indicating a concern for citizen safety and the costs to protect demonstrators. In reality, it is an effort to further limit free speech and silence the patriot movement. The last major public demonstration and gathering is held by Eli and Patrick with a record-breaking three million people who converge on Washington to hear them and others within the movement speak.

The incidence of violence, neighbor against neighbor escalates, in part because the government offers $500 to any citizen who turns in another for violation of any of the new laws. The government creates a Big Brother spy environment, encouraging distrust and suspicion of those around us. Eventually, food becomes scarce, prices escalate by commodities manipulation, people will grow hungry, and crimes against humanity will rise. To control the expected violence, Nadir orders the US Army to prepare troops for civil patrolling in cities across America.

The issue of food shortages grows into a crisis as a result of a number of actions by the government to control production and people. A new law on the books forbids private citizens from establishing gardens for personal consumption and anyone caught growing food receives various degrees of penalties. In addition, government take-over of most commercial food production creates rationing for the first time since World War II. Since most people have never experienced any sort of rationing, fear fosters a backlash of violence, initially against the government, eventually neighbor against neighbor.

Many people, sensing the beginnings of real crisis, walk away from their homes, loading up their vehicles with necessities and heading for remote areas, setting up communal camps comprised of many people of all ages and skills. They survive with generators, and by digging wells and purifying water from streams, building cabins and remaining off the grid and out of sight. In a matter of days they go from modern twenty-first century high tech families to survivalists from the Depression days. The irony is that they fare far better than those who hunker down to survive under the thumb of government and the chaos that surrounds them.

Those families who have long been stockpiling food and supplies and ridiculed for being alarmists are in fully prepared mode, feeling smug and secure while around them people are in calamity, ill equipped for meager survival.

Drug cartel wars in Mexico continue to erode the US/Mexico border, and warfare explodes in many cities around Mexico, putting expats and tourists at risk with killings, robberies and kidnappings out of control. As a result, some U.S. troops from the DMZ zone in Korea and from Europe are withdrawn and returned to the U.S., assigned to guard the border and aid Mexican officials capture drug runners. Encampments are set up along the full span of the border, from California through Texas.

The email notification went off and startled Mackenzie. She went to her computer and there was an email from Eli. "Mac, I am passing along some information that won't hit the media for months but I think it should be part of your notes. See where you can fit it in. I got word from an Administration source that two of the aides to President Nadir have held two secret meetings with members of the liberal media. The purpose of the meeting was to address several sensitive issues that Nadir did not want spread in the media. They were told of the topics to avoid. Thereafter, the media met with other colleagues and crafted a plan to keep certain topics off limits. Part of their plan has been to pick out some noted Conservative talking head and trash him or her, drawing attention away from any damaging news about Nadir."

"Mackenzie, I also have learned that there will be an effort, either by Congressional legislation, or perhaps executive order, to bypass the Electoral College. This would mean that only large, typically liberal states would have a voice in the 2012 election. You realize that things are not going well for Nadir, so this is his way to assure his re-election."

"I tell you Mac, there is something so other-worldly, so dark and evil going on. There are times that I wish I knew nothing. Life would be so much easier. But then I know you know that. Please make use of the information as best you can."

Mackenzie leaned back in her chair, silent, numb. She suddenly thought she had misunderstood Eli's email, so she re-read it. Alas no, she had not made a mistake. She sat there trying to recall a time like this, in her lifetime or in American history. She recalled nothing so far outside our laws. LBJ was a bad guy, but a piker in comparison to this man. She shook her head as if to clear it of the information, so she could focus on her work at hand.

Mac sat back down at the table with all her notes and just stared at the papers. She thought to herself, "This is so insidious, too enormous and far-reaching; I don't know how we can stop it." She suddenly felt very cold, but forced herself to put her attention and efforts back to the work at hand. There was plenty of time to revisit Eli's email.

Our economy will continue to decline with many unexpected problems. Our beloved city and national parks and open spaces around the country will be closed due to lack of funds for maintenance, with trails eroding, grasses turning to weeds, trash uncollected and campgrounds locked up.

The long anticipated hyper-inflation will kick in late in 2011 with prices skyrocketing for everything. Gas will reach $7 a gallon leaving far fewer cars on the road as people turn to buses for their primary means of transportation. Budget cuts to schools will leave many in unsafe conditions, many others closing and classroom sizes beyond any degree of effectiveness. Many parents will opt to remove their children from school and manage their learning at home.

Mackenzie was deep in concentration, overwhelmed by the images of life in the near future. Her head ached and she felt exhausted, as if she had lived through all of these events. She looked up and noticed it was nearly dark outside. She had been lost in this effort for several hours; she was starving, and wondered where David had been all this time.

She wandered into the kitchen, met by smells of something wonderful in the oven. She went to the back of the house to find David sitting in his recliner, sound asleep, with book on his lap. She decided not to wake him, opting to take a hot shower in the hope of reviving herself from what she shall now refer to as her 'futurestupor.'

Once showered and dressed she emerged to find David still napping, so she kissed him on the forehead and he woke with a smile and stretch. "So, my lady has come up for air! Just in time for dinner too. How is it going honey? You seemed a million miles away so did not want to disturb you."

"Oh David, this is very depressing stuff. I can recall so many times growing up and even as an adult that I wished I could see into the future. How fortunate I could not. Now I see the future, and it is ugly, frightening, and even terrifying. Frankly, I dread it; to such a degree that we need to talk about what we are going to do, where we can go, because honey, we can't stay here."

David frowned, "Honey don't you think that is a bit extreme? I mean, together we can handle most anything I can think of, and we'd not need to flee."

Mac sighed, "David, normally I'd agree with you. Not this time. Not with what is going to happen. This is not going to be the America we know and love. I only pray to God I am wrong and that Kate and I had gas, or heartburn and it caused us to have nightmares. Because if I am right? Well, this country is going to hell, and it will be lead by Satan himself, in the physical form of Ivan Schwartz. No, we can't remain here. I am thinking I should sell my house soon, even if at a loss, so we can pick up and go."

"Hold that thought. Dinner is almost ready. Let's have a drink in the kitchen while I finish things off."

Mac and David sipped a cocktail and chatted as he prepared their meal. It was clear to David that Mac was under a great deal of stress and he wanted to come up with some ideas that would give them a break from the pressures.

"Sweetheart, I have the germ of an idea here. I'd like to suggest that we create a schedule, right here and now, wherein you take every other day off, or every third day, and we do something fun and relaxing. You are not going to avoid some degree of depression if we don't build in R&R for you, for us. So with that in mind, I'm thinking that tomorrow would be a good day for a spa spoiling, with massage, mani-pedi, facial, and then an early dinner out with me. Then in 3 days we could take a drive if the weather is cooperative, and hit some wineries and have lunch. You can design your own day, have it alone or together, but we must build in breaks."

"Now that is a perfect idea," Mac said with a smile. "I do need to take breaks or I am going to lose it. This is just too intense to sit days on end writing about. So the spa it is. A massage sounds heavenly. Good grief, where have you been all my life? And how in the world did you learn so much about women in your line of work? How is it that you know just what I need just when I need it? How?"

David was chortling with gusto. "You know, if you asked all the women I have known and dated they would all say I was lousy as a boyfriend. I was all about work. I was all about me. I was afraid of intimacy. They'd all agree on everything, and indicate those were the reasons they dumped me. I was useless. But now; well now things are different. I am mature. I am in love and with those feelings I am far more intuitive and sensitive to my woman. So having spent a lifetime as a jerk, you got me at just the right time. You'd have hated me before.

I surprise myself every day now. Who knew I could be a prince instead of a pea?"

They both enjoyed a hearty laugh, realizing how lucky they both were at this advanced stage of their lives.

The next morning David made the spa arrangements for late morning, letting Mac sleep in. He woke her in time to enjoy a leisurely, light breakfast before he drove her to the spa. Mac started off her day with a facial, and mani-pedi. She had the most marvelous treatment of a full body scrub with oils, sea salt and ground almonds while laying on a marble slab. Then the attendant used a huge and powerful hose to beat the mixture off her body. The end result was skin like a baby's butt. After the scrub she had an hour long massage that was heaven. By the time her hair and makeup were done, David was parked outside ready to take her to dinner.

When Mac emerged from the spa, her hair just done, her skin glowing, her makeup artfully applied, in a stylish outfit she brought with her, she felt like a new woman, relaxed and pretty. David's reaction was confirmation that how she felt was how she looked and he was very approving. They headed to a new restaurant only open for a few months and it was drop-dead gorgeous.

Mac was amazed, "Wow this looks like a high end New York restaurant. It is magnificent." They walked through embossed glass doors into a curved entrance and were lead across a glass walkway with lights flickering beneath, across a glass bridge with water running under it, and into a stunning dining room. The East wall faced the river and was two stories high. Tables were widely spaced offering privacy. Lighted glass pedestals were spaced throughout the room, each displaying a magnificent piece of glass art.

The service was impeccable, and each spoon, plate, and tiny service tray was perfection, as was each course brought to the table. No detail had been left to chance—exquisite presentation.

They had a marvelous seafood dinner in this luxurious restaurant on the river, with a good bottle of champagne and lavish coffees for dessert. It was a divine day of rest, relaxation and restoration.

Mac sighed in utter contentment, "This has been such an incredible day. Thank you so much David. It is exactly what I needed. I feel so refreshed, so together, and now this restaurant blows me away. You are one fabulous man and I love you for giving me this special day so that I can return to that heavy task."

The following morning Mackenzie awoke early, quietly slipped out of bed and went to the kitchen to fix the coffee and feed the dogs. It was a beautiful sunny day, expected to be in the 50s. She was actually eager to begin her writing; she felt rested and had a fresh outlook for tackling the information.

She took her cup of coffee into her office, turned on the computer and checked her email. There was a message marked urgent from Al. She was shocked to receive a message from him but eager to see what was on his mind.

His message was mind-bending to say the least. "Dear Mackenzie:

"I was in Europe for a few days in meetings with some of my contacts. A group came up that you are probably familiar with, but new information was been made available to me that fits with what we are all working on now. I'll give you basic details and leave it to you to do some further digging.

"You have no doubt heard of the Illuminati. It has historical significance from its founding in 1776 by a Bavarian. Many mysteries surround this group that most felt was extinct, but in fact is thriving and very active now. It is not a coincidence either that it is linked to the Bilderberg Group, and to many of the names that are in the news. You should know there is a special connection between Nadir and the Illuminati, and that most of his Cabinet and key advisors are out of the Illuminati, Bilderberg, or Schwartz's group, or the Council on Foreign Relations. I suggest you dig into the latter and those who belong."

"Nadir is long connected with both Bilderberg and Illuminati, and you probably did not know that the Bush family is as well. In the news over the last few months has been comments made by Henry Kissinger and Gordon Brown, among others, in support of One World Order. Kissinger delivered a report to Bilderberg back in the 1970s. It was his recommendation on how to bring about global population control.

In it he proposes forced abortions on young girls, single women and those with more than two children. He goes on to propose various forms of control by putting certain chemicals and ingredients into the food and water supplies of the world. Why? Because Bilderberg desires a population reduction of 70% in order to create their ideal global community. Sick isn't it?"

"You will find that Bilderberg has long been active, and functions in total secrecy, working toward world dominance. However their primary objective is One World Government. What does that look like? All countries of the world united under one leader. But the world would look very different, with a good deal of the population being killed off, leaving a young fit collection of workers, little more than slaves or serfs."

"There are several organizations in this and other countries seeking to achieve One World Order and Government, and the Illuminati is one of the more powerful among them. As the name suggests, it is a group of elites, mostly from Europe, but many Americans have been admitted, including Damin Nadir. There is a cross connection in every direction with some surprising names associated with one group or another. But the common thread since the early 1900's has been One World domination and government."

"Anyway, I think you will find information within these entities that will explain Nadir's rapid rise to fame and victory, and how his actions foretell the future of America, long in the planning."

"Nadir is the candidate they have all been waiting for. He has been prepared, indoctrinated and directed toward his role now, by radicals, socialists and Communists."

"I expect to meet with you in New York before long according to Eli. Please keep this information to yourself. It is one thing to know one or two pieces of the information but to know much of it and then figure out where it all fits can be hazardous to one's health. In that regard, print this out and delete it from your computer; hide the printout. Oh and one more thing Mackenzie, there is a man who is giving a talk at the University of Washington in a couple of days. This is one you need to take in. I can't urge you enough, it is a must. Call the UW and ask about tickets to see Lindsay Williams."

Wow, thought Mac. Her coffee was cold, so she reheated it and returned to re-read this astonishing email. This whole business was like the plot for a cheesy spy novel. How could there be so many secret organizations, so many maneuvers and plans to forever change the world, and citizens of the world so ignorant of what has been going on for so many years? How can that be? How was it possible for so many people in so many countries to be totally oblivious to their fate?

Mac knew that this information changed her understanding of the visions, and of what she had already discovered. She put in a call to the University and picked up two tickets to the lecture, and then returned to her writing and research.

During the remainder of 2010 the stability of America will continue to decline, resulting from many factors, some of them outgrowth of past events, some from manipulated and manufactured events. Chief among the influences over U.S. stability will be the devaluation of the dollar to upwards of fifty percent. That will mean that a family earning $50,000 a year will have buying power of around $25,000. The natural fallout from that will put mortgages and loans at risk, as people are unable to put food on the table and pay their debts. People will be forced to take second jobs in an effort to make up for their lost buying power.

The new head of the World Bank, Robert Zoellick, is a man whose career has been associated with entities that have undergone monumental economic crisis, such as Fannie Mae, Goldman Sachs, and Department of the Treasury. His involvement with the Federal Bank suggests difficult times for all Americans, as much of the world backs off dollars as a reserve currency, and sells off U.S. financial instruments. The most disturbing fact about Robert Zoellick is his membership in the Bilderberg group. Most people do not realize that the Federal Bank system is privately owned, not under any government agency or supervision for that matter. It is owned by twelve international banking families whose involvement traces back to the early 1900s when the Fed was formed under President Wilson. Zoellick by virtue of his association with Bilderberg, supports one world order, and controls the purse strings for the world.

As the year moves along there will be many states forced to declare bankruptcy. Detroit, Michigan was once, back in the sixties, the poster child for government assistance, reinvestment, subsidies, welfare and home to the world's most successful automotive industry. Detroit went from a thriving urban center with the highest per capita income in the entire country, to a city of utter destruction that looks like the center of a Middle East war zone. Once the auto industry was destroyed, the city was left with the subsidized welfare, Muslims and the unemployed.

Enormous government buildings empty, neighborhoods burned down or ripped apart, occupied by wild dogs and gangs on the roam, commerce gone and most neighborhoods boarded up, no business, nothing on shelves to be purchased or looted. California will move in that same direction with unemployment rising to between twenty and thirty percent; the operating fund drained; the government will issue IOU's for everything from tax returns and salaries to payment on State bills.

California, another example of long-term liberal management to achieve the Left's utopian concept, is a dismal failure. Other states join the lineup, and with them all, a vision of collapsing infrastructure, welfare out of control, businesses closing, home foreclosures growing, joined by enormous commercial projects in foreclosure, creating yet another multi-layered economic crisis.

Derivatives will continue to thrive (with about $100 trillion invested in them) and with their success for the few, heartache and demise will be left for the many. Most people, having no clue of just what a derivative is, are oblivious to their existence or impact on all of our lives. Mac understood that a derivative is an individual or group 'betting' on a certain outcome or performance. They hold no paper, no interest in a project or issue (by way of investment of any kind), but merely put up huge sums to bet that something will or won't happen within some aspect of our economy.

In the case of the housing market, trillions were bet that the low-graded loans would not be repaid, the debtors would default, and foreclosures would abound. They had nothing to lose and gained vast profits on the country's demise. These same people are betting on the elimination of the dollar among other ills within our economy. These people, like Schwartz, are crapshooters who risk little for enormous gains at the demise of ordinary people.

As the American outlook turns ever bleaker the rest of the World will suffer as well. U.S. inflation will skyrocket in tandem with the dollar's devaluation, and inflation will spread world-wide, like a pebble skipped across a pond. With the fall of Greece begins a domino effect, eventually followed by Spain, Ireland and other countries that experience twenty percent unemployment, mammoth debt and dwindling GDP. Spain's problems began when trying to create a new stratum of green jobs in tandem with cap/tax energy regulations. The outcome proved disastrous, foretelling what is to come in the U.S. if we go down that path.

With uber-inflation, resulting from the devaluation of the dollar, prices of everything will go up. Gas is likely to reach $7 over the next two years and could keep climbing. Interest rates will go up of necessity to battle against a deepening recession, further tightening the financial market and leaving most people unable to acquire cash for any purpose.

The World Health Organization will seek to control population growth, with guidelines given to each country, calling for forced abortions on unmarried pregnant women and those with more than two children, at the behest of Bilderberg. This form of population control was long ago proposed by Henry Kissinger, to address the Bilderberg objective of reducing the world population by at least thirty percent.

As inflation and economic chaos spreads across America people will get further caught up in greed and corruption. Many turn away from our founding values and God. Our government is so adamant about separating "church and state" they go so far as to issue executive orders to cover all religious icons, and remove them where possible. We will come to a time when no image of God can be seen anywhere. Immorality, portrayed by Hollywood and the entertainment industry, takes an upper hand in an effort to sublimate all religious factors.

In religious terms, the 'lamestream' media is the false prophet, spreading 'propaganda' and news bites created to confuse, mislead and misinform. Along those lines, we will learn that Afghanistan, Pakistan and Yemen are being used by the Administration as diversions to engage our attention and concerns away from the real issues and work being undertaken in Washington.

Mackenzie's head was spinning and throbbing. The more she learned, the more she pieced together, the angrier she became. She could see nothing but treason and betrayal embedded in every aspect of this government and their actions.

Mac decided to take some time off. She found David out in the yard and told him of her idea. "Honey, there is a speech being given in Seattle day after tomorrow and I got tickets for us both. How about we take the train up there tomorrow morning and spend the day meandering around Seattle? The weather is supposed to be great. I thought we could hit Pike Place Market, have a good seafood dinner, maybe take a boat tour around, and then hit the presentation the next morning, and take the train back in the early evening. Up for that?"

"Now that sounds like a good idea, though I am not sure I really want to go to the presentation. But what the heck, I can handle it. One thing though, I'd rather drive up so we can come and go as we wish, and I happen to know that the return train leaves around two o'clock. So sure, let's do it. I love spontaneous activities. Heck, why not leave now?"

"The only problem with now is that we need to get someone over here to look after the pups. But I'll make a call and if that is solved, sure, let's go now. I'll call on the dogs, and you call on a hotel room okay?"

Thirty minutes later there was a friend headed over to look out for the dogs and David had a suite lined up near the Market. They packed up, and an hour later they were on the road. Mackenzie leaned back in her seat and sighed relief to be away from her work. She seemed unable to handle more than a day at a time on this work. Now they were headed north for a couple of fun days.

Mac tried to stay awake but found herself dozing, leaving David to his own company for most of the trip. It was dark by the time they arrived at their hotel. David had considered stopping for dinner on the way up, but the options were just not appealing without going far off the beaten path. They dressed casually and headed to the waterfront for seafood and a stroll along the water.

David could see that Mac was distracted but did not want to press the matter. "Honey is there anything I can do to lift that weight a tad?"

"I'm sorry my dear, I do feel a weight. Getting away from it is not all that easy. The details are seared in my brain and I can't shake them off. And you know, one thing keeps coming back to me. I am so worried for my son and his family. He is so ill-prepared for what is coming. He just won't take information from me and regard it as useful or helpful; he regards it as invasion of his privacy, or butting in to his business. I don't know how to warn him and inspire him to take action now so he is not caught in the mess that is facing us. He and his family are in the worst possible position and there is just nothing I can do to make it better. I am terrified for them. But of course, it is also the weight of the whole nasty business."

"You know David, when I had those visions with Kate, and we made our notes, it was all fragments of concepts, bits and pieces of information, and all disparate, not fitting together. I could easily handle things then. Now I've got the big picture, and it has me so depressed. So no honey, there is no way to lift some of the weight, other than to be with me, be supportive, and make sure we get time for each other. That keeps me grounded and sane, I hope." Mac laughed.

They enjoyed their meal, walk, nightcap and night in the charming boutique hotel. After coffee and poached eggs in their room, they drove to the University campus and headed to the auditorium. The auditorium was filling quickly, so they took their seats near the front of the room near the stage, center right.

David leaned over and asked, "Just what is it we are going to hear. Who is the speaker? What's going on and how did we come to be here?"

Mac replied, "Well, I got an email a few days ago giving me a good deal of information, and some things to research. Within that information was a strong urging to get tickets to this presentation. To tell you the truth, I am not sure what it is about. But the person recommending this would not have pressed the matter if it was not regarded as valuable."

Before long several people took their seats on the stage, and one by one they spoke briefly about their sponsoring organization, or introducing another person. There were two or three religious leaders, one of which was from another state. Finally a woman from the University introduced the speaker, William Lindsey, noting that Mr. Lindsey was a former non-denominational chaplain who worked on the pipeline in Alaska and was retained by heads of that operation to provide spiritual counsel.

Mr. Lindsey stood at the microphone and began his speech and to Mac's utter amazement and disbelief, he was talking about what was going to happen in America and elsewhere in the coming two or three years.

He prefaced his comments by telling of his time in Alaska, and of his opportunity to interact with some of what he referred to as "the elites" with whom he established some friendships that continue to this day.

His comments were searing, adding more validity to Mac's research and visions. She took notes fast and furious as he began his mind-bending presentation, that had Illuminati stamped all over it.

Mr. Lindsey, "I have, over the years, been warned by the elites to not expose information about them, for if I did, I'd be most unhappy about what would happen. They made it very clear that certain topics were off limits at all times with all people. But in recent months, I have been allowed to divulge some of their plans. You see, they may not think or act like we do, nor do they have compassion like we do, but they do have a conscience. So it is their desire that people be warned of what is to come. Now, they will never come out and just say it clearly. They will only give subtle clues. I hope to make things a bit more clear today."

With that he expounded on the decades-long plans of the Illuminati, or as he called them, elites. Their plans have been carried out for many decades, orchestrating exactly what they want to happen, be it war, economic crisis, falls of governments, health issues. They have total control, and all of it has been played out to achieve their ultimate goal of One World Government.

"Ladies and Gentlemen, America will fall. It must fall. It is at the core of the elites' plan. In this moment, there is no relief, no recovery for many years. There will be war—it is already planned."

He proceeded to stun the packed auditorium with information about the Illuminati, a select and exclusive group of powerful people from various countries, who long ago determined that they could bring about great change in the world, a change that would create a socially balanced population under the guidance and direction of one government. They held numerous meetings, consulted various experts, and arrived at their long term plan. They knew that certain conditions must exist; certain events must take place for their plan to eventually take place.

The Illuminati was not alone, but joined with many allied organizations with equally as long a history of working toward One World Government, or as they referred to it, One World Order.

He referenced details that Mackenzie knew, either from her research or visions so in a strange way, she found some comfort in learning similar information to what she had uncovered.

As he went on he explained that according to the elites, America had to fall. If it remained strong economically, spiritually, and physically, it would stand in the way of their goals. They maintained that they now had the ideal President in place, supported by people in the Administration who shared those same goals, regardless of the direction from whence they came.

War, he said, was already planned, as had been many previous wars. The wars provided the elites with control over countries and outcome, acquisitions of land, and vast wealth into their coffers. But the coming war, the last war on their agenda, was to involve the U.S., at a time when our resources and energies were dispersed and stretched thin. It would start with a citizen revolt, elevated from there by Communists, and then a multi-national force invades the U.S. and within a matter of days it is over.

The Illuminati has a provisional military force take down the invading force, leaving America defeated, broke, and in chaos; Americans totally immobilized from their disbelief and shock.

It is then that the Illuminati are able to launch their one world order. The elements that will be sought to create success in their plan are control of birth rates, and control of deaths most often brought about by removal of healthcare to speed the death of elderly.

Mr. Lindsey divulges some of the factors that are involved and served the successful decline of America, but he never mentions names, not one, indicating that to expose any of the individuals or groups would result in his death.

He noted that the World Bank, the Federal Reserve, Council on Foreign Relations, Bilderberg, and others are all working toward the new One World Order, a concept that goes back centuries, but which took shape and importance during Woodrow Wilson's presidency.

Finally Mr. Lindsey discussed what the rest of the world would look like, noting that the U.S. economy would bottom out, the dollar to be replaced by some other currency, leaving Americans in abject demise and crisis. China would emerge as the strong nation upon which the World Order would rely in certain respects. But he cautioned, make no mistake, the elites were in control and would remain in total control. Nothing would happen that was not driven by them.

David was squirming in his seat. Mac looked at him and he was sweating and grimacing, and she knew he hated every moment of this, as did she. In fact the whole audience was on edge and you could cut the environment with a knife. There were people in the audience who had not a single clue of what had been going on. They were still hopeful and believing in President Nadir. Some people got angry and grumblings elevated to shouting before they were ushered out of the auditorium. Some just got up and walked out.

Mr. Lindsey was aware that he was shocking people, even scaring them. He managed to calm people down with some quotes from famous people that seemed relevant, and then he spoke in a quiet voice about the only way to save ourselves and our country. He said divine intervention was not likely though always possible, and if enough people repented and accepted Jesus into their hearts, he might intervene, but it was not to be counted on. Rather, he said, we needed to rise up and take back our country, remove traitors from office, reverse the things that had been done to separate citizens from God, and force those in political office to honor and adhere to the Constitution. He stressed that we needed to act immediately, as time was running out.

He closed his presentation with a final message about his elites, "The elites fear Americans figuring out what is going on. They fear that Americans will wake up and react before their plan is implemented. They know America is all that stands in their way, and while they can continue to bring the country down, the people need to be weak so they fear Americans will rise up.

The audience stood with a few half hearted claps from among them. But then it was like a light bulb moment, with the light switching on and an awareness spreading through the crowd. Suddenly a huge applause erupted, as if in gratitude and understanding.

David and Mackenzie left the auditorium. It was a sunny day, so they walked to a nearby bench and sat down. Both were silent. Some time passed before either could speak and it was David who spoke first, "My God. I did not believe I could be shocked. I am one of those people who have been asleep. I, of all people! I feel sick to my stomach. I feel guilty for having been asleep at the wheel, and for letting you deal with all of this alone. God Mac, I am so sorry."

Mac took his hand, "David, we have all been asleep. Only a few are awakening to the realities of all of this. But still, most people are just ignorant of the truth and complacent in their lives. And really, those who have awakened can thank my friends Eli and Patrick who have been on air divulging facts, figures, names, and details about much of this. Every day they wail to their world to wake up, get active, battle against apathy and indifference. They are the ones who have educated many, but still far too few to turn the tide; to really win."

"I guess what is so stunning to me is that this man has been silently complicit in what has gone on. Why didn't he speak out decades ago? Why now? I can understand him being scared. I mean a group with so much power? But, a man of God remaining silent bothers me. Then again, it is after all, God who is in charge. God enables the Illuminati, God keeps people silent, or proactive; he allows people to choose evil. This truly is the ultimate battle of good and evil, God and the antichrist."

David nodded in agreement before he asked, "Who exactly is this guy? Do you know anything about him? Does anyone you know? He could be pulling our leg to get people to rush out and sell everything they own for nickels on the dollar."

Mac smiled, "Nope that is not who he is. I did check him out and have spoken with people who know him and refer to him as an honorable man, a truly good guy. He has been on a short leash, but in the last decade or so he and one of the Illuminati became good friends. That man is now old, feeble, and dying, and he told Lindsey to spread the word. And so, with some exceptions, he is doing that now. He is providing his information for nothing, which I think speaks volumes."

David said, "Let's get out of here. How about we drive south and find a nice place to eat on the way home, so we can avoid the gridlock here, or has it already started?"

"It's nearly 3 o'clock so the gridlock is already in place. But I am okay with heading out now, as it's only going to get worse, and it would be nice to be home before 9 o'clock. I know of a couple of places in the Tacoma area and south."

They headed out, made their way south to a waterside spot Mac thought David would enjoy. A fine meal, and animated discussion and they were back on the road south.

The next day Mac resumed her work, starting with some more research, and then on to the writing. As she reviewed what she had written, remaining notes to be addressed and all she had learned over the many months, she recalled something Winston Churchill had once said, "Most people stumble over the truth, but they usually manage to pick themselves up and go on anyway." Mac wished that more Americans would so stumble, and then hang around a short time to acquire insight. But she knew it was an uphill battle because the vast majority of Americans were asleep, their warning systems shut down. As such they did not believe evil could take over our country; they did not believe any foreign power had the ability or desire to attack

America; and they held the belief that America was the best country, and always would be, nothing could change that.

Mackenzie now knew that was simply not the case. She knew how hard Eli and Patrick were trying to educate citizens to what was going on, and to what needed to happen if we were to survive. For their efforts they were ridiculed, threatened, made fun of, and belittled—by peers within media, by politicians and by citizens. She knew as well that they were committed and passionate about their work and she prayed they'd remain safe.

Come on girl, back to work. Mac checked her email and once again an email from Al. "Mackenzie, I have been doing some digging into Nadir beyond all that you have found. You said something I believe, about him appearing from nowhere, a blank slate of sorts. I got to thinking about that and have been pressing some contacts for information. I have yet to confirm this as fact, but my source is very reliable. This is how you say, mind bending? My source tells me that Nadir, showing himself to be very bright, and easily taught, was sent by a Communist mentor to Russia when he was a teenager. It was felt that he had the potential to be groomed for big things, and so began the process."

Al continued his message: "At a time when he would have been in college it is said another person, under his name and credentials, was in school, creating an academic foundation for him to use later. Nadir was under the supervision of the KGB. It is why he is said to have a number of passports under different names. He was coached and trained in exactly what he must do, both as an American, as a politician, a candidate and President." The email ended.

Mackenzie let out what could only be described as a primal scream. David came tearing into the office in panic. Mac sat there and began sobbing. David held her, asking "Honey what happened? What's going on? You are scaring me. Tell me."

Mac could not talk but pointed David to the computer screen. He read the email and his face went ashen. "Mac, where is all this coming from? How can some of this, much less all of it, be true? This takes one's understanding of reality into such darkness. I am astounded. How can he write of this? It seems that every day a new monumental secret is divulged to you. How can anyone make sense of this, or decipher truth and fact from fiction?"

"David, I just don't know. I need to talk with my friends in New York. I feel more and more like I am still trapped in the same eternal rabbit hole and am hanging with odd creatures in some twisted nightmare. That said, I have to say, some time ago I learned that Nadir had several passports, none of which he's made public. But it seems just too outrageous, even in this already outrageous scenario, that he could be a KGB recruit. However, it is also true that his primary mentor was an active and loyal Communist who influenced Nadir from childhood."

"But regardless, based on the collection of information, America is under attack by many dark forces and the only thing we do not know is who wins in their efforts to bring us down. We have the Illuminati which is comprised of major leaders from around the world, and based on my investigation that includes the long association of the Rockefellers, Queen Beatrix, President Nadir, Prince Charles, and others. Then there is the Bilderberg group, also in existence for some time, since the 1950s, with the same names associated with it, but also including many from prior Administrations, as well as certain financial leaders."

"Their name comes up often, even though they are shrouded in secrecy of monumental degrees, but for years many people have been dogging them, trying to find out who is involved and what they are up to. I managed to get a list of members, some annual regulars, some only occasional, but get this, look who's on the American list. We have Kissinger, Bernanke head of the Fed, Larry Summers in the Administration, Wallenberg (head of Coke), Tim Geithner, Governor Sanford, George Schultz, Condy Rice, Tom Daschle, Damin Nadir, and Kathleen Sebelius! And that's just a few of them."

"David, these groups share one common objective and that is One World Order which equates to one world government. Many leaders around the world have been talking about this for a long time. I think people hear the term and regard it as innocuous, and distant from our reality. If I told you all I had learned about them you'd think me nuts, or overcome with conspiracy theories. But I will say, they have been working toward their goals for a long time, waiting for the right situation, which they believe they now have. The right leader, the right degree of oblivion among the people, and the other elements they have manipulated have all come together to create the perfect climate. It makes me feel sick to my stomach. Like town criers of old, I feel I should be galloping around town alerting people, then moving to the next town and the next. But we both know some Liberal Loon would shoot me dead, and the horse I rode in on!"

David laughed. "Girl you sure can keep your sense of humor even in the face of all the mess, which we shall now refer to as cridoom, as in, a mix of crisis and doom. So are you going to make it through today without a break?"

"Yeah, I'll persevere and get through the day. Actually I have completed a chapter and just want to review it against my notes. So give me another couple of hours and I'll be ready for a break. Next up is the glimpse at the next couple of years and then things will be ready to send back to the guys. Before it gets too late I need to call back there."

Mac put through a call to Eli. His assistant asked her to hold a moment; that he was wrapping up a call. Soon he came on, "Mac Hi. Good to hear from you. How is the book coming along and how are you doing?"

"Eli hello. I am getting close to finishing the book and getting it off to you. I wanted to talk to you for a few minutes if you have the time?" Eli told her to continue. "Okay, well I have been doing more research. I got an email from Al. Did you get it too? I was blown away by his assertion that Nadir was a KGB operative who had been trained in Russia in preparing him for his position. Is this even possible? He seemed quite sure based on his source. But it is such an outrageous claim. And the other thing, I have been looking into Bilderberg and of course, that has led me to the whole business of secret societies. HELP! I am under water on this stuff."

"Mackenzie, good for you for digging up information on Bilderberg. You will find it hard to learn much about them as they are among the most super-secret entities in modern history. You mention finding alliance with other secret organizations and yes that is true. Some of these secret societies have existed for hundreds of years, some are more modern. Each has a focus or mission. Some broke apart long ago and have re-emerged. If you wish to connect those dots, I can tell you there are a few to look at, in that they have similar people, connections, objectives, and of those in the U.S., all of them are comprised of the wealthiest elite."

"So the groups to look at after Bilderberg would be the Illuminati, Skull and Bones, Freemasons, Bohemian Club, The Trilateral Commission, and The Council on Foreign Relations. Illuminati has ancient roots but came back decades ago. It has included presidents such as both Bushes, royalty such as the Queen of the Netherlands and Prince Charles. Skull and Bones is a secret group at Yale and has existed since the 1800s. Most of the elite who graduate from Yale are members and they stick together thereafter. Freemasons, another group of ancient origin, exists all over the world and its background is checkered, with connection to some very evil deeds. Today, well even Pat and I are not quite sure what they are up to but we believe it is not good. But it is important to remember that the general membership has no idea what is going on in the top echelon."

Eli continued, "The Bohemian Club is located in Northern California outside the wine country. It is a large piece of land, patrolled, isolated, fenced, and has been around for over 100 years. Many Presidents, government officials and captains of industry have been members, and while their true mission is not known, we do know they carry out what I'd call cultish activities, even animal sacrifices. Nasty business."

"The Illuminati is international. The top of the group is quite small—perhaps a dozen to twenty. Bilderberg has about 100 to 150, and they always invite new people with new areas of expertise to bring to the table. Add to those groups, the Black Dragons in Japan, which was formed in the early 1900s, and now is an international body consisting of M16, Pentagon officials, NSA, Japanese military intelligence, Serbian Secret Police and others. They are not about power, money and control, but work to create a world free of war. I'd call them the good guys. They work with Yakuza which is a huge Japanese gang, as well as the Green and Red Society of China, which contains a large gang element too. This network is a cabal comprised of individual cabals. They are a dangerous lot, but for the Black Dragons. One more thing though. These groups are convinced that if enough fear, trauma, crisis, and difficulties are brought to bear on Americans, we will readily give up our freedoms and rights for security. They rule by fear."

"So there you have it. We know some but not all. But there is no doubt that the Illuminati and Bilderberg seek to destroy America in working toward their One World Government. Now you ask about Nadir and the KGB. That is something I can't comment on. I'd suggest that we leave that topic alone. First, we have seen clues, and heard rumors, but we can't verify in a traditional sense. It is a path we should not go down. Mac I expect that you have stepped into more than one hornet's nest, and knowing you, I am confident that you are feeling the weight of it all, and are stressed by the combined significance. Finish your work. Try to keep balanced and don't let all of this overwhelm you. Sure it's easy to say but I emphasize the need for you to try to keep things in perspective. Above all, remember God is in charge."

"As written in Revelations, 'Then I saw the beast and the Kings of the Earth and their armies gathered together to make war against the rider on his horse and his army. The anti-Christ will deceive the world into believing he is God, then, turn the world armies against Christ in the final battle of Armageddon."

"It is God's schedule, his divine purpose, his power," Eli cautioned.

"Thank you Eli. I am feeling as you describe. I frankly am horrified that such evil forces are at work, and seemingly making huge headway, thanks to a relatively gullible population. But I will work hard to get done and keep my wits about me. I may be off base here, but from all I have learned, from what you have said, it seems that all of history has been preordained. It is as if we are merely pawns, or actors, playing roles in a script that was created long ago. Does this mean we have no free will, no choices, or no self-determination? The implications of it all are enormous, such that I doubt the vast majority of people would grasp it or even believe it."

"Ah Mackenzie, that is the question. I am not sure I can answer that for you in any meaningful way. It is complicated, and to get to the root of it all, we'd have to spend a very long time, discussing controversial matters that have never achieved unanimous agreement. But simplistically I'd say we do have free will, to a point, and we can and do make choices every day. Among us, many do battle against the Will of God and often fail; while others place their faith and trust in God's Will to lead them on the right path. This of course does not explain the existence of these elitist groups and their historical intervention in actions of governments."

"Have you spoken with Kate, shared this any of information with her? She called me yesterday, and I was quite surprised that she was argumentative and testy with me. She also spoke with Patrick, and while she was not argumentative, she expressed some feelings that suggest she is quite bitter about you moving along. I take it as more of a jealousy thing."

"Oh my. I need to call her. I have sent her emails and left a couple of messages but not heard from her. I will call her today I promise. She and I need to work through whatever it is that is going on. Honestly, she is behaving like a brat, in my opinion. Well Eli, I should get back to work. I want to get this to you soon. Take care and God bless you for the work you and Pat are doing. Keep up the good work. I hear the comments being made that are cruel; don't let them get you down. Your work is too important. Oh before I hang up, what is the word on coming back to New York?"

"Janice, my secretary, is working on that now. You'll get details in a day or two, Eli responded. "Okay Mac, we'll talk soon."

Mac slipped back in her chair and sighed. Eli always calmed her soul and spirit, made her feel at peace. He might be a Witness, but he was more like an angel. Back to work. Mackenzie was determined to put to paper the concepts of their visions for 2010 and 2011, and then regroup for the balance of the visions and her research. First, Kate.

Mac rang Kate's number. "Kate I've tried to reach you. Are you okay?" Kate answered abruptly, "I'm fine. Just busy."

Mac said, "Well girlfriend, we really need to get together and talk. I'd like to clear the air and solve the problems, whatever they are. So

I was thinking, how about we take a day together, do a spa day, or go to the beach, or something like that? What do you think?"

"Mac you just don't understand that I am very busy. Unlike you, I can't just go off for a day on the spur of the moment. Besides, John and I are going to take a vacation for a week, so there is no time a spa day."

"OK, so how about dinner one night this week? How do you expect we are to get our friendship back on track if you aren't willing to give some time to figuring things out?"

"Mac I am sorry. Like I told you before, we don't seem to be on the same page, about this work, about God or much of anything. I have had lots of time to think about it, I've talked with family and friends, and the consensus is that we are of two different worlds. They don't want me to get into trouble or be hurt as you have been. Early on it was fun and exciting. Now it is not and I want to focus on my family. We are going into end times and I don't wish to waste any time from my family."

"Kate, I would have thought that our friendship of several years was worth protecting, nurturing, and keeping strong. I just don't get it, really. Our differences have been the strength that binds us. We have been close, sharing everything. And until mere weeks ago, all that remained the same. What exactly prompted this change of heart. How have we gone from best friends to this mess in such a short time?"

"Mac, I still regard you as a casual friend. I care about you. But it is clear, to me at least, that we are going to the end times and my focus and priorities have changed. It is important for me to devote my free time to God and my family, and prepare for what is to come. I think you should do the same. You have not gotten your house in order with God."

"Wow. Well not much I can say to all of that. I want you to know that I love you Kate. I should also mention that I am reading the Bible, I am feeling close to God, and when I get through with all of this, I am going to get baptized. Also, one more thing, I have done a lot of research and I do not believe Armageddon is coming soon. I believe it will be a manufactured version to put the fear of God into us all, but not the real thing. Kate, I feel like a part of my heart is being taken away. I can't imagine our not sharing, not laughing, not shopping. I am not going to bug you, but I pray you will reconsider and come to realize that our friendship is just as important as family, but in a different way. I am going to keep in touch, like it or not and I guarantee one of these days you are going to be dying to go shopping, hang out over lunch and chat. Just you wait. Meanwhile, take care of yourself and know I love you like a sister."

"Thanks Mac. Maybe you are right, and I promise I'll pray on this for guidance. You take care of yourself. I hope things are going well with David. Listen Mac, I've got a client here, and I need to go. Bye."

Mac was dismayed, and frankly annoyed, she'd not been able to touch Kate at a deeper level. But she believed they'd find their way back to their friendship in time. Things were stressful now but she'd not give up on her friend. She'd just give her some space and time.

The story for 2010 appears to be in order Mac thought. She felt a huge relief to put to bed the next to the last chapter. Champagne with dinner seemed in order. Now all she had to do was to deal with the traumas to come. But that could wait. Tonight was for relaxing.

####

CHAPTER TWELVE

Evil (ignorance) is like a shadow. It has no real substance of its own, it is simply a lack of light. You cannot cause a shadow to disappear by trying to fight it, stamp on it, by railing against it, or any other form of emotional or physical resistance. In order to cause a shadow to disappear, you must shine light on it.

Shakti Gawain

If all of this seems like a great deal of trouble, think what's at stake. We are faced with the most evil enemy mankind has known in his long climb from the swamp to the stars. There can be no security anywhere in the free world if there is no fiscal and economic stability within the United States. Those who ask us to trade our freedom for the soup kitchen of the welfare state are architects of a policy of accommodation.

Ronald Reagan
40th US President, b. 1911-2004

Mackenzie sat staring off in space. She had a check mark through most of them pages of notes, down now to the last batch of that comprise the visions over the next couple of years. She'd dreaded this time, knowing how difficult it would be to put into words all the information she had acquired that pointed to such a terrible series of events.

But there was no way out of this but through it, and so she picked up her remaining papers and began to pour through them. One thing she was sure of, from all her sources, conversations with men of God, her Biblical readings, and research, there were probably as many concepts of Armageddon and End Times as there were people who had studied the subject. She knew that she was far from a knowledge base that could provide a clear picture of time and place, but she also knew her job was to relate the various images seen, and combine them with her research and the probabilities from both.

"I wish Kate was here to bounce some ideas around with," Mac thought. But she just needed to proceed—Kate was out of the picture by choice.

For some years Americans had lived well, free of tribulations experienced by most of the rest of the world. No matter how poor an American was, he or she was rich in comparison to others in emerging countries. We had become soft. We were absorbed with our narrow worlds—what was happening in our families, neighborhoods, friends and work. We worked more, played less and most people seemed stressed, or at the least, dissatisfied, without knowing why. But life was good so we pushed aside any concerns. However, life changed, imperceptibly at first, eventually with quite a punch—for many. If we were Christians we found ourselves under assault by those who claimed our icons, faith, and words of God were an offense to others. The separation of church and state became a convenient excuse for outrageous decisions. We didn't realize that all those assaults had slowly eroded the symbols of our Christian heritage and founding fathers. Still, there were continual accommodations for Muslims and select other groups.

The Nadir Administration will continue to remove all icons of Christian religion, including images of Christ, crosses, sculptures and paintings of Biblical times, and of course, all references to God on government buildings, documents, currency; all done so as not to offend other religions. Gone too was the annual Prayer Breakfast at the White House.

God some time ago took a backseat in our lives, His level of importance overshadowed by varying personal priorities. Once He was relegated to a lesser position, the degree of corporate corruption, immorality lead by Hollywood, greed evidenced by the outrageous thefts on Wall Street, and of course, the cheating, lies and corruption of government skyrocketed. Our culture has been and will continue to be in crisis, resembling Sodom and Gomorrah. But still we deny, avoid, ignore.

It is no wonder that we are ripe for a not so subtle takeover. As Mr. Lindsey pointed out, we are in store for dire times, created for the most part by the Illuminati. But we can't deny that our avarice, laziness, apathy and blindness have, all along, been huge factors in our change of direction and priorities. It continues in that vein.

The year of our Lord, 2011, sees a continuation of political division, bitter battles, and a seemingly pointless exercise to gain control over the out of control spending and Congress's machinegun approach to legislation. It will not be without specific intent, for the continuing chaos in Washington keeps Americans on either side of the political spectrum up in arms, arguing against or for one policy after another. Americans quickly became accustomed to diversions without realizing their purpose.

Americans place a great deal of hope in the new Republican-led Congress, but find over time that the Majority party is more geared to disappoint than to meeting campaign promises. Many voters wonder if there is any way to achieve the dramatic change desired by most, while others come to terms with the improbability of substantive change.

The European Union is itself in chaos with the Euro all but gone. Their ratio of debt to GDP becomes much too close, from their own wild spending. The EU is driven into decline partly from bailing out Greece; in addition there are external forces at work to minimalize Europe. The Illuminati createth and the Illuminati taketh away. Now that they have gotten a host of countries to give up their sovereignty, it will be a minor step to move them into an even larger government-controlled scenario.

Around the world there is tension and concern, as each country comes to terms with the fallout of the global economic decline; the world hyper edgy, and has its collective eye on those leaders who are unstable. Japan has its attention focused on North Korea, finding it necessary to shoot down a nuclear-armed missile. Israel launches an attack on Iran, after Iran steps up its threats to wipe out Israel. The attacks escalate world tensions as countries divide up for or against Israel.

All eyes continue to be on America, for as she fares, so too do other nations. Things go badly in America, a continuation of how they have gone over the last two years. The economy, having seen a bit of an uptick, is overwhelmed by inflation. The ire and unrest across the nation is palpable. To deal with the people's anger, the Administration takes several bold moves. First, there is a total clamp-down (silence) on conservative talk programming, on both television and radio. Private possession of all guns is outlawed. Access to our own money is limited to small amounts per day. Curfews are put in place in all states; and travel is limited.

Eli Gabriel and Patrick Hennessy continue reporting and wailing to their global audience. In time, government increases pressure to kill their shows. Continuing escalating pressure results in both broadcast companies being fined for each day Eli and Pat's shows air. The company decides to support both men, but it proves a strain on everyone and a very expensive proposition.

There are so many new laws on the books, so many demands made of private citizens; people across the nation are irate, upset, and vow to do battle. Government, not wanting to miss any opportunity, decides to capitalize on all the resentment by offering rewards for turning people and businesses in for breaking and/or not conforming to the rules; such as limits to water consumption, or use of electricity; growing a personal garden; or internet activity critical of the Administration. Life gets ugly as people 'get even' with their neighbors, or worse, rely on the rewards as a means of propping up their monthly budgets.

The North American Union becomes a reality, with money allocated to building highways from various points in Mexico through the U.S. to Canada. The monetary systems of all three countries are replaced with the Amero. The changes create a decline in the standard of living of all three countries, since the Amero is not competitive with other currencies for some time into the future. The resulting open borders create a nightmare of illegal alien traffic, including terrorists. Muslim ghettos spring up in numerous cities, and racial tensions become untenable.

The governments of several countries, the United States included, will decide that population growth is out of control, resulting from United Nations reports, and urgings from members of Bilderberg. A secret plan, formed many years ago to decrease global population, a plan that was initially written and delivered to the Bilderberg group in the 1970s by Henry Kissinger, is to be reactivated. Since the report's origins, Illuminati has experimented with some of the elements of the proposal, but the decision is made to implement the plan in far greater concentration. Their plan includes forced abortions, denying senior citizens treatments for major illness and disease, and adding birth control to water supplies (a practice in existence since the 1990s).

Critical to the Illuminati and Bilderberg population plan is the creation of a global disease, a pandemic that moves quickly, pass from person to person and prove deadly to a huge number of people worldwide. They have for many years experimented in small remote areas of Europe and Asia, but their plan takes center stage on a global basis.

President Nadir spends more and more time traveling abroad, in meetings with various leaders, but also attending private meetings of which the media is not be invited or aware. Such meetings include heads of Illuminati and Bilderberg, who advise him on his upcoming plans, and what needs to happen in the United States for both groups to move forward. In the course of his global meetings, he manages to offend, anger and confuse many foreign leaders; of which few take him seriously. He appears to be the brunt of many jokes and disrespect. Relationships the world over will become increasingly strained, with an undercurrent that few in the U.S. understand.

It is difficult to talk of the future without going back time and again to Illuminati and Bilderberg groups. All visions, and all current events, point to a master plan under the control of both groups. To achieve their ultimate goal of One World Government, they scheduled four events that would serve to merge multiple countries, and simultaneously dispose of their individual sovereignty—with open borders, one central government, one currency, one bank. Their first target was to merge Europe into the EU, which successfully evolved from the European Economic Council some decades ago. Their second goal has been the American Union, comprised of Canada, the U.S. and Mexico; the foundation for which was laid through the North American Free Trade Association (NAFTA). The Union is expected to be a reality within four or five years, with one form of currency, one bank (likely the FED and its field offices), and a new Constitution that covers all three countries. With these changes, all signs point to an elimination of American Free Speech, which does not exist in either Canada or Mexico and is one of the thorns in Nadir's side. He desires to clamp down on excessive or extreme free speech that attacks his Administration and his programs.

Mackenzie rubbed her eyes, stretched, and realized she could not take one more minute of this mess. She went to the kitchen to fix some iced tea. The phone rang and it was David. "Hi, babe. I am running a couple of errands and was wondering if you'd like to take a break tonight for a casual dinner out and maybe a movie?"

Mac started laughing loudly, "Honey you have got to be psychic! I just pushed away from the desk, unable to take any more forward thinking. It is just too brutal to take in big doses. So the answer to your question is a resounding YES. I can be ready in, hmm, ten minutes? Is that too long?" She kept laughing.

David was amused, "Well gee, I was thinking of something more like an hour or two. Can you occupy yourself away from the computer for that long?" "Absolutely. I am going to take a bubble bath and relax. I'll be ready when you get here, or two hours, which ever comes last."

Mackenzie took her tea to the bathroom, drew a hot tub of water, added bubbles and oil and climbed in just as the phone rang. "Hi Mom, it's Jamie. How about you come by tomorrow, early evening. We've meant to get you over, but we're always so tired. Can you come over so I can show you something?" Mac was happy to hear from her son, "Hi Honey, sure I can come by. Care to share what the deal is? Oh, and I am going to bring my friend David if that's okay?" "Sure thing. So how about 7? We'll have a drink," Jamie replied. Mac said, "Sure honey. We'll be there. Look forward to seeing you all."

She sank into the hot bubbly water and rested her head against the tub pillow wondering what her son was so excited to show her. She reveled in the hot water and let the stress and tension flow out of her body. As she lay there, eyes closed, she drifted off into a strange zone between being asleep and awake, much like a meditative state. Mac saw herself walking in a field of wild flowers on a high cliff overlooking the Gorge. It was a gorgeous early summer day with a light wind causing the flowers to bob back and forth. Walking slowly, savoring the view, the breeze, the warmth of the sun, and the fragrance of the thousands of flowers, she sat on a spot of grass, in peace and stillness enjoying the serenity. She could hear a voice off in the distance so opened her eyes and looked around to see if someone was around. At first she saw nothing, but could still hear the voice. Then off in the distance, just over a knoll, Mac could see a man facing in her direction, waving. She could not make out his features, had no idea who he was, but she waved back. She was curious but returned to her quiet space and beautiful surroundings.

The voice persisted, now a bit more audible and the man was calling her name. Again, she heard her name. She looked back to where the man stood and whether by wind or speaking louder, she heard him clearly, saying "You must remain strong. You must hold God in your heart and know you are fulfilling his wishes. Be strong."

Mackenzie stood, feeling both comfort and fear, and began walking in the direction of the man, but he was no longer there. She shivered, feeling cold, and opened her eyes to find herself in a lukewarm tub having dosed off in exhaustion. She ran some hot water, not quite ready to exit the tub, and recalled the images and events of her brief dream. She thought it was a message, a sign that she must finish her work; that she must get closer to God and keep a strong faith in what she was doing. It was almost as if God had spoken to her, providing encouragement.

Mac got out of the tub, fixed her hair and dressed for a casual evening out with David. She was downstairs sipping a glass of wine when he bounded through the door. "M'lady, you look rested, relaxed and lovely. Had a good day?"

"I took some time off and had a long hot bubble bath. It was just what I needed. Now I am starved and ready to go. Where are we going?" Mac asked. "Oh yes, my son called and invited us over for a drink tomorrow evening. Okay with you?"

"Absolutely okay with me. Ah, the dining location is a secret. You'll be happy, don't worry."

They spent the evening dining at a new, off the main drag restaurant with creative delicious cuisine, then off to a movie. It was a carefree, relaxing, fun evening that Mac needed, and she was looking forward to the same type of fun evening for years to come.

On the following morning, cup of coffee in hand, Mac returned to her computer to check her email. There was a note from Eli asking her to call as soon as she was up, so she put in a call.

"Hi, Eli. Got your message. What's up?"

"Mac, good to hear from you. Pat and I had a meeting last night and decided it is time for you and Kate to get back here. How much more do you have to write? And what's the situation with Kate?"

"Eli, I'll be done with the book in about a week. I am at a point now where things are so intense and overwhelming; I seem to manage a day at a time, with breaks in-between. I've never done anything so emotionally draining. Plus those new things that came up from Al; and I've been doing more research. That said, I'll be done here shortly, a few more days. But as for Kate, I don't think she'll come back with me. We had a talk, and she said that she decided her responsibility is to her family. Eli, she believes that the End Times are near and she is preparing."

"Okay, Mac you need to be strong." Mac needed to tell him about her dream. "Eli, I was soaking in the tub last evening, and nodded off. I was in a field of flowers out in the Gorge and while sitting there I heard a voice and saw a man barely visible off in the distance. He waved and eventually I could hear him clearly as he said 'Mackenzie you must be strong.' and at that moment I felt a peace come over me I'd not felt in a long time. It was as if an angel was talking to me."

Eli laughed, "Mac, God works in mysterious ways. He knows you are in a bad place and he knows your work is important. Trust in his word and go forward in peace. I know that the information you are working with is depressing, stressful, and alarming. You are almost done so hang in there. This book is going to help a lot of people, bring them into the light of awareness, and show them a way forward."

"Now if you are going to be done in a few days, you'll be ready to bring your work with you in a week or two, right? My assistant made the travel plans for you but had held off alerting you till she confirmed our schedule."

"Are there any requirements you want her to deal with such as a favorite hotel?" Mac indicated she would be fine with whatever they worked out for her.

"Great. Now about Kate," Eli continued. "I am not really surprised. I had a sense that we'd go this direction. Kate's not used to dealing with the depths of such evil, danger and darkness. It is one thing to read about it, quite another to face it head on. You are used to dealing with evil, but not as much with the word of God. In short order, the switch will take place. You will survive this Mac. So will Kate. She knows that, but she also feels a need to surround herself with comfort and all that she knows and trusts. We must not judge. We are all on the same path, just a different pace, sometimes taking side trips."

"Mac, just dive in and get that work finished. You must know that it will be okay. You will be okay. I know this is easy to say, but you must rise above the evil that you are dealing with in an effort to expose it and inform people. You must come at it from above, empowered by right. You are helping people learn and prepare. You are spreading the word of repentance, which is our salvation. Now you ask Kate if she wants to come and if not, accept that, know it is her decision and right for her. Jennifer will be in touch with you tomorrow with the details for your trip. Do you want to bring your bodyguard with you? I think that would be a good idea actually. So plan on that. Got to run my friend. Pat says Hi and we'll see you and your bodyguard shortly."

Mackenzie was elated that David was going with her. She'd feel safe, plus it would be so much more fun to share New York with him. She'd get someone in to stay with the pooches; and talk with David later in the day so they could make plans.

For now she knew she had to return to the book and press on through the difficult times. She returned to her desk, the computer and her writing.

Attacks continue on Christian values, with the perpetual theme of Separation of Church and State the stated purpose. Moral decay abounds; punishment for crimes weakens as a means of dealing with prison overcrowding. Child rapists, drug dealers, those who commit all but the most violent of crimes will find their way out of prison on one technicality after another, or reduction of sentences.

A constant stream of new legislation is enacted, but Nadir manages to avoid or ignore process and Constitutional law by using executive order and imposing new regulations. The atmosphere grows ever more like cattle drives in the dark of night—never sure just what you'd find in the light of day. Amnesty, providing instant citizenship to some twenty million illegals, remains a battle with strong dissent from across the country. The Fairness Doctrine is revived, but to avoid legislative process, it is turned over to the FCC, aided by new regulations to strengthen their ability to put egregious restrictions on talk radio, and forcing conservative talk shows to close.

Rumors persist in an effort to fill the void of President Nadir's background. One of the more interesting among them is that Nadir was recruited by the CIA for his ability to speak various Middle Eastern languages. Amid the rumors, there are numerous lawsuits brought by citizens against Congress and the White House. The mood of We The People grows ever darker, angrier, and determined.

The phone rang—Mackenzie was irritated at the interruption. "Hello?"

"Mac, can you talk now?" It was Jack and he seemed agitated. "Sure Jack. What's up?"

"Mac, I had lunch today with a friend of mine who works at the White House. I've not had any contact with him for a few years, and knew he was over there for about a year. So he called me and invited me to lunch. I wanted to grill him about what is going on over there, but before I could probe, he started to volunteer information, swearing me to secrecy."

"The story he laid out is remarkable, if not shocking. He said that Nadir was behaving badly, but more like a spoiled brat with a huge ego. Apparently in a staff meeting, he was restless, wandering around the Oval Office, paying no attention to the briefing. Eventually he stopped an Admiral in mid sentence, and complained that his time was being taken up with too many briefings and meetings. He said he did not sign up for this crap. Then apparently an aide whispered something in his ear and he went ballistic, ranting and raving, swearing and storming around."

"Apparently this is not untypical for him; he's been behaving like this for over a year. He generally demands to be left alone, and is often found playing video games, watching television, or hitting golf balls around his office."

Mackenzie said, "Gee, what a shame his time is being taken up with serious stuff, like work. He is a bigger fool than I imagined."

Jack went on, "Now get this. My friend said that on more than one occasion, Nadir's personal physician has been brought to the White House to administer medication, some sort of anti-depressant, which Nadir is apparently taking regularly now. Can you believe, a president on anti-depressants, and God only knows what else. How unstable is this guy?"

"Jack from what you are telling me, it seems he is stressed out and depressed because of the pressures of the job, or the nature of the work, or both," Mac responded. "I mean, what the hell did he think he'd be doing in this job? Oh this makes me furious. He does a stellar job playing golf, flying around in luxury, spending tax payer money, and going on fancy vacations every few weeks, so I guess it is just too much to expect that he might provide leadership and management." Mackenzie was fuming.

"Well, there is more. It seems that he pops pills a bit too frequently on occasion, and renders himself useless," "As if he isn't already," interrupted Mac. "Yes, well, back to the story. On those occasions when he is blotto on drugs, Mrs. Nadir storms into the Oval Office and insists that she is in charge. There have been some major scenes when the Vice President has appeared and been ready to do battle to protect his territory, amid screams and swearing by Mrs. Nadir. Honestly Mac, it sounds like something out of Days of our Lives. This behind the scenes, while Nadir fiddles and Rome burns. No wonder we are in such a mess."

"Jack, do you mind if I use this information? I'd like to include it in something I am writing. This means that the information will eventually go public; but no one will know how I got the information. Is that okay with you?"

"Be my guest Mac. This guy has had a free ride for far too long. Time to pay the piper, and we all know who that is. Anyway pal, I just wanted to share the information with you, and to find out how things are going there? And how is our David?"

"I really am glad you shared the information. It is juicy, but really is shocking. My, how we have declined. I am doing well. Healed from the accident though a big jumpy behind the wheel. And David is spectacular. By the way, we are going to New York in just over a week. I was wondering if you'd like to take that train up and we meet you at our usual place for lunch? Or you could come up in the afternoon and we could have dinner. It would be fun for the three of us to get together."

"Hey now, that would be swell. I've been wanting to see you two together, and to do a bit of teasing of old Dave. But no, really, I'd like that. Do we need to get into any heavy business stuff? If not, how about I bring my wife and we come up for dinner? You pick the night based on your schedule and let me know."

"Okay Jack, count on it. We get in to New York on Saturday night. How about Sunday? I know that evening is free. As soon as I know where we are staying, I'll let you know. We can meet there. You two could stay there as well. Sounds terrific. Thanks so much for the call. We'll talk soon."

Mackenzie leaned back in her chair and smiled. She would be happy to share an evening with her two favorite men, in one of her favorite cities. And the information Jack shared, wow, she thought. Explosive stuff. Now back to the future.

The Bible describes the Tribulation as a time when the Beast foments a global war, out of which emerges One World Church and

Government. The citizens of the world go through a dark, oppressive and dangerous time. In the Bible The Beast strikes against the "Harlot," which is referred to by scholars as the Vatican; and her daughters, as all other churches. There are many signs showing our entry into the Tribulation, and of Armageddon, and End Times.

And certainly the strident efforts to create One World Government fit with biblical prophecy. The question is, who is the Beast? Mac was betting on Ivan Schwartz.

Believers await the ultimate reward for their love of God and devotion to Him and the church, through the Rapture. Rapture is when those with devotion to Jesus and God in their heart, are to rise up to heaven with Jesus. However, 'rapture' does not appear as a word in the Bible. The closest connection is to the Greek word "harpadzo"—to seize, remove or take away; or in the essence of the Bible, to remove the 'church' (people) by Jesus, from the earth.

The events that Kate and Mackenzie had envisioned do not reflect the End. Rather they seem to foretell events that are more manufactured or created, to coincide with certain natural disasters. The end result appears to be Armageddon, which Mackenzie will come to refer to as the "Fateful Faux Arm." From her research Mac has come to realize that there are many theories about just when Armageddon happens.

A new metric, or way of doing and viewing, will spread across the land. No longer will two plus two equal four. Black, we are told, is really white; and white is really black. All rules no longer will apply to our lives, or beliefs, or expectations. All people are off balance internationally, but none more so than in America.

America has to deal with the gradual loss of capitalism and the innovation it fosters. We have to contend with the restriction and loss of several key freedoms. But most of all we have to adapt to a life inexorably changed—from security and comfort to unrest and discomfort, combined with the awareness that it is going to get worse; likely a great deal worse.

Our constitution was written to limit government jurisdiction through the will of the people. We will find the government's powers are no longer responsive to the will of the people, but rather are derived from laws it has passed to expand its powers; as was the case when Hitler ascended to power in Germany. No longer does the 'people's will' and desire equate to restraint of Government; no longer does God or honor of the Constitution hold any significance in the operation of our government.

With the Healthcare plan in effect, senior citizens are subject to the brunt of the deep cuts. As such they find themselves being denied essential medical care and treatments. Rather than looking to a long life at home with home care, or moving to an assisted living facility, they are given options to die. The objective of those building the One World Government is to reduce the U.S. population by 100 million and the overall world population by 300 million. Where better to start than with seniors? A panel, by way of graphs and charts, determines how much longer a person is expected to live, given their age and health. If the patient is diagnosed with severe health issues, the panel rules what if any treatments they can receive, based on their life expectancy. The consensus among government is that there is no need to invest a great deal of money in saving the life of someone who is expected to die in a couple of years.

The events laid out ahead of us are, in some part, orchestrated by humans; intentional, planned, and designed to bring fear, crisis, chaos, and eventual cooperation.

One key component within the full scale of orchestrated events is a national health crisis—a breakout of a virus or disease that is highly toxic and transmutable. It remains unclear whether it is claimed as a terrorist attack to food or water, or if it is domestically instigated, or a so-called natural breakout. Regardless of origin, the crisis enables the government to activate its health army to administer inoculations to all citizens of all ages.

A national inoculation program has always generated wide spread public concern, and this is no exception. For the previous three years two companies in the U.S. have been experimenting with miniaturization of microchips. One company reports a microchip so small it can be administered by a hypodermic needle. The government opts to include the microchip in these mandatory vaccinations, without advising the population. The microchip will serve as identification, and tracking of each person (location, activity, purchases). The government justifies such a program as a national security issue, and a step to improve healthcare and its delivery. It is nothing more than Big Brother and micro-control.

The health crisis creates unparalleled chaos and fear. Thousands are admitted to quarantined hospitals, others confined to their homes. President Nadir calls for a curfew and martial law; and his newly created National Security Force patrols cities and suburbs by vehicle, rural areas by helicopter.

Bilderberg has their own boots on the ground, their troops marshaled into action, preparing for the fall of America. But there are more events that must happen before they can claim victory.

Mackenzie poured over a group of papers about HAARP, some details from the visions, and some from her extensive research. There is a possibility that Bilderberg has or will gain access to the HAARP project, which began as a military experiment between the U.S. Navy and the U.S. Air Force, and has long been headquartered in Alaska. The principle objective of the project was the manipulation of the ionosphere, the uppermost part of our atmosphere, by way of high speed high frequency signals. The program was initiated as a means of improving performance and reliability of various communication systems. One of the many unknown aspects of this project is what influences these signals might have on the atmosphere itself, especially in relation to jet streams, weather patterns and meteorological events.

For Mac the issue of HAARP was unclear but several years of budget cuts had put the project at risk. However, she encountered some buzz about the possibility of Bilderberg somehow gaining influence over the project, perhaps from funding. Be it by design or natural occurrence, the next few years experience a far greater number of major weather events—extreme flooding, record breaking snowfall, avalanches, volcanic eruptions, earthquakes of a magnitude above 7.0, and perhaps the most alarming of all, the solar maximum flares. And thus far, HAARP is said to have the ability to impact all such events.

The solar flares are a key focal point for Bilderberg. Solar flares have been recorded since the mid 1800's. Numerous scientific organizations, publications, scientists and NASA have for several years, been addressing the strong possibility of the 'perfect storm' from a 'solar maximum' between 2011 and 2012. Due to the earth's position to the sun in that timeframe, and a change in the earth's axis, we are especially vulnerable to a major solar event.

In 2008 a NASA craft discovered a hole in the Earth's magnetic field much larger than expected. The magnetic field protects Earth's atmosphere and surface from the thousands of solar flares that happen each year. However, in 2012 conditions are prime for the 'solar maximum.' Solar maximum happens perhaps once in a thousand years. In most instances such flares would not be able to penetrate the earth's atmosphere, and would merely explode in outer space. But in the near future massive flares are expected to penetrate earth's atmosphere. In addition, the volume of flares is likely knock out power grids across the world—outages that could last for many years. As for the flares, NASA reports that one maximum flare hitting earth could evaporate everything within miles, much like a nuclear bomb. Also at risk are the communications satellites. The combined impact of these flares will be regarded as a sign from God that Armageddon is upon us.

This is significant because many studies have been done about Americans, showing that most people would readily give up their freedoms and liberty for security, when presented with dire and threatening conditions. Bilderberg's efforts are directed toward ensuring Americans are filled with enough fear to just give up and accept protection in lieu of their freedom.

Mac leaned back in her chair, and shook her head in disbelief. She had worked hard to not get wrapped up in all the evil, but she was still tired and her head ached. She sat staring out the window, snippets of images flashing before her reflecting what she had written.

David came into the room and interrupted Mac's concentration. It was a welcome relief. "Hi Honey. I was at the gym and brought home some goodies for dinner. Interested in a good meal?"

"Are you kidding? I am starving. We need to eat right away, as we are due at my son's in an hour. I have been pouring over all of this and going non-stop. I want to be sure things are done so I can review the manuscript before we leave," Mac replied.

"We? Leave? What's with that? And glad you are hungry, I am about to whip us up something. Now what's with the 'we leave' business?"

"Well, Eli phoned this morning. Based on where I am with the book, he decided it was time to come back there. He also said he thought you should come too. We'll hear from his assistant soon with travel details. I thought it would be great fun to have a few days in New York together. SO many things to do and see, and sharing them would be perfect. Things like taking a carriage ride through the park, going to the theatre, a couple of great meals. You never know what might happen to New York. I want to spend time there with you, and create some marvelous memories."

"Sounds great. Will I get to meet this Eli fellow you are so wild about? And the other one, Pat? I'm up for the trip. Sounds like fun. Will Kate be going with us?"

"David, I doubt it. My last conversation with her was pretty clear about her wanting to be out of this. When I know the details, I will see if I can encourage her to come but Eli said to honor her decision and not pressure her and he is right of course. Now, I am starving, so don't let me keep you from the kitchen." Mac laughed.

David returned to the kitchen to whip up a fast meal while Mac continued with her work. He had come to realize how difficult it was to reconcile her visions with many months of extensive research. He could tell that it was a laborious process. So he was happy to cook or pick up the slack around the house so she could focus, especially since she needed to get finished; not only for her boys in New York, but for her own sanity.

Mac was driven to work as fast and furious as she could. She had been on some aspect of research and writing for well over a year, and as much as she loved to write, she was ready to bid farewell to this project for Eli and Pat.

Thomas Jefferson long ago urged citizens to bind the government with the chains of the Constitution. Mac knew that Americans had for too long abdicated their responsibility to hold government accountable, to hold their feet to the fire, and to demand actions that were above reproach. The Bible talks about people with their eyes closed, unaware, unseeing. How to awaken them, how to light a fire that will cause them to see, truly see, all that is going on?

Mac was frustrated. She feared that the amount of things going on now and in the future, were overwhelming, whether observed or read about. But then, that was the Administration's point in all of this—to be so overwhelming that people's eyes would cloud over, their minds numb from overload. Mac decided that she needed one more in-person conversation with a scholar, if she could get an appointment within the next day or two. She placed a call to a friend Tom Gordon, a local minister.

"Tom, this is Mackenzie. Is it too late to chat for a minute? I know I've been remiss in not keeping in touch. If I told you how crazy the last many months have been you'd not even believe me, and anyway, I'd have to kill you. Suffice to say, I've been up to 'stuff,' from hat to spats as they say. I know you are busy too, but is there any chance that you'd have an hour for me, say tomorrow?"

"Ah Mackenzie, so are you telling me your life resembles a whack-a-mole course? Somehow I can relate. I am very busy, but never too busy to give you an hour or three. Tomorrow? Let me check my calendar. Hmm, well, how about 1 o'clock? I have two whole hours without obligation, and now they are yours. Should I be prepared for something in particular? People don't usually contact me to chat about the Blazers, or weather."

"Tom you are a dear friend. Thanks so much, the time is perfect. Prepare, well yes, I think that might be a good idea. I am working on a project about which I can't tell you much, but I am up against a wall right now. I am dealing with possibilities, with a forward view over the next couple of years or so, the heavy stuff about Tribulation to End Times. The difference is that I don't want to actually deal with those events, but other events that might mock them, events that could be created to look like them. Do you understand?"

"Of course. I keep up too you know. I'd even go so far as to bet that my thoughts are not far off from yours, my concerns similar too. I think I can help. I'll ponder it between now and then of course. So Mackenzie, are you having any fun between all of your activities? You work too hard. You should be thinking about golf, cruises, playing bridge, easy stuff with no pressure. You sound tense. Well, you can tell me whatever you like, or not, and I'll help as much as I can. So I'll see you tomorrow, and have a good evening Mac. Goodnight."

Mac put down her work for the evening and went to get ready to go visit her son. She then went into the kitchen, "I swear, what does a woman have to do around here to get a cocktail? I have waited and waited, and now my tongue is hanging out. Help! I beg you, a cocktail for these parched lips!" She began laughing and could not stop. "I swear I am getting goofier and goofier. By the time this project is done, I'll be ready for the farm."

"Okay girl, here's something to tide you over. Dinner will be ready soon. One olive or five? And goofy is good. I like goofy."

"I just made an appointment to go see a friend of mine, Tom Gordon. He's a local minister, very wise and he's one of the few ministers around here who sees the big picture. I think he'll be helpful in the final pieces that are left to be done. I am taking the rest of the night off."

"I did not check my email to see if there is anything from Eli's assistant. I'll be right back," Mac said as she briskly dashed off.

She came back a few minutes later, announcing, "We are set. She sent an email with details. We go in seven days, and it looks like we'll be there for five. I am sure that Eli is leaving us with some time for fun. Anyway, she said that all the arrangements are made. We are staying in a posh hotel near the office, they are flying us first class, bless them. I had better check in with Kate before dinner."

She picked up the phone and dialed. "Hi John, is Kate there? Kate it's Mac. How are you doing honey? Good, glad you are feeling better. Listen, I had an email from Eli's assistant with details about going back to New York. So before I reply I wanted to know if you want to go too?

You could have John come along too if you like. David is coming. They could do some fun stuff while we meet with the guys. They are talking about coming back there in a week, so what do you say?"

"Oh Mac, I can't just drop everything and travel on short notice. And John is so busy at work, he can't get away. Besides, we are taking a few days to run down to Arizona. That is our thing. Your thing is all the politics and intrigue and you share that with David. I just got caught up in the excitement, but in doing so I was not honoring my needs, being true to myself, and my beliefs for that matter. I want to be friends Mac, but separate from all of this stuff. I can't do it. And John has been pretty adamant about it too, he does not want me putting me or our family at risk. You thrive on danger I believe. I am revolted by it."

"Now listen Mac, I know I am disappointing you, but I do not want to be judged and I don't want any more pressure from you or Eli. I love my country just as you do. I am a patriot just as are you. I want to protect my country, as you do. But I can't go down the road you are on. I've prayed about it now for weeks. If, as the Bible says, we are going to enter Armageddon and End Times, then I I want to remain on task, which includes daily prayer, and remaining close with my family. Please try to understand Mac, and again, don't pressure me."

"Kate, I do understand, truly. I don't feel I am pressuring you, merely wanting to know if you wish to be included. I would not go forward without asking you that. I get where you are coming from. I don't want you to do anything that is not comfortable for you. So given your comments, I won't ask again, and will assume that you are not interested participating. David and I will go to New York in a week, and once back, let's make a serious effort for the four of us to get together and go out to dinner, catch up. Okay? It's very important to me that we stay friends, so I am not going to give up on that. As for your needs, I respect you for being clear, and for honoring yourself and family. David is calling me for dinner, so best go. By the way, do you have any interest in knowing about the information I have gathered during recent research?"

"Nope. I don't want my mind clogged up with all that stuff. Sorry, but that is how I see it. It is clutter, and I don't want clutter now. I am sorting through everything, cleaning out, from my mind to my linen closet. Take care Mac. Yes, by all means let's get together when you get back; as long as there are no political conversations, okay?"

"You've got it Kate. Night." Mac hung up the phone and sat there, somewhat puzzled, somewhat disappointed, and quite a bit irked. But she knew that she had to honor Kate's wishes.

"I am starving. Is it soup yet?" Mac asked David. "I just spoke with Kate and things are crystal clear. She wants no part of any of this, not now, not ever. So of course she does not want to go to New York. We agreed to remain friends, with no further discussion of any of the problems and issues presently on the table. I know she must do what she must do, but it is irksome to me in all honesty."

"Now Mac. Kate has been on again and off again, for some time now. She was never keen on any of this from what you told me. And I know for a fact that John was very unhappy with her involvement with you in the business in New York. I feel confident John put his foot down on the matter. Hey, they have a large family and they need to do their own thing. You have a right to feel irked, but don't let it dictate your feelings about Kate. She is still your good friend, at least I hope so. And I have a feeling that once you deliver the book to your guys in New York, this chapter will be closed and things will get back to a more normal interaction; assuming anything normal can ever happen again."

"Now then madam, dinner is ready. How about setting the table while I dish up; and don't forget the wine glasses."

Mac and David enjoyed a delicious meal and a nice glass of wine. It was relaxing and put Mac in good spirits. They put the dishes in the sink and dashed out the door with the dogs and headed to Mac's son's home. Fortunately it was a short drive and they arrived just a few minutes after 7.

Jamie opened the door and greeted them, giving Mac a hug. "David this is my son Jamie, and his wife Jen. This is my good friend David Valor. Hey, you painted in here. It looks great. Love the colors."

Jamie said, "Mom, David, what can I get you to drink?" Drinks were delivered amid casual conversation, when Jamie said, grinning from ear to ear, "Mom I've got something to show you. You will be blown away."

"Well now, this is a big mystery and I've been wondering what the secret is. Please tell me it is a birth announcement and I'm finally going to be a grandma. Okay, tell me."

"Mom, don't start. We told you we weren't going to have kids. No it is something I've always wanted. Come with me."

So David and Mac took their drinks in hand and followed Jamie to the garage. There, glistening in the overhead light, was the long coveted 1964 Lincoln Continental convertible, in a rich wine with black leather interior.

"Oh Jamie, this is simply stunning. What a gorgeous car. Did you get in fully restored like this? Wow I am so happy for you."

"No, it needed work, so I have been spending free time in doing some restoration. The motor was in good shape, but the body needed work, and it needed a new paint job, and new leather interior, plus I jazzed up the engine a bit. Want to take a spin?"

"Absolutely, we'd love to. I'd love to drive it if you don't mind."

They drove around the hillsides and side roads around Jamie's neighborhood for a brief time, the car tightly hugging the road on sharp turns, the engine purring. Mac knew her son had lusted after this car since he was a teenager. She was thrilled for him, but also worried that they kept spending money. He just refused to take her advice—to save, get out of debt, and lower their living costs.

Back at the house they chatted about the car, Jamie's plans to take a road trip in the car, his work, and their summer plans. Mac and David left, amid hugs and congratulations on the great car.

On the drive back home, David said, "He is a fine young man. I can see why you are so proud of him. Handsome, smart, and a charmer; he is very poised and gracious. You did a fine job raising him."

"Thanks dear. To tell you the truth, I feel like I let him down in some way. He made so many wrong choices, and I have always felt that had I done a better job he would not have chosen as he did."

"Listen Mac, I know lots of people who have provided the best possible lives and love to their kids, and the kids still go haywire.

It perhaps is peer pressure, a sign of the times, but I don't see it as a parental failure."

"Perhaps you are right David. But how do I justify and explain the many many years of minimal contact from him? I feel like I am butting in if I contact them very often, just a nuisance. I keep hoping he will want to be in contact, to share time, to be of help, but we never get there. It is painful, and has been for a long time. I just try to keep it light and leave them alone. I am happy for him getting the car of his dreams, but so damn worried about their financial situation. I've tried to get them to see what is coming, but they either can't or don't want to, and so they have made no effort to get their lives in order. It's frustrating and worrisome. Jamie has always been one to want instant gratification, never able to wait, save and pay cash for his next acquisition. He is into stuff, lots of stuff."

They arrived home and decided to retire early, and watch some TV in their room. They finished their wine in bed, Mac wrapped in David's arms, where she now felt safer than ever in her life. When morning came Mac felt rested and ready to tackle the project, and the appointment with her friend Tom Gordon.

That morning David headed out early to the gym, and then errands. Mac made some notes, answered emails, showered and dressed, and by noon was headed out to meet Tom. She had a couple of stops, but still arrived at Tom's office a few minutes before one o'clock. She entered the offices which seemed empty, so she called out. A few moments later, Tom came down the hallway to welcome her.

"Mackenzie, it's so good to see you. It's been a while, and by that I mean, since you graced Sunday services. I expect you to correct that situation soon Mac. Now then I have a surprise for you."

He took her by the arm and escorted her down the hall to his office. While walking he said, "Mac you indicated what you wanted to talk about, with certain limitations, such as not really Armageddon, but sort of like it, and so forth. So I got to thinking about a friend of mine that I believe can be far more helpful than can I. So, Mac meet my friend Gerald Evans; Gerald this is Mackenzie Honor. Mac, Gerry has his PhD in Economics and history, and while I am happy to contribute where it makes sense, I am going to enjoy being quiet and letting you two talk. Mackenzie why don't you start by telling Gerry exactly what you are having a problem with and what sort of information you need. I am here to contribute too. I thought between the three of us we could arrive as some solutions for you Mac."

"Tom this is a pleasant surprise and indeed, Gerry's area of expertise may be just the answer now." Mac proceeded to explain to Gerry and Tom that she had found a vast amount of information that boded ill for America in the future. She needed to wrap up a report that had both biblical and political implications, but did not want to be in a position of predicting when Armageddon would happen and exactly how and where. "Frankly I've not been able to decipherer enough information within the Bible about these events, and most of my reading reflects a great deal of confusion over when and where, though the warning signs are pretty clear. In addition, the scholarly experts seem to have vastly different views on the subject."

Gerry smiled as he responded, "May I call you Mac? I fully understand your dilemma. And I hope I can be of help. I am well aware of what is going on in this country and around the world, probably because I am well aware of history. As oft quoted, if we do not learn from history then we are inclined to repeat it, mistakes and all."

"Essentially what we have in the United States is the ideal climate to produce a perfect storm and it is closing in on us. So let's use a hypothetical example, based on today's facts and tomorrow's likelihood. Let's say that in a couple years time, certain conditions in this country worsen—that would be a list of things, and if you don't mind, I'll use Tom's chalk board here, as you may wish to write these down."

He proceeded to write the following list on the chalk board:

- States forced to make massive increases in taxes due to demands of Federal government, budgetary problems and welfare costs
- Taxes increase from the Federal government to cover healthcare and myriad social programs creating a huge deficit
- Dollar devalues further, due to extensive printing of money, and inflation

- Foreign interests refuse to take on any more American debt or buy our bonds
- Stock market takes a nose dive
- Several states go into bankruptcy
- Tax revolt by citizens
- Job losses have escalated
- Economic indicators are dire, in the US and globally
- Government spending has crippled the country
- Inflation has skyrocketed
- The government is spending more than the whole economy produces

Gerry continued, "Now, this is a short list on some things we are facing, and they all have reference to numerous places in history. So you have a foundation that is like a house of cards that could cave with the slightest pressure. Not on this list but of huge financial impact is the collapse of our infrastructure, which is happening now."

"Add to the myriad of problems at least one major natural disaster such as Katrina, oil prices doubling or tripling, some sort of military action involving the Middle East, the government unable to borrow more money to meet current loan interest and debts, and we have the perfect storm. The outcome from even some of this happening within a year of each other would be a collapse of the country. The Middle East is a powder keg ready to blow sky high, and if or when it does, the whole world will be enormously affected in the worst possible ways."

"This country is on the precipice of total collapse as it is. We are being replaced as the world leader and protector of freedom and liberty. We have lost our leadership position in education, innovation, manufacturing, and most every other category. We are looked down on from countries that envied us, because we have proven to the world that we do not place enough importance and regard for our own economy to protect it. Most educated people around the world know more of our history than do our own citizens, but those people can't imagine we'd be so negligent in not learning such basics."

"Now, you wish to see some correlation between what is our fate with the prophecies of the Bible. I am not a Biblical scholar, but I have been told that North America does not appear in the prophecies; rather they believe the reference is to the European area, or the Far East, as areas that will assume leadership. That means to me that North America will have already perished, or will have been relegated to such a low position as to be of no relevance to what will happen."

"If I am correct about that, we are facing conditions that no one can fathom now. We could be reduced to a country resembling the poorest parts of India, or Africa. Unfortunately for this country, we have been served up lessons time and time again, showing us how badly things can end if we opt to follow a particular course. There are examples from ancient history through modern times, and as recent as the last twenty years. But we have two things that have proven disastrous. We have elected the wrong people to public office and then passed them the torch without the requisite accountability. And as citizens we have settled in to a comfortable life, choosing to ignore the warning signs, or to keep an eye on our interests. Most people do not seem to understand that this country operates on our money, coming out of our pockets. Many don't seem to understand that we pay taxes, and that money goes to fund all that government does."

"People instead seem to think that money appears from somewhere and the job gets done and they don't connect the dots. We don't pay attention to the Fed, to our foreign aid, or any uses and abuses of our money; sort of like 'life is good, so let's leave well enough alone.' Well of course, things can't stay good without good intentions and deeds. We are so far removed from both of those, we may never return. Most people do not realize that in the time President Nadir has been in office, which is just over one year, he has grown the deficit from $6.3 trillion to $8.2 trillion, and it is due to rise to $20.3 trillion in just under ten years. It's unfathomable so of course, most people don't tune in. But it equates to an enormous debt for each person in this country, probably indefinitely."

"I'd say that if scholars are right that America is not reflected in prophecies, we are in for some truly bleak times, sooner than later. You I am sure can imagine what those times might look like. I hope this has been a bit helpful and not redundant to what you have learned on your own."

Mackenzie had made notes, so she was struck by the notion that North America was not a critical factor in the period through Armageddon and End Times. He was correct on one thing, if that is true, then America was already done.

"Gerry, thank you so much. You have confirmed some things I knew, but the concept you presented about North America not being a factor in Armageddon is rather stunning. The implications are, well, terrifying. Have any of those you have spoken with given you any idea of a timeframe for this?"

"They don't deal in specific timeframes Mac, but my view of our current situation and the basic economic issues suggest that we are going to realize much of this within five years. Of course, there are many variables, given this Administration, which could shorten that timeline. I understand your angst, and share it. We need a miracle; and that is probably the one thing Americans can do now—pray for a miracle."

Tom spoke up, "Mac, we have spoken on occasion about Biblical matters and the confusion over End Times. It is more or less like economics in that there are varying groups who believe one scenario, but many others have altogether different views. No one seems to have the ideal answer. Most believe we are close, but does that mean one year, five years or twenty years? Who knows? The signs are all there, but until One World Government is a reality, we are likely not going to see End Times. It is after all, God's plan, not ours."

Mac nodded in understanding. "I appreciate your time, both of you. It helps to hear different perspectives before I wrap up these issues. You have an autographed book coming your way when this is published. Now I had best get back to work. Good to see you Tom, and so nice to meet you Gerry. Hope to see you both later. God Bless you both. Bye."

Mac returned home and decided to just get down to business. She still had a lot of sorting, organizing and writing to do. She decided to focus on her notes from today's meeting and incorporate them with her existing text.

The afternoon turned to evening and she realized David had not been around and since the dogs were in the office he was not in the house. He might have gone to a movie, or was doing some shopping, so she went back to her work. But by 7 o'clock she was getting worried. She was checking through the house when the phone rang. It was David! "Honey hi. Listen something has happened. I'm at the hospital. Can you come get me? No, I'll explain everything when I see you. Don't worry, I am okay, just a few scratches and cuts. But if you could come now that would be great."

Mackenzie grabbed her bag and keys and headed over to the hospital. The drive seemed to take forever and she was a wreck by the time she arrived. She went straight to the ER and asked the whereabouts of David Valor. The nurse directed her to a room to the side. There was David, far worse the wear then he had said on the phone.

"David! What has happened? Did you have an accident? You look awful. Oh my, tell me what happened?"

"Now Mac, calm down. Like I said, nothing broken, just scrapes, cuts and bruises. Yes, I'll tell you. No I did not have an accident, at least, not in the sense of an auto accident. I was over on Broadway. I stopped for a coffee and was walking down the street. I saw a little sandwich shop and decided to cross over and grab a bite. I was sipping my coffee, walking in the cross walk toward the shop. A car pulled out of a parking space about 4 cars down from the corner, squealed its wheels and headed for me. I saw it coming and began to run, but it swerved left and hit my side, knocking me about ten feet. It sped off, but I managed to get the make of the car and part of the license plate. The police have been here and taken a statement. I can leave now."

"Oh, David. They are here again. They know you now. Oh David what are we going to do? I have been going around as if there was no more danger. This is the worst. What are we going to do? I am so sorry honey. I never wanted anything to happen to you."

"Mac, I never for a moment thought we were free of those goons. When they showed up at the beach it was clear we were in their crosshairs. I am going to have to think about this though and try to figure out how to get rid of them. It will require something bold and possibly dangerous. We'll see. But it is clear that they were following me and like a dummy I never paid any attention; I let my guard down. They were parked only half a block from where I got coffee. Let's go home. I left the car on the street; maybe we should go by there and pick it up. I am fine to drive. I don't want to leave the car overnight."

They drove to Broadway in silence, both deep in thought. Mackenzie dropped David at his car and asked, "Are you positive you can handle driving? I think it would be okay to leave it overnight. Just be sure, okay?"

"I'm okay hun. I'll drive slowly. How about picking up some takeout for us? Neither of us wants to mess with cooking. Don't worry Mac please. We'll put our heads together and figure something out tomorrow. Tonight I want to relax. Now go home and I'll see you shortly."

Mac drove home, her mind racing. She picked up some Chinese food and sat in the kitchen waiting for David. He arrived, looking pale and banged up. When she gave him a hug he winced from pain. So they sat in the kitchen with their Chinese food and some beer. Mac wanted to keep the conversation light, at least for tonight. She related her meeting with Tom and Gerry and she suddenly realized how funny it was that this duo of friends had those names.

After dinner David said he wanted a shower, so Mac cleaned up the kitchen, let the dogs out in the yard, tidied up and then went around the house making sure that everything was locked up. By the time she was nearly done, David came out in robe and slippers to double check all the locks. "You know, I am going to get some wood from the garage and block a couple of windows here in the back. Then we'll keep the security system on 24/7. I'll be right back."

They went to bed early and watched some television, talking quietly for a time, but David was soon asleep. They'd deal with the issue in the morning.

The next morning David was up before Mac and had coffee and breakfast ready. He let the dogs out but they did not go for their usual walk. Mac joined them, sleepy from tossing and turning.

Over breakfast they began talking about the matter of safety. David said he'd been thinking about it since he got up. "I have an idea. It's bold and potentially dangerous, but it might put a stop to this intimidation. It's something you have to do, with the help of your guys in New York, and I suggest we do it while back there, if they agree."

"Tell me, don't keep me in suspense. If it works I don't care if it's dangerous."

"I think you need to go on one of their shows, be it radio or television. You need to tell your story to their huge audience, exactly what has transpired and name names. That outs them. We need photos of as many involved as possible, so it means television, with Eli. Could you do that? The other part of the equation is that we might go away for a while. No place far, but what if we rented a house in Bend, or up in Washington, just for a few months? The deal is that we'd have to essentially find a place immediately and get our stuff there along with the dogs. So here's the deal, if you agree. I'll find us a house, something nice and comfortable and will take care of all those arrangements. Can you get your friend to take our belongings and the dogs and go to the home and stay there for a week? We'll go straight there from New York. How does that sound?"

"Wow, that is a huge plan. But you know it might work. We leave a car in the garage, the house locked up with the security on, I notify security that the house will be empty so any signs of movement is a break in. Yes I am pretty sure my friend will do it, if she is available. She needs to leave here a couple of days before we go to New York. So first, you find us a place. It should be out from a major metro area, Bend would be fun. Or if not Bend, then something north of Seattle, like Edmonds, or even Bellingham, both of which are fun little towns. Once you find a place I'll get the travel plan going. After we finish up breakfast, I'll call Eli and see if he'd do this."

Mackenzie put in a call to Eli. "Hi Eli. Listen, we've had another incident here. That makes three out here. David has come up with an idea that might bring an end to this, but it requires your agreement and assistance. The idea is when I am back in New York in a few days, you have me on the show to be interviewed, and during the interview I tell about the threats, intimidation and attacks, name names, show pictures and out the whole bunch of them. It fits with what you are dealing with on your show, and the personalization might make a big impact with your viewers. What do you think? Oh and the other part is that David is looking for a house for us to rent for a few months, away from here. I have a friend that would take all our belongings and my dogs and move into the house before we leave for New York, then we'd go from New York straight there, assuming we can be sure we are not being tailed."

"Geez Mac. I, well, I. Wow, this is a mess isn't it? I thought we could pull this off without bringing harm to you. What happened to you this time?"

"David was hit by a car, crossing the street. It was parked in the area where he was shopping. As he started across the street the car pulled out into the street and headed for him. He ran but the car swerved in his direction, clipping him and knocking him several feet."

"And this is your bodyguard! Well, yes we need to do something outside the box. Sure, I'll interview you. Do you want to be identified or in silhouette? I'll set it up for one of the days you are here. Send me an email with a list of names. I can get photos of them all."

"Eli if we are going to do this, then let's be bold about it. They know who I am, so no point in hiding now. Let's go for it with gusto. I'll also email you a list of events in order. Perhaps being outted will call off the dogs. Once I know where we are going I'm going to change our reservations to a different airport, then we'll rent a car and drive to the location. Oh and I spoke with Kate. She is out, totally. I told her I very much understood."

"Okay Mac. Let's get this done. I've allowed for a few days to explore New York with your David. We'll fit the interview into one of those days. Please give me a call when you know where you will be going. Don't send me an email. With all that is going on can you finish the book? Actually, what we'll do is finish it here. Pat and I have additional information that we want in the book and rather than send you notes, we can do it here. So write things up to the last week of coverage, sometime in the third quarter of 2012. Now Mac, you be very careful. Don't take any risks and keep a low profile for the next few days before you head back here. I'll look for a call from you in a day or two. Be careful, both of you."

Mac rang off and went to see if David was having any luck. "I have options," he said. "I went online and found a nice place in Bend for rent furnished by the month, and one up in Edmonds. I have not looked at Bellingham yet. But here are photos. What do you think? Would you like to go farther away?

"Both houses look nice. I like the setting of the one in Bend, but prefer the interior of the one in Edmonds. The thing about Edmonds is that we can take a ferry from there and go exploring. So let's do Edmonds and I'll change our return reservations into Seattle. So tie down the home in Edmonds and I'll get things organized for the dogs and my stuff. You should get your own stuff together. We'll be there for maybe three months? That means it will be into summer so plan accordingly. Honey, what about New York? You can't really go all banged up and feeling sore."

"Listen here, you just try to stop me. I am going, period. No more discussion. I'll be better each day and in a couple of days it won't be an issue anyway."

With some sense of urgency both Mac and David proceeded to make changes to their lives and schedules, in the hope of preventing further problems. Mac was hopeful that the appearance with Eli would do the job, but after all the near-misses how would they know for sure? Anyway, no amount of precaution or effort was too much.

Mac spent the day organizing belongings, packing, gathering up some personal items and kitchen things. David loaded up the van, and by day's end they had most of their things ready to roll. Mac's friend Mary would be over in the morning, dropped off by her daughter, and ready to make the trip. David gave both dogs a bath so they'd be clean and ready for their trip.

This would give Mac three days to get the book finished. And it gave David some down time so he could rest and recover from the injuries.

The next morning Mary arrived. David had prepared a map for her, gave her a wad of money, a cell phone, and with the garage door closed, loaded everyone into the van and did the farewells. David had just come back from a walk around the area and saw no cars loitering, no cars parked except those that belonged to neighbors. So Mary left the garage and headed on her way. Mac's stomach was in knots, so worried that Mary would be followed. But David had her leave the back way and take an odd route to the freeway. She prayed Mary and the dogs would arrive safely. The owner of the home would be meeting them with keys later that afternoon.

David announced that he was going to the club for a steam and a swim to limber up. It was a perfect time for Mac to get down to writing without interruption. She sat at the computer and once again began writing.

It is 2011 and the mood of the people grows ever fiercer. There is massive unrest and animosity across the country. Rumors of a revolution spread, people close up their lives and leave for parts unknown, to get off the grid. As for the government? Most people have come to regard the Administration as little more than the new Mafia; Congress, their goons and bag men. It resembles the old days of crime-ridden Louisiana, or the long time crime scene of Chicago.

Fear of war multiplies with the realization that it could take place in this country. Many people prepare to flee, but the nagging question persists—to where? Where in the World can one be safe, away from the evil influences, governments run amuck, inflation, crime and unstable economies? Some people just won't leave the United States, so they opt to move into the mountains of the Northwest, or New Mexico. Those who feel a need to get out of the U.S will head to the mountains of Mexico. Still others with plenty of money choose to travel to New Zealand. Many people still can't comprehend what is about to happen and still believe things will work out as Nadir promised; they will remain in place, in a stupor of ignorance and complacency. Those are the ones caught unaware and who will suffer the most.

With the spreading fear, people begin hoarding—food, money, gasoline and propane, most anything that supports survival. Those with liquid assets, such as savings and stocks, cash out; purchasing gold and silver, putting it into hiding. Banks continue to fail, leaving the country with the Federal Reserve Bank and its subsidiaries, which are not trusted, and for good reason. As in the Bible, the borrower will be a slave to the lender.

Senior citizens face head-on the devastating impact of the new healthcare reform. With a swoosh of the presidential pen, seniors will no longer be given joint replacements, dialysis, heart surgery, medications or treatment for diabetes, or for a long list of other illnesses and diseases. They feel betrayed and at a loss to know how to save their lives. They come to realize that they have been discarded as the first wave of population reduction. As a result people will be dying in record numbers at ages comparable to fifty years ago.

Eli Gabriel and Patrick Hennessy are attacked by mainstream media, politicians, political commentators, and various organizations under the control of Ivan Schwartz. Pressure is put on their employers to fire them. As the year goes on it becomes clear that their jobs are in jeopardy, and both begin making plans of their own.

Both men continue wailing to their audience, warning them, imploring them to repent, to turn to Jesus, to confess with their mouths and believe with their hearts. At the same time they both unleash a stream of fiery condemnation from their mouths toward their enemies, divulging the darkness and evil that fills the empty souls of those who control events and people. They expose their deeds and intentions, and show how they are working to tear down America and the rest of the world, in order to create their One World Government.

The scripture states that Armageddon will occur once one world government has been created which will be lead by the antichrist who walks among us, waiting for his time to rise to his throne.

There is a new paradigm, a new metric that becomes the law of land. Gone are the days when man can work to achieve unlimited wealth. People are expected to share their prosperity, with the rich giving to those less fortunate. President Nadir refers to them as middle class, but most of the middle class disappears due to the loss of jobs, or the fleeing of people to other countries. So in reality, the rich are giving to the poor. The economic prosperity dwindles for the country, a result of business being controlled and led by the government, no longer by the private sector. Capitalism dies a slow and unbearable death, taking dreams, hopes and prosperity with it.

Christians, church leaders, those who hold Jesus in their heart believe that if the evil forces that have taken over other's lives, but repent, we'd avoid the times of tribulation. Winston Churchill said,

"A man does what he must—in spite of personal consequences, in spite of obstacles and dangers and pressures—and that is the basis of all human morality." But, pure evil does not exist as part of human morality, and can't repent. There is no soul, no heart, no conscience, no remorse, and no sense of wrong. Therefore, pleas to such people prove pointless—they persist down their path of destruction because it is what they want, what they have planned for and then the end is justified in their minds by any means.

That leaves We The People, who must repent for agreeing with the Devil, for allowing the destruction of our nation, for selling out the riches of God and church. We must turn from our wicked ways, be they in business, government, church, or in our personal lives.

"For God sent not his Son into the world to condemn the world; but that the world through him might be saved."

"That whosoever believeth in him should not perish, but have eternal life."

Mackenzie stopped, looked at the computer screen, and sat in silence for several minutes. It is done, she thought, and let out an enormous sigh of relief. It is done, but for the last days. She felt there should be some sort of celebration, something special to acknowledge the closure of this chapter of her life, this book most difficult to write. But it was not over yet, no, not yet by far. She turned off the computer with a grand wave of her hand.

Mac and David spent the remaining day preparing for their trip, sending off lists to Eli, making notes for Mac to use in her interview, and collecting a few notes from Mac's research to take with her. They called Mary to make sure all was well, the dogs were safe, and she was secure in the rental home.

On the appointed day a driver picked them up and whisked them off to the airport. Within a couple of hours they were comfortably seated in first class and preparing for takeoff.

The flight passed quickly with a decent meal, some good wine, a movie and nap. Eli had arranged for a driver to collect them and deliver them to their hotel in Manhattan. Once settled in their lovely suite,

David decided they should get cleaned up and take a walk to before they met Jack for dinner.

Mackenzie responded, "Oh I'd love that. I have to admit that my memories of my last trip here color my enthusiasm for wandering the streets of New York. But with you with me, well, we'll be fine. So yes, let's walk. Jack made a reservation for us, so we'll meet them there. One thing honey, I have an appointment with Eli tomorrow. I don't want to be a baby, but I really need you to go with me. I just don't want to be out and about alone. I know that makes me pretty wimpy, but after all that happened before, I don't feel very secure."

"Mac my love, I had no intention whatsoever of leaving you alone to go anywhere. I am here to see that you are safe, to hopefully share some good times with you, but most of all, to make sure you leave here in one piece without any scratches. Okay? We won't discuss it again. It is a given."

New York remained a contradiction, part glamorous, part tattered and worn. But it was an exciting city, so David and Mackenzie enjoyed their walk, their meal, the ambiance of their upscale neighborhood, and the elegance of their hotel. They had a lovely evening with Jack and his wife Elaine. No business, just recalling lots of good times over the years, and discussion about retirement and what they all wanted from this next phase in their lives. They were staying at the same hotel, so had a night cap in the bar and then hugged and went to their own rooms.

Breakfast was by room service as they both got ready for the meeting. They were in a cab headed to Eli's office with plenty of time to spare, even with the dense traffic congestion.

Thirty minutes later they were escorted to Eli's office. "Mac, I am so happy to see you in one piece, no remaining signs of all the traumas I see. And you must be David. I am Eli and welcome to New York. Please, have a seat. David you look like you lost a battle with a bat. What happened?"

"Eli, I brought David along because, frankly, I am not comfortable going out alone after all that has happened. David was victim to another hit and run, not an accident for sure. Eli, he can wait outside if you'd prefer. But I have to be honest, I have had to share information with him, because he has been charged with protecting me, and he needed to know against what and whom. I hope you don't mind, but it was a matter of practicality and necessity."

"Not to worry Mac. And David may as well stay here with us. Pat will be over shortly. But I'd like to get down to business. You have five days here. I expect that you can compose the last few pages in a day or so, and that is number one priority. The next thing we need to deal with is your interview. Today is Tuesday. I'd like to do the interview on Thursday. That leaves Friday and Saturday for you two to be on your own and do as you wish before flying back. And on that note, have you taken care of housing for a while?"

David spoke up, "Eli, we have secured a very pleasant house north of Seattle, and Mac's friend drove up there with our belongings and Mac's dogs a few days ago. She has money and a cell phone and we have communicated with her. All is well. She has one of the cars with her, and we'll send her back by train or plane once we get up there. I hated to uproot Mac after all that she's been through, but it seemed like a prudent thing to do, as extra precaution."

"Excellent," Eli said. "Now, in order to make the last bit of writing as easy as possible, Pat and I have made notes in one document, put it on disk, and you can take I back to your hotel. However, Pat and I want to discuss some of the information before you get to work. And David might as well hang around, because we are going to be talking about our departure, and plans that you two should make, and I hope Kate and her family as well."

"Now, it has recently come to our attention that Nadir secretly created a new program that puts our coastlines, oceans, and other bodies of water under control of a newly formed commission. That commission is accountable to the United Nations, and essentially the action abolishes U.S. sovereignty, leaving us to adhere to UN rules, regulations and sanctions. This will impact waterway commerce too. In addition, one of our sources reported that other secret meetings have been held with foreign entities for the purpose of negotiating the future sale of national lands mostly in the West, and even some of our bodies of water. This is so incomprehensible and disgusting, I can barely even talk of it. The reason for the potential sales? To raise more money to enact yet more social programs and fulfill their social "justice" plans."

"Now, Mac you have no doubt been hearing about the pressures on our employers? Well the tension is building; the threats to us and our families have intensified to the point that we have had to hire protection to move about with us, and to guard our homes. This is no way to live. Our wives are frightened, our children are terrified. No matter how driven we are to do our work for God, we can't put our families in jeopardy. Once we lose our jobs, and we will, it will be time for us to relocate. And once we have done that, we'll be back on the air."

"Now, about where we are going. We have struggled with this for some time. But Pat had a phone call the other day from the Governor of Alaska. The state is about to withdraw from the Union, and become an independent nation state. I think Pat said they were going to be called the Alaska Republic. We are not thrilled about all the cold, but we are very encouraged about what is going on there, and we've been invited to continue our broadcasting from there. They have been doing some very exciting advanced planning unbeknownst to most, and they will be completely self-sufficient for many decades."

"Pat and I have talked, and we'd like you two, your families, Kate and her family to all join us there. I am telling you now, because at some point we are going to announce to our followers where we are going, and encourage patriots who have God in their heart to join us. We'd like you all to have your lives in order just as you want them, before we make any announcement. And we don't know just when that will be, but it will happen probably within six months or so. Our bosses have pretty much indicated they can hang on only so long, and that time grows near."

David was paying close attention to all Eli was saying, and asked "Eli, why have you chosen Alaska? Why not some other state or country? And how many people do you think will follow you there? Finally, when do you suggest we make our plans, and once made do we move immediately, or wait for some predetermined point?"

Mac felt a lump in her throat as she asked, "Eli, are there no other options? David and I have been talking about Mexico, or New Zealand perhaps. But Alaska? I shiver just thinking about all that ice and snow. I can't imagine my son opting to go with us. His wife would never leave her parents anyway."

Eli nodded understandingly, "Mac, we have looked carefully at the situation, current and future. Alaska is the only place with sufficient resources to carry a sizeable population for many years. There is a stockpile of food there; the state has launched two satellites to meet all communication needs; it has endless supplies of energy resources; there is plenty of water and space; and the state is well removed geographically from the mainland, plus we don't see Russia as posing any problems. It meets all the criteria. Now you don't have to follow us. I encourage it because it is a place where I know we will all be safe from the ravages of evil under way."

David nodded his agreement, turning to Mac, "Mac, Eli is right. It is a safe place. It is not permanent necessarily, but we can live a comfortable life there without worry about food, getting around, living freely. We'd have medical care I am sure, right Eli? And should we need to get back to the lower 48, we can do that. I think it makes sense. Better safe and secure than scraping by in Mexico, which is likely to be as big a mess as here."

Mac nodded. She was stunned by the news, and it was going to take her some time to get her mind around it all.

"Well one good thing, my fur coat will come in handy, as will my various snow boots. But I am going to have to embrace the concept in baby steps," Mac laughed. "Especially since I have imagined us living la dolce vita in Mexico, with endless sun and warm weather. But Mexico is in turmoil, dangerous, unstable, and tied closely to the fate of America. I can see we'd be trading one fire for another."

Patrick arrived, introductions were made, David's presence explained, and they all sat down to a serious conversation. Pat explained further about what they were going through. He said, "We expected difficulties, we had no reservations about serving God's wishes, and we will continue as long as listeners and the stations will have us. Once that is not possible here, we will move and begin anew. One thing is important to understand. Just because bad things happen to this country, we can't give up, we can't turn our back on God, and we must continue to battle the elements of evil. Eli and I will be doing that but from Alaska, not here."

They had a discussion about notes on the disk, and the information that Eli and Patrick wanted in the final chapter. After going over all the details, Eli spoke. "David, we can't demand anything of you or Mackenzie. But we hope you will feel good about joining us in the new Alaska Republic. If you decide it is a good move for you, then I'd like you to coordinate with my assistant. She has information on some areas with great housing, not far from a decent size community. I'd also suggest that you both do some online research on the pros and cons of the areas up there, based on your own needs and desires. You probably will want to go up there and check out some of the areas while looking for housing. Keep in mind that some areas are so remote they are only accessible by small plane, or boat."

"My guess is that you'll want to be in reasonable proximity to Anchorage, just because it has the most amenities to offer. But whatever you decide, Pat and I are behind you 100 percent. We know you will decide what is best for you both."

"Now, I think you should get busy on this last chapter Mac. You can bring it with you when we do the interview, so please plan on being here by 2 o'clock. We'll go on the air at 3 o'clock. Do you have any more information for me for this interview? Do you have any specific questions you want me to ask?"

"Yes, I have a folder here for you. These are notes I have made, copies of some of the materials I sent via email, and some questions. I have a copy for myself to refresh my memory, and I'll look things over that morning. David and I have some things we want to do on Friday and Saturday, and we'll head out on Sunday morning. Our flight leaves at 10:48 a.m."

"Okay Mac, that is good. I'll have a car at the hotel for you at 8:00 that morning. Also, we'll be able to chat briefly on Thursday before I go on, but please know that once I am on, I won't be able to visit. If anything comes up or you have any questions, give either of us a call.

Now, we need to get back to our work. Take care of yourselves. Oh and are there any questions or concerns now?"

David spoke up, "I can't say what we will decide right now, but we will be checking things out. Right now I feel a bit overwhelmed. But Mac and I will get things straightened out. Thanks for your time, both of you. How long do you think we have to decide and make plans? Is there some event that will put things into action? Mac do you have any questions?"

"No. I too am a bit overwhelmed. For now I just need to focus on the last bit of writing. One thing though, is there anything very shocking on the disk that I may find upsetting or difficult to deal with?"

Pat responded, "Mac I think you've been exposed to enough that you'll handle what's on the disk without too much difficulty. It is not a pleasant scenario in the least. But it is a situation that must be known to as many as possible. As for your questions David, we think six months, give or take. We anticipate major events around the loss of our jobs. But there will be other things happening and you'll discover those things with Mac, from the disk."

Eli concurred, saying "Alright then, we are up to date. See you two on Thursday. Good luck with the writing, Mackenzie."

They bid their goodbyes and headed out into the sunshine and fresh air. Mac stood outside the building and breathed in deeply. Her eyes were tearing and David knew she was powerfully affected by much of what the men had told her. "Honey everything is going to be okay. We will be okay. Things will be difficult but we'll make it just fine."

"Oh David, it's not so much what will happen to us, it's what will happen to this country. I have been dealing in details for months now, which has kept me from really truly looking at what is happening to the country; what will happen. That pains me deeply. I love this country, our spirit, our history, our values and freedoms. I've traveled around much of the world, and when I get home I know that this is the most remarkable country in the world. We have lead with valor, inspiration, and compassion. And we have also displayed hubris, and been underhanded. But I believe there has been far more good than bad, at least until the last thirty years. My heart breaks to imagine what it will be like in the coming months and years."

"Yes honey I know. I feel the same way. You are doing all you can to awaken people, to sound the alarm, to get people to repent and embrace Jesus. You can do no more. Eli and Patrick are doing all they can. The more we move people to God, the quicker he will respond. Each of us must take that step; we can't do it for them. How about we find a place for some lunch before we get you back to that laptop of yours?"

Mac spent the next two days drafting the final chapter of the book. It proved to be a painful process that drained her of all energy. David was comforting and understanding, not taking it personally, but being an emotional support. He gave her space, and then worked to provide a lightness of being during the evenings, getting tickets to the theatre, and taking her to delightful places for dinner.

All too quickly Thursday came. David and Mac had a late breakfast and arrived at the studio a few minutes before 2 o'clock. Eli was busy but waved to them while going over the program with his producer. Mac and David sat off to the side of the studio and observed a surprisingly large team of people scurrying around getting ready to go live. Eventually Eli came over, gave Mackenzie a hug, and took the manuscript, handing it to his assistant.

"Mackenzie, you'll be up after the first break. As I said before, I won't be able to visit with you. So I say this now. Patrick and I are indebted to you and Kate, but especially you, for all you have been through to get this book done. You were absolutely the right person for this job, and we are just so sorry that it's been such an ordeal for you. So from the bottom of our hearts, we thank you; and on behalf of God we thank you. I'd like you to take this envelope and put it in your purse. Don't bother to open it till you are on your plane headed West. Promise? Also, I'd like to hear from you every week or so, to let me know how you are doing. We also want to know your final plans and how we might be of help. Now I need to get back with the crew. God bless you both. See you on set shortly Mac." With that he gave her a huge bear hug, shook David's hand with gusto, and dashed back to the set.

The interview went well with Eli asking probing questions that made it possible for Mac to provide enough details about the individuals involved and what they were up to. When the interview was over and they went to break, Eli gave Mac a kiss on the cheek and whispered in her ear, "You can relax now. Your job has been done. Be well Mac."

David and Mackenzie left the studio and went down to the street. The sun was shining, the wind was blowing, and Mackenzie felt as if the weight of the world had been lifted from her shoulders and she'd have to be held down from floating away. Hand in hand they headed to their hotel to decide how they'd spend their remaining two days. They decided to rent a car and drive north following the Hudson River, stopping along the way to visit historical sites. Saturday, weather permitting, they would do a carriage ride through the park, walk up Fifth Avenue, hit a couple of museums and have a glamorous evening on the town at a fancy restaurant and club.

Mac collapsed on their bed and heaved a sigh of relief; her soul felt light, and even though her heart was heavy with the knowledge of what was to come, she felt she was better prepared and that her awareness would help the two of them survive.

###

THE CONCLUSION

In tribulation immediately draw near to God with confidence, and you will receive strength, enlightenment, and instruction.
St. John of the Cross
1542-1591, Spanish Christian Mystic and Poet

Thou are never at any time nearer to God than when under tribulation; which he permits for the purifications and beautifying of thy soul.
Molinos

Oh I Have Slipped The Surly Bonds of Earth...
Put Out My Hand And Touched the Face of God
John Gillespie Magee, pilot., Royal Canadian Air Force

2012—year of myth, legend, prophecy, mystery, anxiety, anticipation—a convergence of natural and manmade forces that will forever alter life as we have known it. The possibilities seem endless, with little indication that we will not be challenged in ways never dreamed of.

After three years of dire events and forces beyond most people's recognition or ability to control, we face a year that is shrouded in darkness and predictions of evil. It is the year Christians believe we will see Armageddon. It is the year that Mayans showed as the end to their calendar. It is the year of odd outer space alignments. It is a year ripe for explosive events and deceptions.

From years of consistent yet subtle manipulation against God and Christian religion, too many people will be separated from God and blinded to Satan. Sin thrives without regard to consequence and levels of violence, man against man, and assumes a demonic component.

Evil forces bind together to achieve the ultimate victory—destruction of America and control of the World.

The mantle of humanity will be under great duress and attack, and nothing will make sense. It's as if everything has been jumbled and turned upside down.

Eli and Patrick continue wailing and warning the world; their message that we need to surrender to Jesus, to repent, blended with news, often unfathomable. They urge us to seek agreement and obedience with God, through desire not obligation. They are passionate in their urgings, telling their audience that all they need is within them.

Sadly it was not enough to stem the tide of destruction. America gives up being grounded in reality, but still swayed by fabulous implications of infinite what-if's. What if the dollar rebounded? What if corporations return to America and we once again manufacture 'stuff?' What if the economic crisis disappeared? What if green technology really did make energy cheap? What if healthcare got cheaper? But it is too late for such wishful speculation!

President Nadir proved his promises are empty, and that he is an ungodly man many likened to Nebuchadnezzar, King of Babylon who destroyed Jerusalem. Nadir's hold over the U.S. will continue to increase, as he gains control over most of the country's main industries, through executive order or legislation. To ensure citizen compliance he has two military-like forces, as boots on the ground to enforce Presidential edicts.

Under Nadir, life grows far more difficult, and uncomfortable. Only seniors who lived through the period following World War II have a true understanding and appreciation for what will be lost—in freedoms and liberty. Younger people have lived without war and have little knowledge or understanding of the country's history and our Founders. But we all hold fear and uncertainty in our hearts, and a sense of foreboding. Those who got the message early have 'disappeared.'

The North American Union becomes a reality, with open borders, a single currency, the trans-continental highway under construction, and negotiations under way for a new constitution and government.

The implications of this union are vast and as yet unclear. People look to the EU's collapse as an indicator and are concerned.

President Nadir and his Administration have shown repeatedly that they have little if any tolerance for dissent and criticism. They have long complained about conservative talk radio and continue to put severe restrictions on free speech until it is fully eliminated within the new Constitution. Severe penalties will be imposed on media and individuals who publicly criticize the Administration and its policies.

2012 and the American Union creates the perfect opportunity for Nadir and his cadre of radical associates to rework the Constitution. Topping the list of Nadir's priorities will be the alteration of the Sixteenth Amendment, thus changing the two-term limit for the Office of President, and enabling Nadir to remain in office for a period of time only he knows.

IWN, Eli and Patrick's employer, decide the time has come. They kill both men's broadcasts, and with little ceremony or apology both men are cast out into the streets of New York. The move creates violent clashes between those who have been calling for the ousting of both men, and those who are followers and supporters. Demonstrations, attacks, and general riots force the police to arrest many as the violence escalates outside the IWN building. Accompanied by their devoted friend Al, the men leave the IWN building by a side entrance to waiting cars. An enraged crowd surges toward them on the attack. Both men suffer abrasions and cuts making their way to the cars.

Al, being jostled about by the raging crowd, jumps on the roof of a car and raises his hands for silence. The rioters ignore him and continue beating on the cars, screaming and yelling. Al shouts loudly and the crowd slowly grows quiet.

"Calm down. Silence! You are attacking men who have spent years warning you of dire times to come. You have subjected them to vitriol, name calling, attacks and threats to them and their families. These are men of God's choosing, whose only desire has been to save this country that they love, and its people; and to bring you to Jesus. They have preached love and repentance and you have ignored them. They have told of dark deeds and maneuvers on the part of our government and you did not believe them. They have wailed numerous warnings for years, and you ridiculed them. Now you wish their harm or worse, death? Shame on you. You have no one to blame for what is to come but yourselves. You have been selfish, you have shunned many chances to save yourselves, and you have embraced evil and distanced yourselves from God. Now you must pay the price. God's wrath will be seen in many ways and you will sting from it, but you were warned. By God, you were warned."

"These two men deserve your gratitude not contempt. These two men have given a great deal to try to help you, but you have been asleep. You were promised much by this Administration, but what has been delivered but pain, suffering, and the ruination of this country? Yes you ignored their warnings. Go home. Embrace your families. Make a plan to survive. And above all, get on your knees and repent, ask God for forgiveness for your sins, and for the salvation of this nation. Pray for these men and their families. We are now left with prayer as our defense against the evil. Use it and don't stop using it."

With that Al leapt down from the car and the crowds stood in silence, gradually breaking into applause. Al got into one of the cars and they moved through the crowd as the people part, creating a path of departure amid more applause.

At the same time, their supporters storm into the IWN building, overwhelming security, and making their way to the executive floors. Hundreds of people charge past security before police arrive to close the building down. Those who make it to the executive floors go from office to office shouting support for Eli and Patrick. Eventually police swarm the area, directing people to depart and arresting a few of the more rowdy demonstrators. Their shouts of support and outrage continue all the way to the street.

The country is now suffering from double-digit inflation, and taxes skyrocket. The Ruling Class suffers no hardship or inconvenience, as is typical. Everyone else is hit hard. There are consumables available, but at prices average people can't afford. The cost of utilities jumps so high people are forced to turn off their heat, and use electricity for barely an hour or two a day, just enough time to prepare a meager meal, and take care of essentials.

The mood of the people turns from apathy to despair and resignation. Those who have fought the long and bitter battle against the evil inherent in the Nadir Administration, go into hiding, or leave the country, in disgust and disappointment.

During the course of 2012 many natural disasters take place in the U.S. and elsewhere, straining the world's ability to respond with assistance. The United States gets hit hard with a series of earthquakes and storms, maxing out response crews, resources, and finances beyond the breaking point. The combined disasters leave hundreds of thousands homeless adding to the chaos, and difficulties experienced by all citizens around the country. It becomes impossible to feed and house those now wandering city streets. The Elites? Well they remain oblivious, indifferent, separated from the problems. This is the price to be paid to achieve their utopian existence.

The combined disasters well serve the plans of Illuminati and Bilderberg. They had decided many years prior that 2012 would be an ideal time to manufacture events regarded as Armageddon. It is their final push to bring the country down. They know that most people, overcome with fear and agony, will quietly and readily give up as they seek assurances of safety and some modicum of support. The Illuminati has long been counting on that human frailty to be evidenced in America.

2012 has long been the Illuminati target year because of the Christian belief that End Times arrive. They knew they could orchestrate a simulation of Tribulation that would bring people to their knees, defeated, weary, seeking basic survival. In addition to their plans, they learned that natural disasters would be greater in number and intensity due to changes in planet alignments. They have access to the HAARP project, and pay for a series of experiments that their experts have assured will result in an increase in natural disasters.

This is also the year that earth and sun alignments are distinctly different, resulting in solar maximum flares that have long been predicted to pierce the outer atmosphere, or ionosphere, leaving the earth's surface at risk of being hit. The experts explain such a strike as similar to 100 atomic bombs hitting in one area at the same time—or, scorched earth far and wide.

Rumors foster terror; terror, violence; and violence fosters death and destruction. It is a part of human character to over-react when confronted with the reality of not having enough—not enough food, water, gas, money, cake, booze, clothing—whatever. When faced with that belief, people go quickly into a 'me me me survival' mode regardless of risk or cost. For decades government agencies have been messing with our food and water supplies, working in secret with Monsanto, genetically altering foods, spiking foods and water with birth control and even mood altering drugs.

Food, the sort that the government ships to Third World Countries and those in crisis, is made sparsely available to the people in the U.S. Unbeknownst to those eager for the handouts, the food was genetically altered prior to its being hidden away for long term storage. Corn contains birth control, as example.

In tandem with the food shortages and distribution, and as part of the Illuminati and Bilderberg plan, a nation-wide health crisis breaks out. The healthcare system is strained far beyond capacity, forcing temporary holding facilities to be opened to quarantine large numbers of people. The death count climbs steadily, and provides the ideal opportunity for President Nadir to declare Martial Law, and to call out his various private security forces. The healthcare Army go door to door to withdraw the sick and put them in quarantine; and to make sure each person in each household is vaccinated. We have no options.

This crisis finally presents the government with the means to force microchips on all citizens. The technology, now highly sophisticated and miniaturized, has been in production for a few years, waiting for the right time. The time is 2012, and they will be implanted with an inoculation. Thereafter any sense of freedom will become a distant memory.

The human mind is so complex—it can endure a great deal, store vast amounts of information, and operate the complex systems of our bodies. But it can move us from reality to fantasy quickly especially when under duress. As a case in point, many of our military officers were put through 'survival' training prior to being shipped over to Vietnam. One survival school was in the high desert outside of San Diego. The training lasted for a few days with various types of survival operations, starting with sea/shore survival, then into the mountains for day/night survival. Part of the program is to feed oneself from the environment. The next day was evading the enemy, where soldiers wearing armbands acted as the enemy, swarming through the dense woods. If the trainee managed to evade the enemy for a day he got a sandwich, after which he and the other officers were taken to the prison compound, where they spent their final day and a half as POW's.

There was processing, interrogation and waiting one's turn. In what was only a few hours, some men's minds gave way to real fear. They lost all touch with reality, whispering among themselves about how things were, back in the States, how they wish they were home, how they longed for a burger, and they hoped they'd live to see their families again.

Mere hours and the mind, in defense from fear, retreated into a dark place where reality could not penetrate. Not all minds, but more than a few. Some men rose to the occasion then, and later when they became real POW's. The knowledge of that experience points to people who become leaders and resisters, and to those who buckle quickly under minimal pressure. It is just another equation and human factor that affects how we deal with the crises.

Nadir, feeling especially victorious and anticipating the enormous takeover with global implications, decides that this Fourth of July, 2012, will be cause for a major celebration, the likes of which have not been seen in Washington for many decades. Staff will stay busy for months preparing for a two-day event that will include a grand ball, fireworks, elaborate feast, barbeque, and entertainment.

The President and his wife have a long list of friends and supporters to whom they are indebted, so the invitations to both events result in hundreds of people pouring into the White House over the two days.

On July Third the back lawn is transformed into an amusement arcade with food stalls serving elegant gourmet versions of carney food. A stage featuring top country western performers, a dance floor, waiters in western garb passing trays of cocktails and finger foods, and a small but spectacular fireworks display.

In the wee hours of July Fourth a level three hurricane enters the Gulf of Mexico, estimated to arrive within twenty-four hours along the Texas coastline. That evening the Nadirs welcome their high profile guests, including members of Illuminati, Bilderbergs, Ivan Schwartz, Drew West head of SEIU, Johann Adler, Cora Lamia, various Middle Eastern dignitaries, staff, Cabinet members and other questionable people. No expense is spared as premium champagne flows freely; tubs of caviar adorn the buffet table, compliments of the Russian Embassy; as well as raw oysters and other delicacies imported from around the world. Dinner is a five-course gourmet feast served by an enormous contingent of waiters in white gloves.

The guests are turned out in gowns and tuxedos, some politely sipping their champagne, some exhibiting hubris in the extreme, loudly demanding this and that. The evening is to end with an extravagant display of fireworks seen across the city.

Just as the fireworks are about to commence, word comes to the White House that a huge earthquake over 8.0 has hit along the Mississippi River, with powerful aftershocks continuing northward. A few minutes later another earthquake hits along the East coast from New York south to Maryland. Reports also come in about objects falling from the sky, hitting in the Pacific Northwest, an area around Kansas, and Southern Florida. News of widespread power outages, fires burning out of control, death and destruction fill the airwaves.

The Nadirs decide to cancel the rest of the evening's festivities, their guests making a mad dash to waiting limos. Mrs. Nadir orders staff to prepare baggage for a long flight and trip. Everyone in the White House are scurrying about, as President Nadir selects his most trusted advisors and invites them to join him on Air Force One, telling them that they have exactly two hours to get their belongings to Andrews Air Force Base for departure and that they will be gone for several weeks.

Within two hours staff, aides, the Nadir family and a few select guests are aboard the Presidential plane awaiting takeoff. Two of the special guests ask the president's aide about where they will be going and when told, they ask to be let off the flight. Nadir personally broadcasts the following announcement on the PA system, "Ladies and gentlemen, we are about to take off. This is your President speaking. We will be heading to a secret location in the Middle East and we will remain there operating the government during the crisis now playing out in this country. If you either do not wish to make this trip, or if you can't support my actions, then I ask that you get off the plane now. We close the doors in less than five minutes. You have till then to make up your mind, or forever hold your tongue. Once airborne you will be told of our destination, and at that point all communication with the outside world is to cease."

A few people depart the plane and standing on the top of the ramp, look out to see fires and smoke. When they get down to the tarmac they all fall on their knees and begin praying, asking God for forgiveness of their personal sins.

Nadir orders doors closed and everyone to prepare for takeoff. One staff person enters the President's private quarters to suggest that he lead everyone in prayer, asking for salvation and redemption, and a safe and speedy return to Washington.

Nadir screams at the aide, "Hell no! I bow to no God other than Mohamed. People on here can pray if they wish, but it will do them no good. Things are as they should be. Most importantly, things are as I want them. So no, there will be no official praying. Now get out and don't come back. We wish to be left alone till we arrive, except to have meals served."

Before the Presidential plane lifts off the tarmac, Eli and Patrick and their families, some friends and colleagues are on a chartered plane out of LaGuardia Airport in New York, headed north to the Alaska Republic. Moments later Air Force One lifts off to parts unknown in the Middle East.

Once in the air Eli phones Mackenzie, "Mac, you've heard the news? The East coast is in trouble, and we've heard reports of fires in the Northwest. Are you near them? Now is the time Mac. Now is the time. You need to get out. Can you get Kate up there with you in short order and all of you fly out soon? Things are collapsing quickly. We just heard that Air Force One was loaded and headed to the Middle East. Figures!"

"Eli, the news is not good here either. We are okay, but there are fires from some sort of hit, probably one of those flares. We made arrangements for a helicopter to take us to a small airfield east of Seattle. I also spoke with Kate and arranged for a helicopter to pick them up at their home and take them to the same airport, along with my son and his family. I expect some others to come with us too. We are all due to meet there and depart by a chartered jet in just under two hours. We've all decided to join you in Alaska, but right now I need to know where? We don't know how long we'll stay but for now, we want to be where you are."

"I am so relieved you have made arrangements and are getting out. We are going into Anchorage. Let's all meet there tomorrow for breakfast and regroup, say 10AM? Be careful Mac. Things have never been more dangerous."

David and Mackenzie and the dogs, safely ensconced in the helicopter, flew over Seattle, somber as they witnessed the deadly scene below them. Even over the noise of the chopper they could hear the desperate screams for help from below. It was near darkness everywhere with plumes of smoke casting an eerie shadow over the sparsely lit area. Tears welled in Mac's eyes. This was her country—this was her home. It was collapsing in front of her. In her darkest thoughts she could never have imagined such a scene.

The helicopter moved on toward its destination. David put his arm around Mackenzie, realizing she was in great pain from the scenes below. He wondered if they'd ever know some semblance of "normal" again.

Kate and her family, Jamie and his family, Mackenzie, David and the dogs arrive by helicopters within forty-five minutes of each other and begin loading their bags on the plane. The area was pitch black, lit by a generator, casting an other-wordly glow over the people moving silently between craft, boxes and bags in hand. Mac and Kate had left messages for others, and a few are due to arrive any time. Thirty minutes and all are on board, waiting a few more minutes for any late arrivals. In twenty more they are airborne headed north to the Alaska Republic.

Everyone is exhausted, sweaty, scared and worried. As such the flight continues in silence, some asleep, some staring out the window at the darkness broken by occasional fires.

By the time they land in Anchorage they are cold, hungry, wanting showers and sleep. Mackenzie gathers the group and gives her speech. "I know we are all tired, hungry, scared, and dealing with anxiety over the unknown, both here and back home. We are fortunate that we have escaped and are together, and safe. We need to stick together, and give support to Eli and Patrick. This move up here is what we choose to make of it. It can be permanent or temporary; it can be joyous or depressing. We may all opt to return home at some point, if there is something to return to; or we may decide to go elsewhere. But we are here now, and let's do all we can to support each other. We have difficult times ahead, but they are likely to be far less difficult than if we had stayed at home, or ventured forth without our family and friends."

"I suggest we all get showers, change, meet Eli and Patrick for breakfast, and then get some much needed sleep. We are staying at the Residence Inn for the time being and we are to meet Eli and Pat at the Captain Cook Hotel for breakfast. We should be there in an hour."

An hour later, bathed and in clean clothes, the whole crowd minus dogs arrive at the hotel and join Pat and Eli in a private room for breakfast. They discuss short term plans, where each family will be living, and how they are going to carry on their work. David reported on housing he had found for them, and some options for Kate and John. They made a plan to meet again in a few days once they were settled in and had some basic needs taken care of.

As they were sitting there a news bulletin flashed on the television screen.

Ladies and Gentlemen, this just in from AP Service: PRESIDENT DAMIN NADIR, HIS FAMILY, CABINET AND STAFF HAVE GONE TO DUBAI WHERE THE NEW GOVERNMENT OPERATIONS HAVE BEEN SET UP. SECRET SERVICE AGENTS AND STAFF HAVE SPENT THE LAST TWO MONTHS SETTING

UP A NEW WHITE HOUSE AND GOVERNMENT OPERATION. A WHITE HOUSE SPOKESPERSON SAID THERE WOULD BE A STATEMENT FROM THE PRESIDENT AT 7 PM, EASTERN STANDARD TIME.

CNN AND FOX NEWS REPORT DESTRUCTION ACROSS THE UNITED STATES. MASSIVE NUMBERS OF INJURED AND HOMELESS, POWER OUTAGES, HOSPITALS OVERFLOWING— WE AWAIT CONFIRMED NUMBERS. A VOID IN LEADERSHIP IS CREATING CHAOS WITH GOVERNORS CALLING UP THE NATIONAL GUARD. A SPOKESPERSON FROM CORA LAMIA'S OFFICE, IN A HYSTERICAL PLEA, IS BEGGING COUNTRIES TO HELP AMERICA, AND FOR THE PRESIDENT TO RETURN.

The Tribulation, manmade or real, has begun. Nothing will remain as it was. Aid from countries around the world trickle in to various ports and airfields. Citizens will be lined up for hours for food and water. Life is changed, but Americans will endure.

The price to be paid is for man's mismanagement of earth and its resources; blindness; greed and ignorance; apathy and arrogance; and allowing the satanic invasion to gain control, speeding human demise and suffering.

Satan's victory is temporary. Americans, one by one, in small and enormous groups, fall to their knees and begin praying to God, confessing their sins, asking for God's blessing in these times of trial and tribulation. They will do this daily, and in so doing, hope will slowly return to their hearts. They know they must endure, but they will begin to realize that one day God in His own time will create anew and we will rise with pure hearts, bringing the American ingenuity, hard work and bold spirit back into play.

The American story is not over, merely changed, and with God's blessing, we will rise again, stronger, centered, and honoring our original Judeo/Christian faith from which we long ago became separated.

###

So now it is time to disassemble the parts of the jigsaw puzzle or to piece another one together, for I find that, having come to the end of my story, my life is just beginning.

Conrad Veidt
German Actor

GLOSSARY

Words should be used as tools of communication, not as a substitute for action.

unknown

Damin	(variant of Damien—Antichrist)
Nadir	(Arabic) lowest point
Cora	Goddess of the Underworld
Lamia	Child eating demon; large shark
Marxism	The opposite of capitalism; *"a theory in which class struggle is a central element in the analysis of social change in Western societies."*
Thugocracy	Rule by a group of thugs
Neocracy	Upstart rule; government by inexperienced, amateurs, neophytes
Meritocracy	System where one is chosen and advanced based on talent and accomplishment
Hegemony	Aggression or expansionism by large nations in an effort to achieve world domination
Cabal	A number of people together, generally to promote their common belief or private view
Aristocracy	Position based on origin
Plutocracy	Position based on wealth
Nepotism	Position based on family connections
Oligarchy	Government by a small group, control for corrupt and selfish purposes
Cronyism	Advantage and opportunity based on friendship
Democracy	Election by popularity

Republic   A government in which supreme power resides in a body of citizens entitled to vote and is exercised by elected officers and representatives responsible to them and governing according to law

Tribulation   Matthew 24:21; short period of time where people who follow God will experience worldwide persecution; and be purified and strengthened by it

Socialism is a philosophy of failure, the creed of ignorance, and the gospel of envy, its inherent virtue is the equal sharing of misery.
Winston Churchill

Would you like to see your manuscript become a book?